EDUCATIONAL PSYCHOLOGY

EDUCATIONAL PSYCHOLOGY

[A REVIEW]

[For BA (Hons.), BEd, and MA Courses]

Dr Manjaree Sengupta

MA [Psychology], MA [Education], PhD [Education]

Retd Professor, Educational Psychology, Department of Education

University of Kalyani, West Bengal, India

New Central Book Agency (P) Ltd

LONDON

HYDERABAD ERNAKULAM BHUBANESWAR

NEW DELHI KOLKATA PUNE GUWAHATI

NCBA

REGD OFFICE

8/1 Chintamoni Das Lane, Kolkata 700 009, India

email: ncbapvtltd@eth.net

OVERSEAS

NCBA (UK) Ltd, 149 Park Avenue North, Northampton, NN3 2HY, UK

email: ncbauk@yahoo.com

EXPORT

NCBA Exports Pvt. Ltd, 212 Shahpur Jat, New Delhi 110 049

email: ncbaexports@ncbapvtltd.com

BRANCHES

2/27 Ansari Road, 1st Floor
Daryaganj, **New Delhi** 110 002
email: ncbadel@ncbapvtltd.com

Shop Nos. 3 & 4, Vinayak Towers
681/B Budhwar Peth, Appa Balwant Chowk
Pune 411 002
email: ncbapune@ncbapvtltd.com

Shop No. 15, Bharati Towers, Ground Floor
Forest Park
Bhubaneswar 751 001
email: ncbabub@ncbapvtltd.com

House No. 3-1-315, 1st Floor
Nimboliadda, Kachiguda, **Hyderabad** 500 027
email: ncbahydb@ncbapvtltd.com

GSS Shopping Complex, 1st Floor
Opposite College Post Office, Convent Road
Ernakulam 682 035
0484-4021054/53

Radhamayee Complex (Second Floor)
Opp. Axis Bank, Panbazar, Jaswanta Road
Guwahati 781 001
email: ncbaguwahati@ncbapvtltd.com

EDUCATIONAL PSYCHOLOGY • Dr Manjaree Sengupta

First Published: 1999

Reprinted: 2006, 2008, 2010, 2014, 2018

PUBLISHER AND TYPESETTER
New Central Book Agency (P) Ltd
8/1 Chintamoni Das Lane, Kolkata 700 009

PRINTER
New Central Book Agency (P) Ltd
Web-Offset Division, Dhulagarh, Sankrail, Howrah

PROJECT TEAM
Prabhat Jas, Subas Maitra and Joydeep Ghosh

ISBN: 978 81 7381 365 8

Price ₹ 385.00

Dedication

This book is dedicated to respected Prabrājikā Vedaprānā —without her blessing and encouragement this venture would have been impossible.

With respect and 'pronam'

Preface

The general aim of this book is to present and explain the fundamental concepts of educational psychology and their pertinence to practical human concerns. It is concerned specially with those who are directly involved in any educational endeavour. In order to understand the role of educational psychology in developing educational practice, it is important that we try to identify the processes underlying them, and apply them in teaching—learning procedure of the present-day educational set up.

The book has been written as a text book to help not only the students of this discipline but also for the teachers teaching them the subject—**Educational Psychology**.

The course in educational psychology should be an experience shared by the teachers and the students (including teacher trainees). The students, in general, who enter in the realm of educational psychology at the higher levels of educational ladder are mature and are equipped with a background of introductory knowledge about the basic sciences. Some even have partial training in psychology, education and sociology during their high school years and college years as well. They are supposed to have developed if not very clear cut—but some explicit or implicit notions of the subject they are going to encounter. But they fail to perceive its relevance with the profession they are in or the operation of their own mental processes. Too often the beginners are familiar with some mere vocabularies, a few isolated facts, some vague ideas and some incoherent thoughts.

Here, a particular mention is necessary about the special students who are teacher-trainees, for whom the in-depth study of educational psychology is compulsory. Even they, while going through the whole course, find it difficult to relate their theoretical and practical knowledge of educational psychology with school teaching. Because school teachers are generally subject teachers and teaching to them is not learning to teach, but for them, "teaching is the distribution of a package of educational material to a procession of consumers : year after year, the same lesson plans, just new names on the seating chart".* The teacher's duty is not to prepare a person (student) but to prepare an examinee. Therefore, knowledge of educational psychology is not for them to develop an insight into the improvement of teaching-learning situation but a heavy burden to throw off the shoulder after the training period is over. It is an appendage, not related to their job and what they are supposed to perform in the school.

---

* Harry Shearer. Telegraph. Saturday, 17th July, 1999, Vol. XVIII, No. 11.

With these confusing considerations in mind this book attempts to help the teachers, teacher-students and students in general who undergo the course to attain some broader objectives of the course related with human behaviour, human relationships, human abilities, human developments and development of human personality in social environment. This book, therefore, attempts to highlight some special characteristics, furnish broader objectives (in the Introductory chapter) which try to eliminate the apparent grievances mentioned above. The author admits that a student's learning is an individual accomplishment, and that the platform of the professor and the text book, ultimately can serve only as adjunct, a reinforcement to the learning process. But the author hopes that her humble attempt to write this book with in-depth analysis of the topics selected, will help the students to obtain an accurate orientation of his own and enable him to relate them with life situations, provide a perspective with which he will be able to identify the educational peroblems to be dealt with effectively.

Educational psychology is a discipline which encompasses every spectrum of life and living, growing and developing, preparing and providing opportunities to create, making decisions and solving complex problems. It helps the learner to learn and learn to teach. Therefore, it has a vast scope and runs parallel to general psychology course touching every aspect of life. As a text book with specific objectives, referred to above, the present book has been restricted to the fundamentals of some interrelated topics solely necessary to suit the aims of educational endeavour—both formal and informal, both individual and institutional. More concentrated treatment of the field as a "behavioural science" than a general social science, has been emphasized. At the same time mechanical behavioural approach is less regarded and cognitive and affective, humanistic and depth psychological view points are more attended to in order to make behaviour more socially interactional—to make learning more personal as well as professional, sophisticated and interesting. Further this book stresses and ensures the importance of theories in educational psychology supported by research results to establish them—tries to refer to experiments in their theoretical contexts. It is believed that without adequate awareness of the theoretical contexts in which they are rooted the results of individual experiments can not be understood properly and often seem trivial, insignificant and sometimes unconvincing. Although theories evolve from the experiments carried individually or co-operatively, within a single culture or cross-culturally—the collection and integration of experimental studies, in turn, provide data for forwarding the basis of suggesting further more accurate investigations. Therefore, emphasis is laid here, on analysis and critically examine the theoretical conclusions of each topic. In order to serve the single purpose of intensive discussion of the topics related to teaching-learning parameter, the vast course could not be compiled in a single text book. So, some related topics only are selected by the author for that specific purpose. The author regrets her deficiency on this account and begs to appologize to the readers concerned. The author agrees that individual instructor will have his own scientific preferences which may not be in complete accord with those selected for this book. The author tries to point out that in sampling the current psychological scene related integrally with education, she has, of course, stressed those theories and research studies which seemed to her—in the light of the present and future trends in the field—to have great significance and value in the educational programmes of the present and coming generations.

There are many individuals—friends and students who have been of great assistance to the author in preparing this volume. Their helpful criticism and appreciation had been of immense help to write this book. While I have tried to incorporate of all their suggestions (including the suggestion of the reviewer of the press, for which I thank him a lot), but in many cases due to the lack of relevance to the context or for some other reasons all could not be contained in. The inadequacies (which I believe, still exist) in the contexts of the text are claimed by the author.

Finally, the author would like to express her deeply regarded thanks to her son and daughter particularly and friends and relatives in general, for the encouragement and push she received from them for completing this book. Last and not least, my hearty thanks and gratitude has been rendered to my publisher and the whole team connected with the publication of this book.

59/1A Hindusthan Park
Calcutta 700 029
17. 7. 1999

Manjaree Sengupta

CONTENTS

CHAPTER 1

Introduction

India is a vast country, the second largest land of population explosion, suffering from a dreadful disease of indigence and poverty. India is an agricultural country with rural base, inhabited mostly by land-based villagers and other small scale workers. Barring certain groups of rich agriculturists—who have flourished through cooperative farming—people are generally poor and moderately fed.

The section of people living below the poverty line are manual labourers, daily wage earners and others who live mostly in more or less starved condition. To go in search of food is their day's work. They survive in terms of no-work-no-food basis. Their life is characterised by hunger, poverty, lack of shelter, dearth of minimum clothing to protect the body from varying weathers, absence of any medical help, absence of the basic necessities of life and living. Even their survival is a big question mark. They face frequent child death, incurable diseases and adopt various sorts of malpractices just to survive. Therefore, education is a misnomer for them and for their children. For a hungry man food and not education is a must.

The people of this country have been socio-economically divided into three major social classes—the poor, the middle class and the rich. The poor class live through manual labour or through the development of one skill which is handed over from generation to generation. Therefore, education for them is mostly informal, immitative and hereditarily acquired. They need no special training as the same method has been repeated day by day. Sometimes they use sophisticated tools, if necessary and found useful. However, they are also conscious about the new machines which are helpful and are self-educated through mass communication programmes of television and other media. This is how now they are familiar with the mechanization process, with the corresponding advancement of global technology. So a kind of indirect education has gradually crept in at the rural level.

The rich and middle class people are mainly service-oriented and industry dependent for earning their livelihood. It is these two social classes who enjoy the benefits of formal education. But the overall picture of the social class structure of India reflects that Indian population in majority are land cultivators, because India is primarily an agricultural country and even many of the industries in India are agro-based. A major portion of Indian population is rural; they live in villages, mostly in mud houses or some in pucca buildings (those who are comparatively wealthier) and are provided by agricultural crops. As agriculture is weather-bound many people who thrive on it stay without any earning when the crop season is over. They need other jobs during the interim gap periods and in the resultant lean months they work mainly as manual labourers. Some of them who have some extra savings try to run rural shops to provide them. It is this class who send their children to school to get at least some sort of formal education which would help their business and trade. All of them have their roots in villages and visit urban areas only when necessary—either for some temporary work or for some small projects, just as a stop-gap measure.

The urban life and culture is totally different. A large portion of upper and middle class people are engulfed by the urbanized culture. They receive school and higher education and run mainly after salaried jobs in offices and industries. These jobs are work-oriented and demand general education of a moderate standard. They live in the cities and small towns and moderately big townships, receive school education compulsorily. They constitute the middle–class group as a whole. The aim of their learning is to equip themselves to get a handsome salaried job in order to provide themselves and their families. This urban section of middle–class youth comprise the population who attend formal education centres and training institutions, with the sole ambition of getting a secure job. As the social opportunities vary, the institutionalized training continually undergo changes as regards their aims and objectives, organization and management methods and procedures, evaluation and application of the products they produce. They also vary as time and technology change, as new research results are handed over and come into operation and as scientific investigations advance.

Gradually from the late nineteenth century to the late twentieth century, educational system witnessed the ushering in of the factory idea in schools and equated schooling with industrial and commercial work culture. The students coming out of their schools are like factory products. All educated youths who somehow climb over the high steps of the institutionalized ladder and acquire the general degree—a passport to enter service—are considered competent to fit in the offices and factories, industrial enterprises and educational institutions and can avail of the salaried jobs plus security. But the problem remains, since the jobs available are far shorter than the number of people considered fit for them. The inevitable consequence is unemployment and its disastrous appearance. Moreover, at present, the rural youths have also started qualifying themselves to be included to swim in the same stream, making the problem more acute. This has become the frightening picture of unemployed, frustrated youths of industrial society which has taken the place of agricultural life style in India.

Employment for all is the cry of the day in our country. Employment for every youth is a democratic right too. Nevertheless, increasing unemployment has become a major problem all over the world, but not as acute as in the developing countries. Our education system has also been framed in such way that it feeds the need. The ultimate aim of our young people today is to find out a salaried job and remain satisfied with it. There ends all education. Youths today are least bothered about the broad-based aims of education of making a complete man or building a wholesome personality.

With the advancement of technology of twentieth century, more and more industries were being set up changing the status of the socio-economy of the country as well as the educational systems. A strong bond has been established between commercial work and education. Hence education has become all the more service-oriented and not total. Young generation of the twenty–first century will face more of unemployment with increasing population and less job opportunities due to more sophisticated mechanization.

In order to tackle this problem, a change in attitude in planning educational system will be necessary. The aims of education in this context cannot remain restricted to the attainment of a specific qualification fit to be utilized in industries or commercial office establishments, i.e. attaining a specific standard. It should take the role of a guide and cannot be utilized only as a means of livelihood.

Education is modification of behaviour of man. It is a way of life and living. Therefore, it cannot have a short term aim only. Education is a life-long process, a continuous affair. It shapes a man and the scientific treatment of education helps in the vital process of man-making. Scientific attitude, scientific research and their successful application in educational procedures have earned attention of the educational scientists. As a result, classrooms came to be treated as scientific laboratories, where plans, methods and curriculum have been experimented upon. Their endeavour produced specialised and skilled work force necessary for the new era of industrialization. The work-force of a country who push the country forward towards advancement is the product of the country's educational system. Therefore, the necessity arises to reconsider the philosophy and psychology of education; to throw new light into its present state and to its future purposes, tasks, liabilities, responsibilities and ability.

Now that the country is entering into a new century presently, and a worldwide change is in the offing—as evident from the sudden jump from democracy to technocracy—the think tanks of educational system are somewhat confused as to setting new aims of education. They again are looking back to the democratic values and emphatically announce that the general purpose of education is to reshape the 'behaviour' of the young generation of the twentyfirst century in such manner that they fit into today's advanced technological society—a post industrial world society—but, at the same time, do not lose their democratic and national characteristics and values.

Modern education system has not reacted only at the national level but has extended to the international spheres. The world has come in a closer circuit and the young generation is eager for advancement, are ambitious and aspire for self-development, along with the country's socio-economic progress. They are self-actualized persons trying to put effort for technological advance, face global competition, emphasizing efficiency in work. They need planned education providing opportunities to be able to fight against all the odds of the competitive world. The parents today want their children to be achievement-motivated, to have hope of success and fear of failure. This is the group who are concerned with the students' test score and academic brilliance. But, in spite of these motivations the work-culture in our country is showing a downward curve. People are aspirant, but lazy to put active effort and lack competitive zeal. Some think that this is the consequence of our industrialization, where active participation is not essential and passive mechanization leads to withdrawal of effort from the person concerned, thereby staking decision—making and problem—solving which are essential for participating actively in the technological society of modern time. This is the beginning of the post industrial era, a transition in the history of civilization and culture.

This period finger points towards a new turn, a new look into the existing cultural ethos, revival of democratic values with modifications in a very sophisticated mechanical age. So the entire educational system needs to be reshuffled, needs setting new aims, objectives, new planning, considerable thinking and new management. Education now onward will not only be imparted with remote control device but will be an involvement of the participants in planning, programming and executing. This is a cultural-cum-educational revolution, not only at the national level but world over. This aspect we will discuss in more details in the next section. A change in the outlook has already appeared in the horizon a management stance, a professionalism to be practised in the field of education. It is essential not only in work places but also in educational institutions.

Every country, in the present state of affairs needs a better educated flexible work force capable of continual learning. Equally important is that the country needs work places that value those traits and put them to use. Complex changes are going on in our work and schooling. Therefore, organizational innovations are necessary if both the institutions are to regain their competitive edge.

The advent of modern sophisticated technology has placed us at a critical juncture where it is no longer enough to teach students and train workers to perform well on standardized tests and tasks or set examinations. What is needed in both the office and in the classroom is a new system of management and learning, a pragmatic outlook, changed attitude and a new interest and motivation. Now is the time that instead of being passively dependent on machine, which we have to, a system has to be introduced which draws upon and teaches skills in abstract thinking, experimental inquiry and collaborative problem solving. By replacing top-down bureaucratic prescription with a participative interactive approach that has its roots in our democratic tradition and values we have to replan the education system for the coming days so that the system can create a highly skilled work force of decision makers and problem solvers, able to think abstractly but positively and adapt to change.

At this juncture, we cannot afford to stick to the earlier policy of appropriating others' prescribed principles—without testing their utility—in our educational endeavour. Today we have to search the policies which would help us to create productive work force that will enable our country to compete with Western as well as Eastern developed countries and other developing Asian nations. Conventional wisdom suggests that we need to raise student test scores at least to a level on par with those of the students from the countries that are our competitors. This simple solution has become dogma embodied in a wide range of the commissions and reports available from different governmental meets, from time to time. The decisions at the educational level has been taken with an eye to the economic policy actions adopted. That has again established a strong relationship between the pupils and work force so that they meet the national demand.

A few years later the topic and the proposed solutions become rather stale and uninspiring—especially when the world order is changing so fast. The world is geared up for the 21st century. It is clear now that we are well into a new post-industrial era marked by the computer communication revolution, a competitive world market and spectres of severe ecological damage. The centralized control system of scientific management, that once dominated the industrial era work, and have spilled over to influence schools, was becoming dysfunctional for meeting turbulent change of the computer/ electronic era. Some leaders in the industry and education were beginning to recognize that we need alternatives to beurocratic centralism in order to be more creative in dealing with rapid change. Hence is the cry for privatization, liberalization, entrepreneurship type of management, to enable individuals to exhibit their creativity, ability for decision-making and precision and proficiency in problem-solving. This fact is also evident when we compare the government managed schools with those privately managed—the qualitative difference cannot be overlooked. Therefore, the alternative is liberalization or autonomy within limitation in imparting education.

The aim of education is to promote positive motivation, to give a psychological boost to constructive thinking, to combine certain values from our historical and democratic tradition with the power of electronic technology. The age, which our children are passing through, is a confusion for their parents though they know fully well that the 'old order changeth, yielding place to new'. But a high jump from democracy to technocracy is for them a 'crisis for human spirit'—a shift from brain process to computer process.

But all educationists know that as a dynamic process, education keeps pace with life, growth and development of the community and is altered both by changes imposed on it from without and by transformation in its internal structure and intellectual development. However, in spite of the transformation, the basis of education is a general consciousness of the values which govern human life, its history—the change of value system affects the current values within the community. Values can mean both "end-state values", as well as "values-as-means" (Chakraborty, 1993)[1] and when applied in education the first one highlights aim and the second method. As education is inclusive of training and development and improvement of skill the aim signifies the essence and the method signifies the practice to attain Education helps a man not only to 'be' but to 'become' through value orientation which is culture-specific. But culture-specific values are not unrelated with universal values. The universal values infiltrate into different cultures but retain the same unitary character of the transcultural level which gives a parity between different cultural values. So it is the value-as-means which is important in education as it is the applied form of education which goes by the name training. It is through training that the innate

1. Chakraborty S. K. Management by values. Towards Cultural Congruence. Oxford University Press, Calcutta 1993.

behaviour of man is being modified to fit into a given culture, its work situations and in the formation of the ethos of that culture—both subjectively and objectively.

As education of the coming century emphasizes the increased productivity both qualitatively and quantitatively, work and education internationally now conform the challenge of a series of inter-connected global changes. A few of the evidences are :

(1) the computer/electronic revolution that is pushing us into a post–industrial society

(2) the emergence of a competitive global market and fields of work

(3) an ecological crisis resulting from our careless treatment of the natural and human environments

(4) change of attitude in family relationships and child rearing e.g. (a) home vs creche, (b) family vs nursery, (c) active vs passive attention towards children, (d) disciplined vs free social sanction

(5) communication revolution

(6) the emerging centralized office vs office-cum-residence concept etc.

The kind of responses need to be made will be determined by the educationally oriented policy that should be taken to cope with the turbulent change of electronic era. It means making a second major cultural change within the hundred year period just ending. In 1900 we were moving rapidly from a rural agricultural India to an urban, corporate industrial society till the middle of this century. In 2000 we are moving swiftly from factory industrialism to computer driven post–industrialism and high-tech society. Therefore, education has now to be changed from its hiearchical, bureaucratic control system, where "thinking and authority were reserved for technical/administrative cum managerial experts who broke instruction and production into minute prescribed tasks, while people at work were reduced to programmed performances under supervision. Eventually the hierchical style conflicted with such values as equal worth and dignity of persons, the chance to participate as an active subject rather than a mere object, the chance to use one's distinctive capacities to learn, think and grow" (Wirth, A. G. 1992)[2]. The central feature of this corporate industrialism known as Taylorism (after the name of Frederick W. Taylor) a method in the history of management was the system of technocratic control over the less educated workers whose energies were to be welded to the relentless rhythms of 'assembly-line production'—another model borrowed from industry. But as the time changes Taylorist efficiency is becoming dysfunctional for meeting challenges of the new era. Therefore, a new leadership involving a combination of participative values with computer technology is needed to make our education more competitive by releasing creativity and competent decision–making ability and, thereby, improving the quality of life in work and schools. But it also involves a change in the nature and locus of power.

As against the changing world order, the economic growth and social change in India (to cope with the changed order) when economic productivity and the quality of education cannot be separated, we, at the same time, must recognize that human resources are more important than the physical ones. That a work force educated simply on "old school basis" will not be equipped for meeting the challenges of a turbulent change–a change of attitudes would be a crucial factor.

The strong trend now is towards participative work system—an 'informative type'—as the term used in industry management. The informating strategy helps tapping higher human capacities for communicating, collaborating, creating novel situations and "making value judgements as well as giving people in the work place access to relevant information so that they can become active agents in trouble shooting, suggesting innovations and making decisions and consequent functional efficiency." (Wirth, 1992). If we follow this strategy in the functioning of educational psychology, it will yield desirable result as it provides a framework of learning where people can experience participatory and creative ability to come into operation. In the informative type system, the learners in the school—like employees in the production category —will be able to perform "a broad range of tasks, maintaining their own quality control and other participatory activities like goal setting, budgeting, problem solving and decision making

---

2. Wirth, A. G. Education and Work for the Year 2000. Jossey-Bass Publishers. Sanfransico, 1992.

so that work is performed by self-directed teams leading towards sophistication and sharpening of skills". Twentyfirst century educational strategies will be "nothing less than revolution in the role of the teacher and the management of schools" as reported by CED (Committee for the Economic Development, 1985) of U.S.A. The new educational policy of the coming years of technological sophistica-tion is bound to focus on individualization of all the agencies–individual school, individual teacher and individual learner to make room for meaningful improvement in quality and produc-tivity. The 'informate', rather than 'automate' model would be more workable to open up decentralized system leading to liberalized education for all. Education should cater to the needs of higher order learning to think critically, anatytically, to co-operate and communicate as well as to complete and to solve problems, to assume responsibilities and 'to learn to learn'. The output measures are to be conducted, teacher effectiveness in the autonomy to be provided, and creativity assessed. For students, collaborative learning, divergent thinking and acquisition of higher order conceptual skills using symbolic analysis, the ability to handle complexity with constructive abstract analysis and, above all, the ability to communicate and collaborate by means of new technology and dialogue is the need of the post–industrial society of the coming century.

Here comes the role of psychology in controlling educational issues. Psychology provides the insight about the individual learner. As the issues, goals, methods, aids, curricula and the students bodies in the society change, innovations in psychology offer a boost to welcome the transition and trim the blue-print prescribed. Modern educational psychology contains the changed mood of the individual student and his environment and is concerned about issues like coding, creativity, mechanically devised educational aids, about effects of reinforcement and feed-back, instructional innovations, open classroom and open universities, bilingual teaching (English and regional language), computers and so on which are making learning activities far more diversified, offering teachers far more options. Considering all the issues, one unified principle underlies all learning activities where psychology comes to help immensely even in the restructurized organization of school system. While offering new stances in the organization of education for the forthcoming change these basic traditional principles have to be considered in learning situations : (Cronbach, 1977)[3] , viz.

Behaviour is purposive : In each act, one sees a sequence of interpretation, provisional trial and response to consequences. Whenever the person actively engages himself in a problematic situation, learning occurs.

Development is cumulative : Social demands set developmental tasks for the person at each age. These generate needs that provide the core of motivation to learn.

Mental ability is achieved : "Intelligence" is simply behaviour in which concepts, techniques and attitudes, working together, enable the person to cope with what is unfamiliar. Transfer value is the chief criterion for judging instruction.

These three principles constitute the basic structure of educational psychology of the future. Therefore, the essential step in the struggle to restructure education involves a convergence of new attitude towards time and with new attitudes towards action. In spite of the fact that our traditional culture has been subjected to intense and prolonged bombardment of technological, social and psychological changes and that the change is accelerating, we witness everywhere in the hi-tech society evidence that the old industrial era structure can no longer cope with futurism of tomorrow, yet the basic human structure remains the same. Even in the super-industrial civilization, child development follows the same pattern only in a changed social order. In this situation the teacher is to select what kind of human abilities, skills and growth patterns need to be encouraged in students to enable him to be a creative problem–solver and decision–maker in the restructurized organization.

Psychology has great deal to offer in the study and teaching of the future. As time advances, mode of living advances, international relations deepens, change occurs in human life. Therefore, time and change are inextricably linked and, affects human minds. Thus even in many of the core concerns of psychology, such as child development, including personality development, growth and maturation, motivation and learning, abilities and skill—all dealing with processual thinking, a time perspective that includes past, present and

3. Cronbach, L. J. Educational Psychology, 3rd ed. Harcourt Brace Jovanorich, Inc. 1977.

future (Toffler, 1976)[4] , the change of attitude is enormous. There remain a need to shift time perspective more towards future with an anchor in the past and present; to develop an epistemology to take account of the openness, uncertainty and problematics of the future, and to broaden the psychological concern with the meaning of human life. The dominant style of behaviouristic psychology of 1950s may turn out to be "a narrow, artificial and relatively sterile approach to the understanding of men. Human Sapien is not simply another animal. Nor are we machines, nor are we static" (op. cit). A major task of psychology is to help humans learn how to learn and how to discover, and perhaps to help expand, the human potentials dynamically. Modern life-oriented education starts in an individual's life right from the school age. Therefore, school is the starting point in continuing the journey of education. There the teachers play the pivotal role in developing student's knowledge of the world, of the life and their ways of understanding and adjusting with it. By doing so the teachers develop their own "personal educational psychology" (Lindgren, 1980)[5] consisting of reality-based understanding of the how and why of human behaviour, which, in turn, facilitates intellectual and social growth, development of ego-strength and all-round developed personality of the students.

The personal psychology will also help developing and understanding of the psychological realities of teaching and learning.

This book, therefore, is more than a text book of educational psychology. It lays emphasis on progressive, pragmatic and futuristic education through better understanding of psychological foundations of education. It is hoped that the teachers, parents and others who are interested in building the children of the twenty-first century in a changed life style, may receive some knowledge about a sound understanding of the psychology of growth and development, the ways in which learning take place, what the basic aptitudes, abilities and skills are and the effects of the personal and social environment for learning, personality development and teaching the new generation.

---

4. Toffler, Alvin : Learning for Tomorrow : The role of the Future in Education. A.D. Publishing Committee, U.S.A. 1974.
5. Lindgren, Henry Clay. Educational Psychology in the class room. Oxford University Press. N. Y. 1980.

CHAPTER II

Educational Psychology

Educational psychology has become a separate discipline altogether as it poses itself in the present time. The individuals who are interested in teaching profession and those who are already in it, as for example, the classroom teachers or educational managers-cum-administrators have become more and more interested in the development of broader and more general themes of educational psychology. A number of eminent scholars and scientists have in the process contributed to the development of educational psychology as a major applied field within the context of psychology.

A brief historical treking along the developmental path of educational psychology as it reaches the modern age, would probably be relevant here. Before the emergence of psychology as a discipline in its own right, and of educational psychology as a branch of that discipline—speculation and observation concerning the relation of human nature to the educational process were not uncommon. In the West, this feature can be traced from pre-Socratic period of classical Greece, where Democritus in fifth Century B. C. advanced his idea of education. He wrote about the importance of education in man's continuity of life process as well as considered the influence of the home and family upon the child. He held that the father's self control and the process of educating himself served to teach the children.

Eventually there arose the importance of child rearing process in educational psychology. Stress was laid upon such matters as training in the management of property by sharing it with the children. In India the same kind of imparting education by the father to the son was a social a practice. Moulding the son in accordance with the identity of the father —even to be absolutely identified with the son to enter into the son during death as presented in Mahabharata (ref. Bidur —Judhisthir story) is an example of the same process. That is, in fact, the essence of patriarchal society. In Arya Society in

India, however, education was confined to a particular stratum or class, whose formal education started only at the age of 12 after a formal initiation, who became Brahmmacharins. They were totally separated from the family for a particular period of life—sent to the Guru's (i.e. teacher's) Ashram, where they were trained to acquire various skills and given special trainings to lead life and later to attain self realization, the ultimate aim of education. The concept of mind and its training was more of philosophical nature, than of psychological one.

Much later, psychology replaced philosophical concept after a great deal of research work carried on throughout the nineteenth and twentieth century. Other great names in the field of education of classical period in West were Socrates, the epitome of education, followed by Plato and Aristotle. They were gems of post-Socratic period dating back to fourth century B. C. From Plato and Aristotle onward we got glimpses of modern education and its relation to psychological factors. Scattered throughout their works Aristotle and Plato discussed the following issues such as, (as compiled by Lindgren, 1965) "the ends of education, the ideals of the educated man, the disadvantages of being educated, the kinds of education that are appropriate to different kinds of people, the training of the body and the cultivation of bodily skills, the formation of a good character, the possibilitics and limits of moral education, the influence of the family in the training, the role of the state in moral education, the effect upon character of music, poetry and other arts; the profession of teaching and the relation of teacher and students, the means and methods of teaching; the nature of learning; the order of learning, the emotional aspect of learning; learning apart from teachers and the acquisition of techniques." (Lindgren, 1965).[1]

Almost the same kind of educational system was operative in ancient India and we see the greatest teacher Krishna teaching the most obedient disciple Arjuna in Gita and imparting the kind of education embodying the ethos of Indian social thoughts and Indian idealism.

Aristotle's psychological views relevant to the educational matters are presented more systematically, logically and in

1. Lindgren, Henry, Clay : A brief History of Educational Psychology. John Wiley and Sons Inc. N. Y. 1965.

greater details than as forwarded either by Socrates or Plato. Aristotle's views encouraged the working of faculty psychology and emphasized more of intellectual and rational processes than the emotional ones. Aristotle laid the foundation for the main psychological doctrines taught and accepted by the learned world for the next two centuries to come. They were subsequently modified by the later psychologists throughout the developmental period of history of educational psychology.

In the hands of seventeenth century philosophers, specially Descartes, mind was equated with innate ideas which did not arise from experience, rather the ideas are considered as the basis of true knowledge. The scientific character of psychology remained a doom at that period. But very soon John Locke, in the same century, renowned as empiricist, initiated the first wide and continued protest against the form of faculty psychology current in his time. He argued that the faculties do not function by themselves, knowledge is gained when the mind becomes functional as it comes in contact with the external environment. At birth the human mind does not perform but is potentially sensitive to impressions from outside through the senses. "Through the empirical process of experience he receives sensory experiences from which simple experiences are built into complex ideas, through the internal activity of reflection, and ideas".... They arose from sensory impressions and from the processes of reflection. Thus arise all knowledge, all values, all learning. This learning by experience come to be known as empiricism.

The interactional processes between one's self and environment involved in learning laid the foundation of modern psychology—the non–faculty point of view turned into behaviouristic character. And psychology—instead of being defined as science of mind (psyche+logos)—achieved a scientific status and, finally, came to be defined as the science of human behaviour.

Modern psychology, a science of behaviour like all other sciences, has its origin in the feeling of curiosity of the primitive man. His curious inquiry about the nature and its events ultimately gave rise to physical and biosciences of modern age. The same curiosity about his own thinking, feeling and willing, dreaming and imagining gave rise to an inquiry into the menfal process, which gradually helped the emergence of the science of psychology. According to the modern definition of psychology, mind can be analysed functionally into different mental processes—cognitive, conative and emotive and is expressed through behaviour of the interacting person. Hence psychology is a science of behaviour.

Psychology emerged as a scientific discipline as and when Withhelm Wundt—the founder of experimental psychology—established the first psychological laboratory at Leipzig in Germany in the year 1879. From that time onward the learned world witnessed a host of renowned psychologists working in different aspects of mental performances and a long intellectual pursuit of psychological discoveries ensured. This led more and more to the application of theories, branching, specialization, specification of methods as well as more and more qualitative and quantitative sophistication of techniques. One such branching encompasses the educational field and has been termed as Educational Psychology which emerged as a separate discipline, involving the general principles of experimental psychology applied in the field of education. A great name in the history of educational thoughts in the early 19th century was Pestalozzi who psychologised education by emphasizing upon 'education' as a process of drawing out the functional mind of the individual.

The next great advance in educational psychology came about mid–nineteenth century when Johann Frederich Herbart, a German professor, formulated an approach to education based directly and avowedly upon psychology. From the end part of nineteenth century till the beginning of twentieth century a number of famous psychologists started working in different lines of education applying the principles and techniques of general psychology. Among them mention may be made of Francis Galton, the oldest of the founders of educational psychology. He conducted the first experiemental investigation of associationism, tests on reaction time and sensory acuity. Stanley Hall, meanwhile, published his papers using the questionnaire to investigate the minds of children. In 1885 Ebbinghans published his study on memory and, within the span of six years, events of importance like objective measurement, child psychology and learning experiments, all took place.

To add to the list enriching the movement was Galton's studies on nature-nurture problem, mental inheritance of ability, studies of twins, widespread realizations of individual differences in the psychological sense, various mental and physical developments as well as use of psychological tests and their statistical interpretation (particularly the correlational studies which was later followed by Karl Pearson), rating scales and questionnaires. "His most important theoretical contribution was the distinction in the 'Structure of mind' between a general broad ability of intelligence and special abilities entering only into narrower ranges of activity" (ibid).

The next major contributor to the foundation of educational psychology was Alfred Binet in the field of intelligence testing. With assistance of Theophile Simon, he developed the first Binet Scale. Then comes John Dewey whose contribution is rather noteworthy in the field of educational philosophy than in the general psychological field. After Dewey, from the year 1900 to some ten or twelve years more, educational psychology remained more or less in incubation till Edward L. Thorndike came out with his revolutionary 'laws of learning'. He was possibly the first man to be called an educational psychologist in the modern sense of the term. He studied the art and science of learning very systematically and consistently. Then joined Woodworth with Thorndike and together they worked on transfer of training at the turn of the century. Thorndike then published three volumes of Educational Psychology between 1913-14 consisting of his original work arising from experiemental research. His studies in various related fields of education opened up new vistas to be treked by later educational psychologists.

Scope of the field

Educational psychology embraced over the years various fields of education e.g. intelligence testing, mental abilities, achievement testing, child psychology, developmental psychology, school performance, mental deficiency, curriculum, personality, character, educational measurement and so on and so forth. In 1910, the Journal of Educational Psychology was first published, to reveal experimental researches on various psychological issues regarding education and their interpretations.

In the recent past the field of educational psychology has become more complex as the vision of what it encompasses has broadened. Originally concerned with learning and measurement its scope has been extended with each succeeding generation to the point where now the newest extension is in social-educational field and a new branch emerged in educational psychology known as educational social psychology (Lindgren, 1965).

In conclusion, we may note that the aim of educational psychology is to apply psychological concepts and principles in order to improve educational practice. Educational psychology that has evolved as a new discipline tends to represent all the areas within psychology in general. These include some distinct areas dealing with human development, individual difference in ability, aptitude and temperament, perception, motivation, learning, thinking, problem-solving, psychopathology, the dynamics of personality and group interactional processes.

The educational scientists have employed two strategies for applying psychology in education. Consequently, two kinds of researches had been advanced in the field of educational psychology; the first is the direct experimental investigation of learning in laboratory and school settings. The second has been an attempt to distil from basic psychological research the educational proceedings to be employed in teaching-learning situation, implication of learning in its broader perspective (formal and informal learning), and also human nature and its interactions. In this process educational psychology deals not only with the individual's own psychology and its functioning, but also an awareness of his interacting counterpart, the changing environment—both physical and social.

Any educational endeavour is actually a learning situation; the task of educational psychology is to study the learner in that situation. The first learning situation outside the family a child (or a learner) encounters is the school, which is again teaching-learnin, condition oriented. The teacher's duty in this setting is to apply the general propositions received from psychology and apply them in the classroom. But not one single strategy employed so far had yielded any fruitful result. A more practical oriented strategy is required in order to synthesize the learner, the teacher the instructional techniques and the educational managers on the one hand and producing qualified students to meet the demand of the day, on the other.

The world we live in today is shaped to a considerable degree by the decisions people make—individually and collectively. Any decision–making needs possessing some knowledge and use them in solving problems. In other words, the kind of perceiving, thinking and evaluating that goes into the problem solving has to be considered. Historically, possession of knowledge and its utilization are learned during the developmental years of the children through interacting with parents, employers, religious and political leaders as well as teachers in the classroom. The interaction with the teachers is no less important in the process of our lifelong learning even if the exposure to school be brief and transitory (this is stated considering the number of dropouts at the school level in our country). It has an impact in their lives, nevertheless.

Specially in the developing countries like India and South Asia the involvement of young people with teachers and schools is certainly increasing as revealed by survey reports at Governmental level for the last two decades. Teachers do.play an active role in the teaching–learning system. It will not be unreasonable to say that the kind of future we and our children will experience is influenced more by teachers than by any other professional groups.

The world of tomorrow will be shaped not only by what today's children are learning from their teachers, but also by the 'way' they are learning it, for it is the way knowledge is presented that determines how children will learn to solve problems. Thus according to Lindgren (1980)[2], the 'how' of teaching includes not only teaching methods, but also teachers' attitudes and values, and full range of teachers' classroom behaviours. They serve as 'models' whose way of thinking, behaving, attitudes, advice and manner, the process of acquiring and imparting knowledge are imitated in more ways than they can imagine. Hence they are influential far beyond their immediate awareness. Therefore, it is necessary that the teachers know consciously their personal psychology in order to understand the psychology of their students.

2. Lindgren, H. Educational Psychology in the Classroom. Sixth Edition; Oxford University Press. N. Y. 1980.

What is Educational Psychology ? A text book point of view

Educational Psychology may be defind as the study of the human mind and behaviour with relation to teaching-learning process (Magoon and Garrison, 1976)[3]. Educational Psychology involves all the people who learn and help learning, teach and help teaching. Hence educators, psychologists, teachers, learners, parents and friends, workers and bosses, relatives and associates all form part and parcel of this process, because all of us try to learn and teach. We learn nearly all our life and watch others learn. We try to teach each other, trying to arrange conditions to achieve success in life. In the process we try to modify in same way our aims and objectives, beliefs, values, attitudes, aspirations, practices and skills. Sometimes we do it unaware and, therefore, fail to approach in a systematic and effective way. But when the same thing is being done consciously and with a voluntary effort the process becomes professional and sophisticated—teaching becomes institutionalized. But the classroom, in spite of undergoing a conscious formal processing, is not immune to the deficiencies mentioned above. As we inquire and wonder "why" such things happen even when we follow a set rule, there remains the scope to discover what other kinds of arrangements have a greater probability of success. "This is what texts in educational psychology are about" (Anderson and Faust, 1973)[4]

Educational psychologist believes that the answer to such "why" question can be given with a thorough knowledge of the psychological principles underlying all learning activities. So, how does psychological inquiries contribute to education is the theme of educational psychology. The psychologist observes systematically about the traditional educational practices and ideas, their strength and weaknesses, and improve upon them, if necessary. They evaluate methods and techniques, offers concepts for the teachers and curriculum-makers to consider while framing plans. That endeavour helps the educator to become applied scientists, who would make judgment about

3. Magoon Robert A. and Kart C. Garrison. Educational Psychology—An Integrated view. Second edition, Charles E. Merril Publishing company. Columbus, Ohio. A Bell and Howell Company, 1976).

4. Anderson, C. Richards and Gerold, W. Faust : Educational Psychology : The Science of Instruction and Learning, Dodd, Mead & Co., N. Y., 1975

values and assumptions, about taking educational decisions, encouraging use of advanced educational technology to enrich the educative process. Educational psychology as a behavioural science contributes to the soundness of both traditional and uptodate technology.

The subject matter of educational psychology, though restricted to teaching-learning domain only, is an applied field of the broader principles of psychology, which deals with human behaviour, in general. According to the behaviouristic concepts in education the term behaviour can be subclassified into such terms as exploratory, impulsive, involuntary, learned, reflexive, purposeful, emotional, patternized risk taking, reinforced, modified and shaped behaviour, and extinction of a behaviour. The aims of educational psychology are understanding, predicting and controlling behaviour in learning situations. So far as learning process is concerned, three sections of psychology contributed most in evolving the scope of it. These three styles have been distinguished as behaviouristic, humanistic and cognitive-developmental. As Cronbach (1977)[5] writes : "Behaviourism seeks to develop firm conclusions from objective evidence, and avoids discussion of internal psychological processes." This view is a product of the protest lodged by Watson long ago in the history of psychology when psychology used to be defined as the science of soul or mind, derived from the word psyche. Soon the scientists and educators realized that the mind, as such, is difficult to study, observable behaviour is more easily analyzed as a clue to person's ideas, knowledge, feelings and other inert mental processes.

Humanistic psychology emphasizes inner feelings and interpretations. Wishing to explain broad phenomena, the humanist accepts wide variety of data, including naturalistic observation. "The cognitive-developmental psychologist sees the person as actively engaging his environment, thinking about his experience, and growing as a result."

Educational Psychology—Behaviouristic aspect

All psychologists observe behaviuor of the learner. Strict behaviourist in the learning situation will only restrict his observation on what is seen, and what can be recorded

5. Cronbach, Lee. J. Educational Psychology, 3rd, Harcourt Brace Jovanovich, Inc. N.Y., 1977.

objectively. The strict behaviourist relies only on responses given to a stimulus, where reasoning is cautious and conclusions are limited to observable behaviour; i.e. he notices only what the learner 'does' without any reference to inner mental states. "He concentrates on aspects of the situation that can be experiementally altered and controlled" (Becker et al, 1975)[6].

A major figure in the behaviouristic school is B. F. Skinner (1968, 1970)[7]. Much of his research on operant conditioning, which was carried on by his followers subsequently, was based mainly on how rewards—which he called 'reinforcers'—affect responses.

The behaviouristic emphasis is summed up in the following assumptions or working hypotheses (Cronbach, 1977, p. 20) (ibid)

* The environment can be unambiguously characterized in terms of stimuli.
* Behaviour can be unambiguously characterized in terms of responses. (After a stimulus is presented, an observer can say that the response did or did not occur).
* A class of stimuli called 'reinforcers' can be identified. (The reinforcer may be grains in the pigeon's cup or the teacher's nod of approval following the student's response to a question. A reinforcer makes the response it follows more likely in future).
* Learning can be completely characterized in terms of couplings among stimuli, responses and reinforcers.
* Unless there is definite evidence to the contrary, any type of behaviour is assumed to be learned, to be open to change when the conditions are altered, to be trainable, and to be extinguishable (in the sense that a habit can be wiped out). (Cronbach 1977), (ibid).

Psychologists in the behaviouristic tradition had had great success in dealing with some difficult practical problems.

6. Becker. W. C. Engelmann, S. and Thomas D. R. Teaching 2. Cognitive learning and instruction. Chicago. Science Research Associates, (1975).

7. Skinner, B. F. The Technology of Teaching. N. Y. Appleton-Century-Crofts. 1968—Contingency management in the classroom. Education. 1970, 83-100.

When the reinforcement conditions can be controlled and the desired outcome is definite, behaviouristic techniques can work remarkably well. But it has its weakness too. Exceptional emphasis on objective behaviour speaks nothing about the subjective aspect of experience. Behaviouristic technique may operate successfully and effectively in a research setting or in labortory condition, but broad and long term conditions are ignored by the strict behaviourist. The behaviourists hardly examine the learner's total school career—their study of learning conditions are piecemeal. Moreover, the learner's purpose and his self-fulfilment are hard to discuss in behaviouristic language. These questions were raised by the critics of behaviourism.

As a result, a second line of behaviourism emerged in the field of educational psychology which is known as neo-behaviourism. It takes up a broad range of phenomena, and does consider cognitive process. The neo-behaviourists reinterpreted the concept of learning and behaviour, expanded the usage of reinforcement. 'They recognized that reinforcement involves a subjective feeling — it provides information as well as pleasure'. A person learns to anticipate the consequences of his behaviour when learning gradually becomes complex, and he learns to change his behaviour accordingly which is more than stimulus–response connection.

Educational Psychology—Humanistic aspect

Humanistic approach is more humane, more subjective and involves more mentalistic concepts than the objectivity oriented behaviouristic viewpoint. They accept all the terms and language which are discarded by the behaviourists. Humanistic psychology is particularly interested in the inner states of mental processes, man's feelings, aspirations, motives and motivation. The humanists are very much concerned with the 'self' of the individual, his self-awareness and self-esteem. They see each person as a self-directing, integrated being, evolving in a unique direction as he interprets his experiences. Observation is also a method for the humanist, and he recognizes the subject as a self-observant. Their prime data rests on what a person says about his present feelings and recollection of past experiences. They count much on a person's image of world—take them as unit rather than breaking them up as single action into stimulus and response.

Among contemporary humanistic psychologists, one of the most eminent is Erik Erikson who based his studies of American Indian tribes and of such men as Luther and Gandhi. His famous work is on 'identity' (Identity : Youth and Crisis, 1968)[8]. The same view has been corroborated by Abraham Maslow, who took similar position, equating healthy development with "self-actualization". (Maslow 1973)[9]. The humanistic psychologists examine the human conditions in life situations and do not restrict their observations to the well-controlled conditions only. They prefer to observe the human behaviour in its natural setting at par with the traditions of natural scientists. For this they base their observations on biographical and anthropological studies of the whole culture or on interviews that examine the sources of a person's lifestyle, and even on his own introspection and reflections. They study the individual's impressions in a social context, his value judgment of educative importance and the values that he himself incorporates. The humanists have strong views about good life and good society and, within this limitation, they are permissive on an individual's self-determinism. It may sound romantic but in fact the humanistic psychologists are considered more democratic than the behaviouristic ones. The behaviourist-humanistic dialectic is alive in the minds of most educational psychologists when they plan an education system.

Educational Psychology— a Cognitive-Developmental view

The exponent of this theory is Lee. J. Cronbach. He explains his theory first by analysing the terms involved. The first one, i.e. cognitive part, "stresses the active 'intellectual' functioning of the person. The second stresses that behaviour develops in a 'cumulative fashion'. Any behaviour means not only a reaction to the present circumstances but the past experiences are equally important to constitute such behaviour. An experience when is converted into behaviour involves both cognitive and affective aspect. By 'cognitive' we mean understanding, reasoning, interpretation, and intellectual analysis—'to become acquainted with'. "Affective" is associated with emotions, preferences, interests and positive

8. Erikson, Erik. Identity : Youth and Crisis. N. Y. Norton. 196
9. Maslow, A. What is a Taoist Teacher ? in L. J. Rubin, ed. Facts and Feelings in the Classroom. N. Y. Walker, 1973, pp. 150-67.

and negative feelings. The contrast between the two meanings is apparent so far as an experience is concerned; any experience is coloured both with cognitive and affective elements i.e. a cognitive experience is also affective in nature. The nature of cognitive behaviour changes as a person develops. Behaviour and attitudes evolve in part through encounters with the world; hence the developmental psychologists compare persons living in different conditions in their natural settings, like the humanistic psychologists. The developmental psychologists, therefore, classify children, for example, either in terms of social-class background, or in terms of age groups or in terms of parent's style of child-rearing etc. These psychologists employ sometimes standardized conditions for making age-to-age or group-to-group comparisons like that of the behaviourists. But even in doing so the internal mental processes are equally attended to by the cognitive-developmental style. For example, external behaviour plus encoding, self-criticism and identification and such other mental processes are duly considered.

Educational psychology considers all the above approaches in determining behaviour of the learners and teachers. It helps the teachers to plan their lessons, to program their instructions, to develop insight or regarding their students. The central implications of educational psychology leads us to ensure that :

(1) Behaviour is purposive—that whenever a person is actively engaged in tackling a problem-situation, learning takes place.

(2) Personality Development is cumulative—that "societal demands set developmental tasks for the person at each age level. These generate needs that provide the core of motivation" (Cronbach, 1977) i.e. motivations are culturally determined which are constituents of personality.

(3) Abilities are expressed through behaviour which enable the persons to acquire new knowledge through intelligence where concepts, techniques and attitudes work together to know the unfamiliar.

(4) Educational psychology helps teaching to be scientific, technical and professional.

It is true that the essence of teaching involves emotions, values, instantaneous judgement, and intuition which science cannot provide, because these cannot be standardized. But teaching is also a skill, which can be improved through application of scientific techniques. Some new techniques have been directly inspired by research on behaviour. A good example is computer-aided instruction. The rationale for computer-assisted instruction rests in part on the principle of feedback or reinforcement. Clear-cut signals about the appropriateness of responses shape response patterns. The first developments were programmed instructional materials in printed forms. Nowadays the computer offers considerably better flexibility than the printed page—a technologically controlled education.

(5) Decision making, problem solving can be made easy with the application management models forwarded by modern technology (e.g. 'automated' vs informate' model).

This chapter encompasses following concepts in order to introduce educational psychology as a discipline :

Educational research
Educational technology
Computer-assisted instruction
Value judgements
Behaviourism
Behaviour control
Reinforcer
Neobehaviourism
Humanistic psychology
Cognitive-Developmental Style
Cognitive/affective.

Aims and Objectives of Educational Psychology

Let us start this section with Gordon Allport's caution : "One aim of education is to make available the wisdom of the past and present so that youth will be equipped to solve the problems of future".

The general aims of educational psychology, as stated before, are understanding, predicting and controlling behaviour in learning situations. As the learning situation includes, teacher, learner, classroom environment and evaluation of their interactions, therefore, each objective can be separately treated. The aims are closely related with the functional aspects of educational psychology. Hence the functional objectives are :

(1) To evaluate educational theories and put to application the workable part of it;

(2) To examine contemporary educational practices and suggest the modifications required;

(3) To critically examine and evaluate contemporary teaching methodology in the light of established principles of learning and motivation in varying conditions of different cultures, different environments and different facilities provided.

(4) To provide methods for researchers who are scientifically studying educational problems.

(5) To assess and modify the principles and practical operations according to the set values, beliefs and attitude of a culture and also to maintain the scope for the changes with time.

In order to point out the aims of educational psychology it is better to remember William James, who—as early as 1898—put an important question in psychology; "What we are about"? Educational psychology should provide such answer to this question as it is through learning, through experiences a behavioural change occurs and makes a man what he is. Educators not only look to educational psychology to learn "what we are" about, but also to learn "what we should be about" in education tomorrow—it is not only to 'be' but to 'become'.

But to achieve it, is a hard task. The world is changing so fast that parents and teachers now see that tomorrow is not a photocopy of yesterday, present is not the replica of the past; learning of their time is totally different from that of nowadays. We need an image of tomorrow's society while teaching today and in framing the aims our image must include the likelihood of radical changes—changes that we are today unable to comprehend. Because the changes that are likely to occur in possible future is not one-sided, not singular, but plural, many-sided and global. Subject to the choices we would make innumerable arrayed options (Magoon, 1976, page 5, ibid) where some lines of development are more likely than others. An eye to this will help the educators to frame future sensible goals at present time. The sensible goals signify that the development of personality or constant individual growth must take into consideration the meaning and purpose of human life. The educationists who set the goals should remember and realize that the homo-sepiens, though primarily animals, are most advanced forms of life. Neither are they to regard people as machines, just a little higher or lower than the computer. Bell (in Magoon, 1976, pp-5) states. "A major task of psychology of the future is to help humans learn how to learn and discover, perhaps to help expand the human potential".

The identification and proper statement of the educational objectives of a lesson is the most important step in instructional planning. When a teacher knows where he is reaching, what is his specific objective, he will be able to decide how he will be designing a lesson. Therefore, getting a clear statement of educational objectives is the first step in the systematic application of psychology to education. The setting of goals in terms of objectives i.e. to understand, to predict and to control behaviour is the behavioural objectives for the teacher. The first behavioural objective for the teacher is understanding the terms "understanding" and "knowing" and these are the key ones of the various educational objectives. While setting instructional materials the teacher should analyse the objectives in behavioural terms, like knowing, understanding and recognizing the importance of the materials presented. Therefore, in setting up educational objectives, the objectives are to be interpreted in such behavioural terms as :

1. Specific statement of properly stated objective.
2. Differentiating between properly stated and improperly stated objectives.
3. Expressing educational goals in terms of behaviourally stated objectives. (Anderson & Faust, 1973)

The test for whether a person—child or adult—"knows", or "understands" a concept means whether he talks or acts appropriately—appropriate to the statement made. In the same way to test whether the person understands a statement made for him, one must witness the fact, watch him talk and act accordingly when confronted with the test situations, or when circumstances arise in the natural course of events. Therefore, a teacher, when imparting a concept to a student, must check all the aspects of concepts—translate them into behaviour (behavioural concepts) and then test his range of understanding (behavioural objective).

The educational objectives, then, help the educator in deciding what is required to evaluate a person's understanding which is in essence, identifying those tests he wants his students to pass after instruction. Such understanding will also pinpoint the 'skills' and 'knowledge' which are involved in the process of understanding. Teaching these are the educational goals interpreted as proper form for statements of educational objectives, whereas instructional objective is to teach a concept or to teach an understanding of a concept. For example a concept of addition involves many things. "An 'understanding' of addition could be broken down into an understanding of part-whole relationships (Objective I), a 'Knowledge' of the sums and columns of rows and numbers (Objective II), an understanding of word problems involving addition (Objective III) and so on". (ibid) Breaking down the objectives into more specific statements removes some of the vagueness, so that objectives are stated behaviourally, in terms of what student is to say or do – in terms of student's behaviour. (for detailed programming the reader may consult "Educational Psychology. The Science of instruction and learning". By Richard C. Anderson and Gerald W. Faust. Dodd, Mead and Company N. Y., Toranto, 1975.)

Teacher's Objectives

The central theme of all education is learning, and the teacher's objective is to guide and stimulate pupils in their educational growth. The teacher should look into the conditions needed for effective learning and its method of application. The main behavioural objective of the teacher is to understand the characteristics of children and adolescents and the basic principles of learning, knowledge about the subject matter and bring all these knowledge into the classroom. Each child comes to the school equipped with experiences gathered from his environment in his own way and peculiar to himself.

He uses his experiences so gathered to accumulate variety of them which he uses again to interpret his new environment and new experiences. Schooling should help them to reshape their concepts whenever necessary so that they may be helpful to reinterpret them in social context, thereby broadening existing concepts, developing new skills, acquire new attitudes and reorganize behaviour. This is how enriched learning takes place.

Today student-teacher objectives are often expressed explicitely as outcomes or learning. Such objectives generally include subject matter, knowledge, and learning-oriented attitudes, appreciations, interests and skills. The main and most important teacher's objective is to help children acquire behaviour patterns that contribute to effective living.

Methods

Educational psychology—being a behavioural science—uses scientific methods of behavioural research. The commonest of all the methods is observation. Educational psychology uses observation not as common–sense view sees it. It uses systematic observation which equates methods with research in the educational field and is also scientific in character. As such, the subject matter of educational psychology is human behaviour and every one can observe behaviour. But educational psychology avoids subjective observation and employs the method objectively to evaluate behaviour and its modification which is a product of learning. An educational psychologist adopts systematic, objective and investigative measures in assessing the effects of learning in the pupils. Such in-depth scientific probes are necessary if we are to explain, predict and control behaviour with any acceptable degree of accuracy. This is in short, scientific observation.

Educational research depends on the use of scientific method which need to follow five steps for its investigation. These steps are :

(1) Formulating the problem,

(2) Stating the hypotheses,

(3) Collection of data from respective fields,

(4) Testing the hypotheses,

(5) Interpreting and reporting the findings, and

(6) Applying the findings. Researches in educational psychology can be conducted in the classroom, in the laboratory or in the outer field as is necessary.

Laboratory research has sometimes been referred to as pure research, while that conducted in the classroom is known as applied research.

The use of scientific methods in educational psychology has produced profound changes in organization and management of school, curriculum, syllabus making, learning materials, audio-visual aids, effective lesson planning and instruction methods. A number of scientific teaching methods have been tried out in the classroom researches to get effectiveness in teaching e.g. discovery method, the learner-centered method, the Socratic method, the project method, the laboratory method or the tutorial method—based upon various conditions with various subject matters and with various kinds of students.

The description of these methods are not discussed in this book, because all these methods have been tried out and tested and gradually renovated to fit into the changing structures of ongoing educational systems at different times and in different kinds of educational institutions. However, the detailed descriptions will be available in books on research methodology—which deal with the introduction, improvement and either rejection or retention of a particular method or combination of them as required by the teacher while imparting instruction. The researchers also use the methods in order to reach to any conclusion following a hypothesis or an assumption they adopt.

CHAPTER III

Growth and Development

A probe into the process of growing up of the children reveals that growth and development is, in fact, a psycho-physical study of the child right from the conception and following prenatal stages before birth through various stages after birth to the stage of post adolescence. The approach of the study is chronological.

Development

When a new baby is born in the family, it is all amusement in that home. According to Gita to exist which did not exist before is known as birth. To be born is an amazing event and to grow is challenging. As soon as a child is born he/she starts undergoing a developmental process in continuation with the life process. It is the beginning of another life process. The study of this growth process is equivalent to the study of childhood and child psychology.

Childhood and Child Psychology

Learning Objectives (From Gibson, 1978)[1] :

This chapter deals with

1. Describing some characteristics of the period of childhood in terms of the importance of development.
2. Identifying the major societal factors that affect child development which are important to the psychologists.
3. Selecting method of research for understanding growth and development of the child.
4. Consideration of ethics and non-ethics in child study.

If we want our nation of the 21st century to be prosperous and advanced and consisting of happy, healthy youngsters and adults, it is essential that we have insight into the factors that contribute to sound development. As the children grow

1. Gibson, J. T. A study of children. Addison Wesby Publishing Co. Inc. N.Y .1978.

the various types of developments present unique opportunities to respond to them in ways that can either deter or facilitate healthy growth—both physically and mentally. By discovering how we can help children learn to use their bodies, to think effectively and to solve problems, to develop healthy attitudes, productive interests and to interact successfully with others would lead to their becoming useful, happy adult citizens of tomorrow.

Urie Bronfenbrenner stressed the importance of studying children when he asked the question "How can we judge the worth of a society? On what basis can we predict how well a nation will prosper" ? His own answer was "the concern of one generation for the next". (Bronfenbrenner[2], 1970). But ironically our misled concern led us to as the Oriya Poet writes in his poem "The Making of Man" (Translation from original Oriya and selected by Jayanta Mahapatra in The Telegraph magazine, Sunday number dated 21st May 1995.)

All of us together build children
Parents shower affection
Children become orphans
Teachers teach,
Children become illiterates
Government provides employment,
Children become unemployed
Priests give sermons
Children become fanatics
Leaders talk patriotism
Children become terrorists
All of us together build men.

These predictions are satirically presented with respect to the present state of the socio-political conditions. If the future needs to be brighter it is time for the educational psychologists to orient their views, methods and techniques to review the developmental processes of the child. Psychologists today are more aware than ever of the importance of early development and its influence on the later life experiences. So it is necessary

2. Bronfenbrenner, U. " Two Words of Childhood" N. Y. Russell Sage Foundation, 1970, p-3.

to look into the developments of various aspects of growing and also the development of effective behaviour of the children from infancy and childhood through adolescence to adulthood.

Growing of a child means progressive changes in body size, getting stronger and heavier than the earlier stage of development, change in behaviour, becoming more and more capable of making intricate responses and solving more and more complex problems. Gradually the child's response pattern changes, develops different sets of attitudes, interests and abilities at different stages of life. All these changes take place as people age through a series of progressively more complex stages. This fact is known as 'maturation' in the developmental terms. Another aspect related to maturation is known as 'learning'. Both of these together influence the process of development.

Maturation

Some changes that take place with age are due simply to our biological inheritance and to the fact that we belong to the homo-sapien group i.e. we are human beings and this differentiate us from all other living creatures. Whatever the environment, a sapling will grow into a tree, a puppy grows to be a dog and a baby will become adult human being. This development is controlled by the genetic materials contained in each cell of our bodies and is sure to take place independent of the varieties of environmental influence in which they grow. The steady development that takes place in spite of the interaction with the environment and regardless of outside influences—which is more or less same for everyone—is termed "maturation". Maturation affects all types of development, behavioural as well as physical. Child psychologists have shown that many behaviours develop through matu-ration. The ability to walk, to speak, to communicate, to think and perform other cognitive functions, to express normal human emotions and to socialize at large are all products of maturational process with minimum learning experience.

Learning

At the same time, from the instant of conception, the developing individual is interacting in certain ways with the environment. When interaction between the child and the outside world leads to changes in behaviour—"learning" takes place. Humans are capable of very simple forms of learning even before birth (Spelt, 1948).[3]

It is extremely difficult, therefore, for the psychologists to determine which behaviours are due to maturation and which to learning. It has been generally agreed upon that maturation and learning are closely interrelated and jointly they exercise their influence on child's development into adult. This interrelationship between these two processes explains the individuality of human behaviour.

A good many researches have been carried on in order to study the effect of maturation only with the identical and fraternal twins, from early twentieth century by Gessell and Thompson, (1929)[4], Strayer (1930)[5], Hilgard (1933)[6] and others.

Maturation helps the developing child to make new kinds of behaviour. Some new behaviours are self-generated. These are called "autogenous" behaviours, which seem to appear spontaneously without preparation or practice. They are also limited to very simple skills. But more complex behaviours need proper maturation as well as special learning experiences. The authors (Stone and Church, 1973)[7] have described the relationship between maturation and learning as : "being in a circular relationship—each feeding into the other". Maturation, in fact, can be termed as a state of "readiness" for the appearance of new and more complex behaviours. In some cases e.g. learning, readiness is the maturational point when the child would be able to make new responses provided he gets suitable learning aids. We call this point as readiness to learn. According to many psychologists children cannot learn until they are ready. But in order that he can make more complex

3. Spelt, D. The Conditioning of Human Fetus in Utero. J. of Experimental Psychology, 38 (1948) 338–346).

4. Gessell, A and H. Thompson, "Learning and Growth in identical an experimental study by the method of co-twin control". J. of Genetic Psychological Monographs. 6 (1929 : 1 – 124).

5. Strayer, L "Language and Growth : the relative efficacy of early deferred vocabulary training studied by the method of co-twin control". J of Genetic Psychological monopgraphs 8 (1930 : 209-219).

6. Hilgard, J "The effect of early and delayed practice on memory and motor performances studied by the method of co-twin control". J of Genetic Psychological Monographs. 4 (1933 : 493 – 567).

7. Stone, L. and J. Church. : Childhood and Adolescence N. Y. Random House, 1973.

responses he needs proper training at the ready-stage of development.

There appears in the maturational process of development some critical or sensitive periods—a fact that the developmental psychologists observed, during which learning new behaviours first becomes possible. They also are of opinion that certain interactions with the environment are required during these critical periods. If appropriate interaction does not take place at this time, the development may either be slowed or gradually stopped. In other words, there are more favourable or less favourable periods in the development of learning different skills, as for example, learning of vocabulary will be more facilitated if the child gets attention and praise during early developmental period of language development and would show amazing skill, whereas a child deprived of it will grow as an introvert and shy of speaking freely. Learning deprivation occurs when caretakers do not provide a child with suitable attention. Certain other types of deprivation during critical periods of development can actually cause permanent damage, such as problems due to socio-economic condition of the parents, religious, ethnic and racial backgrounds. And, more seriously, severe protein malnutrition at early ages can lead to irreversible retardation.

Next, we shall discuss the principles governing the development in general, as presented by different developmental psychologists.

Principles of Child Development

Development does not only see behaviour of any individual child at a particular stage, but also looks into the involvement of all people concerned with the development of the child. It is not only that a child grows and changes his behaviour but it is also necessary how other people around him look at the child's growing up and reconcile with his behavioural changes at each stage. The principles listed below govern all aspects of development—physical, sensory-motor, cognitive, mental, behavioural development as well as social-emotional development etc. The following principles will help the adults around the child to perceive him and his behaviour in the process of development, which at times seem inexplicable to the adults surrounding him.

1. Development proceeds qualitatively from simple to complex

In order to understand this principle, it is first necessary to distinguish between "growth" and "development". All organisms including the humans increase in size as they grow older. Their responsive behaviours also increase in number as time passes on and life situations vary. This is an index of quantitative change and is called growth. These quantitative changes accumulate to form a noticeable change of behaviour pattern—a qualitative change from earlier to the present set of behaviour, which is termed development—a noticeable difference in the pattern of the same behaviour will be marked at this stage. Development progresses qualitatively from simple to complex, from reflexive to habit formation, from unsteady to bold and stable ones. The growth and developmental process starts at the prenatal stage, as and when a single–celled organism at conception grows and develops to a highly complex body structure along with variety of functions. The process by which it takes place is known as development. It continues after the baby is born up to maturational limit.

2. Development proceeds from general to specific

As the child develops, his behaviour becomes more and more intricate and complex leading towards specificity. In the beginning his behaviour remains mass and undifferentiated—a general response to all stimuli. But gradually they get differentiated and specific response is elicited to specific stimulus. For example, the child at birth expresses only three kinds of behaviour—they lie and rest on the bed, they sleep and they cry when they are hungry. The baby again cries when he is uncomfortable due to bed-wetting or something else disturbing him. Gradually this crying response becomes time-specific when he is hungry at intervals. His crying responses due to uncomfortable feeling becomes different from the earlier ones due to the presence of an unfamiliar face or remaining alone in the bed and so on, thus indicating this awareness of making different responses to different stimuli. This happens because development has taken place and the child's behaviour proceeds from general to specific. Again, a baby makes general arm movements long before specific responses for reaching objects. These are the examples of behavioural development. Even in terms of physical development, as the cells of the body change their character, specific kinds of tissues with specific functions are developed — skins, bones, blood etc. Same thing happens during the child's language development.

3. Development proceeds directionally

"The cephalo-caudal" principle refers to the fact that development (as well as growth) always proceeds directionally from head to foot. We see this principle demonstrated in physical growth simply by comparing the changes that take place in the comparative sizes of different parts of the body. At birth baby's heads are large in comparison to the rest of their bodies. As children grow older, the rate of growth increases in the lower extremeties of the body. As this occurs, the head gradually begins to look smaller in relation to the rest of the body.

The other direction in which the body develops is known as "proximo-distal" fashion i.e. it proceeds from areas closest to the central nervous system outward to the extremities of the body. Therefore, arm muscles develop before finger muscles.

4. Development continues throughout life

Development is more or less a continuous process with spurts at some stages. The changes that are controlled by the developmental process are orderly and tend to occur in an unvarying sequence. Therefore, the major changes are, more or less, predictable. Everybody can be expected to sit before standing, to stand before walking Havinghurst (1952)[8] . Other psychologists tried to present some "developmental tasks" of life according to the chronological sequence. According to Havinghurst, each of the major periods of life involves some of the important physical, cognitive, social and emotional tasks which are to be mastered at the proper and accepted developmental stage of the whole life span.

Since development is continuous, what happens at one stage influences all ensuing stages. People change as a result of maturation and experience. Psychoanalytic theorists have pointed out great importance of the experiences the child

8. Havinghurst, P. "Developmental Tasks and Education" 2nd Ed. N.Y. Longman-Green, 1952.

receives in the first year of life. Particular emphasis has been laid on maternal affection he/she gets at that period, the lack or loss of which can be expected to exhibit predictable social problems in later stages of development. It is necessary. therefore, to study the facts of child development in order to understand the behaviour of the adults.

Although the development is continuous and one stage merges gradually to the next one and sometimes are overlapping in character, still development sometimes seem to be discontinuous and saltatory. This happens because development varies from age to age for any given child. For some, it is not very smooth and gradual. Sudden spurts in development appear from time to time, especially during the first two years of life and at puberty. A sudden noticeable change appears at some stage which is entirely different from the previous stage. Taking the first step for walking is such a change, which is an amazing and very satisfying sight for the mother. The rate of development also varies from child to child. Any two children born at the same time can be expected to differ somewhat as to their height, weight or levels of sensory and motor development and so on. This means that each child is unique and tends to grow and develop as per his/her own rate and characteristics. The rate of development is also asynchronous, it varies as to different types of development, e.g. emotional, social or language and concept development.

Developmental Stages

There is relationship between different aspects of development, for example : there is a marked correlation between the rates of physical and mental development. Thus we can surmise that the developmental stages emerged logically from the principles outlined in previous section. According to these principles, the child develops in a systematic and orderly fashion. The concept of the developmental stage becomes most useful when it is used to describe not just one behaviour, but rather an interrelated and unifying set of behaviours associated with a given age level (Wholwill, N.Y., 1973)[9].

---

9. Wholwill, J. "The Study of Behavioral Development". Academic Press, N. Y. 1973.

Inhelder (1953)[10] calls this set of behaviours "a structural whole as opposed to any isolated pieces of behaviour". This view led the psychologists to explore broader aspects of behaviour at various stages of development and generalize the sorts of behaviour expected of children at various age levels. Consequently, some categorical stages could be labelled, as childhood, adolescence etc. along the developmental continuum. The hypothetical divisions are based on the descriptions of the sequences of changes in behaviours at those levels. It is again to be, considered that though development is a life-long process, but viewed ability–wise, each development —physical, mental, sensory-motor language, emotional or social etc. which can be measured quantitatively—ceases as the child reaches certain age level e.g. at the onset of adulthood. The post-natal stages after birth are broadly divided as infancy through childhood, preadolescence, adolesecence to adulthood which provide descriptions and sequential changes at each stage so named. For example, the term "adolescence" brings to mind a particular description and sequence of behaviours different from those of earlier stages at different age levels. Description of developmental stages are based on the "average" person's bahaviour—that is, behaviour expected of most people at any given age. Eventually, these behaviours become age related, i.e. behaviour of the particular age group. Their behaviours designate them as belonging to a particular age group known as e.g. "adolescence". Thus infancy, childhood, adolescence etc. are considered as periods of life i.e. developmental stages. They serve as a kind of concise summation of what is happening to the individuals at that point in their development. Kenistone (1970)[11] described a developmental stage between adolescence and adulthood, which he called "Stage of Youth". Youth, he believes, "is characterized by behaviour associated

---

10. (i) Inhelder, B. "Criteria of the stages of mental development". In J. Tanner and B. Inhelder, eds. "Discussions on child development : A correlation of the Biological, Psychological and Cultural approaches to the Understanding of Human Development and Behaviour". Vol. I of the Proceedings of the First Meeting of the World Health Organization Study group.

(ii) On the Psychological Development of the Child, Geneva, Switzerland : International University Press, 1953, pp. 75-96.

11. Kenistone, K . Youth : A "NEW" stage of Life! The American Scholar, Autumn, 1970 in J. T. Gibson, "Growing Up : A study of children". Addison-Wesby Publishing Company. London, 1978, pp. 68.

with tensions between self and society, pervasive ambivalance alternating estrangement and omnipotentiality".

The developmental stages are, in fact, not simply description of age-related behaviour but according to Piaget (1960)[12] the stages of development describing certain sequence of behaviour—the behaviours that gradually and predictably change in some specific order.

To summarise, we can state that development is unified and cumulative. The child's physiological maturing interacts with his experience. Thus, development has been equated with readiness.

Apart from age-related behaviour, maturity can also be rated in statistical terms, comparing an individual child's behaviour with the "norm" for his grade as the child enters school. Maturity gradually changes its concept from age-related to achievement-related behaviour. This broadens the concept of maturity and refers to the extent to which the children have mastered not only educational skills and knowledge of subject matter but also general competence, social competence, control of emotional behaviour, physical coordination and so on. The achievement-related maturational concept helps us to understand such facts as "early maturer", "physically advanced children for their age", "late maturer", "immature children" and "exceptional and bright children" etc. The extent to which the child exceeds or lags behind the developmental norms for his age tells us great deal about his behaviour. Norms refer not only to physical development but also to social and emotional development as well.

It may further be mentioned that the term maturity conveys two notions from the behavioural point of view :

(a) behaviour that is appropriate to the age of the individual concerned, and

(b) refers to the behavioural standards and expectations of adults. The maturity level, judged from these two aspects, involves an individual child's readiness to engage in "prosocial behaviours" (Lindgren, 1980)[13] like sharing, helping, cooperating, exchange of ideas

12. Piaget, J. "Psychology of Intelligence", Patterson, N. J. : Littlefield and Adams, 1960.

13. Lindgren, H. C. : Educational Psychology in the Classroom, 6th ed. Oxford University Press — N.Y. 1980.

and so on. Much depends on the kind of behaviour they see in adults. Adult models are very important in the development of child's prosocial behaviour and equally important is the role of 'role playing', 'discussion' and 'formal training'.

Developments

It has already been stated that development is a continuous process in an individual's lifetime—from his birth to maturity. After the maturational level has been reached and all developmental skills been achieved to fullest strength by the individual concerned, the small growth processes constituting the developments stop at some levels temporarily, while some of the developments continue till the individual's death. The latter ones are acquired characteristics of the individual which mature as he accumulates and renews his life's experiences.

Though the individual's development is a unified process, yet it can be analysed and differentiated into different kinds, of which five aspects can be lebelled distinctively in spite of their interelationship : Physical, Cognitive, Social, Emotional and Personality developments. Cognitive development refers to activities that involve thinking, perceiving, understanding and all mental abilities including problem-solving. All these activities can be considered "intellectual", that is, involving human intelligence. Physical development is the most basic of all and its progress can be observed and measured most readily. Physical development can be evidenced from the increases in height, weight, development of internal and external organs of the body, changes in the body build, cessation of some and revivation of certain glandular activities, development of secondary sex characteristics, loss of 'baby' teeth and eruption of permanent teeth, the occification of cartilage into bones—short and long ones, lengthening of extremities and so on and so forth. Lindgren (1980) says "physical development is basic because an individual would be able to perform all intricate activities in future involving intellectually, socially and emotionally mature behavior which depends at least in part on the development of certain neurological, glandular, muscular and skeletal structures and functions—in other words, on physical maturation" (page 78). Therefore, all the five developments need teacher's attention individually and in details.

Physical Development

As has been stated earlier, development is unified and cumulative; hence the discussion of physical development cannot be restricted only to the growing in size. Any development implies an all-round developmental behaviour pattern. Yet the study of the significance of physical growth separately is to see how much does it contribute in total personality development of a person from childhood to maturity.

Physiological maturing prepares one to profit from experience. It is important in educational psychology because biological changes—especially in the nervous system—influence what one can learn in future. Children who differ in rate of maturing have different experiences and develop different personalities.

Children grow at different rates and develop different physiques. The direct effect of these differences is seen in the child's ability to play games—solitary or cooperative. The indirect social and psychological effects are even more important, e.g. physical immaturity, poor coordination, or biochemical abnormalities can interfere with any type of social learning. The child who tires readily, for example, will have a shorter span of concentration, will be more upset by difficulty and will be less willing to persevere (Cronbach, 3rd ed. 1977)[14] .

Physical superiority helps beneficially the development of personality and it has been noticed that physically competent children gain social assurance, are more confident and have positive self-concept. The child with a slight physique or poor coordination finds himself mostly unwanted when his playmates are choosing teams. Physical strength and stature are particularly important to the boy whose personality affects all of his social relationships. Stronger boys are generally superior in spirit and appearance and more masculine which attract other people's attention. One's attitude toward one's physical endowments is an element in self-confidence at all ages. A large portion of adolescents are at some time disturbed about one or another physical characteristic. Tallness in girls, shortness in boys, fatness in either sex lead the list of causes of discontent, in general. Hence, there bubbles up a craze for

14. Cronbach, L. J. : Educational Psychology, 3rd ed. Harcourt Brace Jovanovich Inc. N.Y. 1977.

body building, preparation for good look, attractive appearance because body builds are associated with self-image.

In spite of all the facts stated above, physical superiority does not necessarily lead to superior development of personality. Sometimes the large boy is overbearing and unpopular. A relatively small adolescent who is attractive and mature may be popular among his peer group. What is most important is that the effect of a physical characteristic depends upon meaning attached to it by the person and the group.

Patterns and trends in physical growth

Even casual observation reveals that the first two and three years of development are of very rapid growth for the human organism. In order to know the characteristics of these periods of life it is important firstly to identify general principles that can adequately characterize and summarize growth and secondly, to collect normative data regarding the development of particular body parts and functions.

Viewed in its larger perspective, bodily growth occurs through approximately the first twenty years of life in humans. The entire span of overall growth period can be divided into three major subdivisions—infancy and early childhood (upto the fifth year of life), middle and late childhood (upto the age of twelve) and adolescence (upto the age of twenty or little more). Growth is more rapid and more likely to show spurts during both the infancy-early childhood period and the adolescente period than during middle childhood.

The growth systems (Physical)

The first trend that is noticeable in the early physical growth period is the increasing size of the body. Different body parts show somewhat different growth patterns relative to the age of the child. Various organ systems or tissues show respective and regular growth pattern contributing to the increase of the size. The 'body-size' category, which includes the skeleton, muscles and internal organs, show more rapid growth during the first and third developmental period of early life than in the middle childhood. The 'lymphatic system' (thymus, lymph nodes, and intestinal lymphoid mass) reaches an adult level by seven years of age and is even larger during preadolescence before the growth stops, and gradually declines. Similarly, the neural system (head, brain, spinal and intricate nervous network) is almost fully developed by the age of six. In contrast, the reproductive organs grow very slowly until adolescence, at which point their growth is propelled.

The general principle of early development is that development proceeds cephalocaudally—that is, from the cephalic or head region to the caudal or tail region. A fetus is remarkably top heavy and the neonates less so and, until middle adolescence, the proportions of adulthood is not apparent. The early growth and development shows that the functioning of the organism appears in keeping with this direction of physical growth. Infants are able to lift their heads within the first weeks of life but cannot stand until the end of the first year.

The second general principle of the development is that growth proceeds from the proximal or center axis of the body to extremities or more distal regions. This 'proximo-distal' pattern of development is also reflected in the youngster's behavioural competence.

The most intriguing facets of body growth is that there are large individual differences in the 'rate' at which growth occurs. This fact has potential implications for the development of social behaviour. All these are maturational effect of growth which takes place normally as a rule of nature.

Motor Development

The issue of motor development is important to the educational psychologists as it paves the way for later smooth learning on the part of the child. As the child grows physically he or she develops the ability to know and manipulate the environment which is also an indication of rapid growth. This type of motor development is often referred to as perceptual-motor development because it involves many complex perceptual and cognitive processes. Two general principles of motor development in a child are two closely related processes known as "differentiation" and "hierarchic integration". The term differentiation refers to the facts that the child's physical development is characterised by an increasing degree of control and specificity in its motor functions. Varieties of developed motor activities and control are manifested by the young infants very quickly during the growth process which indicate growing motor coordination. First they show good control over arm movements, then hand movements, and, finally, finger movements and so on with increased coordination, increasingly differentiated control over the exercise of other body parts. The individual movements over which the child gains mastery are then "put together" that is, 'integrated', into more complex and sophisticated organisation of behaviour. This process is called the "hierarchic integration" (Heinz Werner 1948)[15] : implying that individual parts of the child's new motor competence are integrated into larger and more coherent whole units of motor behaviour. Thus, the process of 'differentiation' leads to the process of 'hierarchic' integration to complete the growth process in the motor development.

Maturation and learning

The total physical development of a child is influenced by two factors—one maturation and the other learning or experience. The two factors, though labelled separately, as a matter of fact are interwoven to cast influence on the growing process. Maturation refers to the changes that primarily represent an unfolding of the nature of the capacities of the organism (and the species) that are at least relatively independent of special environmental circumstances, training or experience. Maturation is a concept more important than mere chronological aging. Maturation implies the changes involving improvement of behaviour from earlier to later stage of development. This means that maturation takes place automatically as an organismic process in its natural way—in a species-specific way, following two general principles of differentiation and integration. Similarly, the 'learning' factor, which is a product of experience, contributes to the environmental influence. The relative importance of the two factors need not be discussed in the present section as it has already been discussed earlier—that the processes involved in the two factors act together and contribute jointly to form new behaviours. Therefore, this dichotomy appears to be quite simple and it is an agreed fact that a child's behaviour develops through the interaction of his biological and genetic make-up as well as his social and environmental influences. Maturational and learning factors combine for the development of various kinds of behaviour in a child again through the same process of differentiation and integration.

---

15. Werner. H : Comparative Psychology of Mental Development. Chicago : Follet, 1948.

Growth indicates improved motor performances with age. Growth is more than enlargement. Parts of the body change in relative size, glands and their secretion take on new functions and innumerable changes take place in the body's microanatomy and biochemistry. Change in height and weight is most striking in early adolescence. Adolensence sees great increase in height and weight, change from childish to adult body proportions, change in the sexual organs, change in the glandular functions and change in voice. The child, in effect, acquires a new body, which can do new things and admits him to new social relationships. These biological changes extend over several years. It is customary to consider the appearance of adult sexual characteristics (primary and secondary) at the start of adolescence. This development is known as 'puberty', is dramatically signalled for the girl by the first menstruation (menarche), and less suddenly for the boy by the appearance of pubic hair and breaking of voice. The child does not leap into adolescence; the physical and behavioural changes are gradual.

As to the size, height grows rather steadily during childhood, slowing a bit before the spurt at puberty. In middle childhood, the average for the two sexes on most physical measures are about the same. In adolescence the males become taller, heavier, and stronger than females.

The second trend is the 'timing' of adolescent changes. Girls enter the adolescence cycle ahead of boys. The peak growth for the girls come somewhere between age 10 and 15 and most often at about 12—two years ahead of the average boy. The more rapid growth for girls presents special problems during Grades V–VIII. Physically, the typical girl at this time is as mature as the boy two grades ahead (Cronbach, p.153). But as growth is influenced by environmental conditions also, the rate of growth and maturing age differs from culture to culture and from country to country (due to the influence of varying climate and weather).

The third prominent trend is individual difference. Both before and after puberty, persons of the same age and sex differ markedly. Some girls enter adolescence at relatively lower age and some do not make the transition until few years later. Among boys even some high school juniors are still children—physically.

But, on an average, most traits that concern teachers have something like a 'normal distribution' following a normal statistical curve. The curves become non-normal only as students begin to bump against the upper end of the scoring scale. Both physical and mental measures are likely to have somewhat symmetrical distributions, high in the middle, when the scale is open-ended. Provided the measures of individual differences are distributed normally, two mistakes the teachers can avoid are :

(1) to consider only the deviations, i.e. individual attention to be paid just to the students who are advanced or who are behind the groups only. The normal curve warns us to consider that, superiority is as common as inferiority,

(2) To think of "superior', "normal" or "inferior" groups as distinct. Statistically considered, nearly all the qualities of the students which are of concern to the teachers have continuous distribution. The general curve shows no gaps in the height distribution, for example, separating "tall" from normal, nor even in the mental distribution, between "bright" and "normal" or "dull". Whenever exceptional children are selected for special treatment, the dividing line is arbitrary. Considerable variations remain within each group. Therefore, the teacher should be cautious to employ only statistical norms because the normal distribution is definitely a useful working concept, but not an exact law (ibid, p. 154).

The child who is advanced in some physical characteristics has a good chance of remaining above average. But, equal differences in size may not be equally important. Being 10 cm (four inches) above the average height may be much more distressing for a girl of 14 than being 10 cm (four inches) below average. On an average, though the physical growth is more or less consistent, but in spite of this consistency, some children spurt in size or strength and others grow normally. Again, illness or emotional upset may impair not only physical development but all learning and social adjustment. Despite the consistency, there are early maturers and late maturers in physical characteristics. What is of importance is that they do not differ in success per se, but they differ as persons. The personality effect in the early maturers become far smoother socially (Clausen, 1975)[16] each success adds confidence and prestige, which helps them further.

Neural Maturation

The neurophysiology and biochemistry of the brain and nervous system change as the child grows older and the changes do influence his or her performance and learning. But knowledge about the internal changes is not so readily available for us as to reach some definite conclusions about their effect. The teacher needs only to be aware of the significance of neural development and of the interpretations of the physiological findings thereupon. It is important to know that the brain changes in size and structure and permits precise control of motor responses through nerve-cell. The microanatomy also changes : nerve-cell endings branch, strengthen and lengthen, more fibers connect the trunk with the brain, and, in general, the system becomes more complexly connected. As the brain changes, new performance becomes possible, hence intellectual growth, even after schooling begins, is probably biological in part (Cronbach, p.159).

The maturational process implies the changes to be unfolding of prepatterned structure that help development, given normal health, nutrition and stimulation. Formally speaking, a maturational process is one where the 'timing' of emergence of some characteristics, and form are primarily controlled by genes (Eichorn and H. Jones. 1958)[17]. But secondarily—and no less importantly, every physical and behavioural characteristic depends to some extent on diet, exercise, material care and other aspects of environment. It is important for the educationist to note that if under normal conditions brain structures unfold in some largely predetermined manner, this should influence the timing of instruction. Neurological studies of humans establish the role of stimulation during the formative period in promoting even biological maturing. Though biological maturing is automatic, however, it becomes improved and varied when earlier

16. Clausen, J. A. "The Social Meaning of Differential Physical and Sexual Maturation". In S. Dragastin and G. H. Elder, eds. Adolescence in the lifecycle : Psychological change and Social Context. Washington D. C. Hemisphere 1975, pp 25-46.

17. Eichorn, D. H. and Jones, H. E. Maturation and Behaviour. In G. J. Seward and J. P. Seward, eds. "Current Psychological Issues" N. Y. Holt. 1958.

stimulation has been provided. Limited amount of stimulation has as much effect as massive stimulation which perhaps overload a child's behaviour. Burton White's (1967)[18] view is that the initial information-processing activities of the child are "plastic". Adjusting environment in the cradle days gives the parent a first opportunity to educate the intellect of his child.

Cognitive Development

Cognition is the general term for all processes (mental) by which a human being becomes aware of his set or environment. Cognitive activities involve thinking, reasoning, perceiving, learning, memorizing and problem-solving, i.e. the activities that can be designated as "intellectual" and the ability behind all these activities is known as cognitive ability. The cognitive activities in a child undergo a process of development. They become more and more complex as the child grows in age. The progressive changes in intellectual growth which take place from birth to adulthood are assumed to follow a definable sequence. Three main theories of cognitive development dominate developmental psychology at the moment, those of Piaget and Bruner and Flavell, which we shall discuss in the latter section of this chapter.

For considering cognitive development, we first start with the cognitive abilities based on intellect. Binet describes and defines intelligence in 3 parts—

(i) the tendency to take and maintain direction.

(ii) the capacity to make adaptation for the purpose of attaining a desired end.

(iii) the power of auto-criticism.

The first point has to do with accepting task and keeping one's mind on it. The second point contrasts intelligent behaviour with acting out of habit, with little analysis of the immediate solution. The third emphasizes that better performers prevent errors before they occur or catch them promptly when they are made.

How does the intellectual performance change? What processes enter into effective performance at various ages?

18. White B. L. "An Experimental Approach to the effects of experience on Early Human Behaviour" In j. P. Hill, ed. Minnesta Symposia on Child Psychology Vol. 1, Minncepolis Univ. of Minnesots Press 1967, p. 201-26.

How does the child master these processes ? The changes that occur in intellectual development are gradual—transition is not abrupt, though it is accepted that the stage of operational thought begins at age 11—actually it means that the stage starts around the age 11.

Intelligence, as defined by Binet, in the first part of it has motivational as well as intellectual components.

(1) The child has to be willing to try; with each added experience of pay off following a big of effort, his willingness to try is strengthened,

(2) To set his own direction, he has to visualize goals—from simple goals of childhood to more complex goals of adulthood

(3) With increasing age the child is able to think about more original goals, and he learns to point his efforts toward a goal. The second part of the definition of intelligence consists in maintaining direction and in order to operate it he must resolve a large task into intermediate tasks and give himself an instruction for each step of the journey.

The third element—"Self criticism"—likewise has both emotional and intellectual components. Emotional readiness to review one's impulses obviously grows out of relations with authority in early childhood. The intellectual component includes knowing how to recognize a good performance and knowing the difference between functional criticism and niggling perfectionism.

The second of Binet's elements—analysis and adaptation —is the centre of Piaget's theory to which we now turn.

Although Piaget is a highly original thinker, his work is a direct outgrowth of Binet's. Piaget started his work in Binet's laboratory, testing the reasoning of school children. Both were interested in why children make mistakes and in how children control their responses to reach excellent performance. Piaget watched individual children in infancy to see how more mature mental operations come into being. Piaget's interpretations have had great influence on developmental psychologists in all countries, particularly since 1960. During the same period an experimental cognitive psychology was being formulated—almost independently—mostly in British and American laboratories. These theorists described "information processing" in a language different from Piaget's, but the concepts are close to those of the developmental psychologists.

Construction of Schemata

Piaget's observation was that mental "structures" developed out of the child's physical experiences (actions). As Piaget puts it, the child gradually assembles a "construction of reality" in his mind, and uses it to interpret new events. The child experiences that an object appears, disappears and again reappears. When the same phenomena are repeated an idea of disappearance and reappearance is formed as a residue of the series of experiences. As a person gains control of physical actions he also stores up an image or "scheme"—a residue of dozens of physical performances.

Psychologists use the Greek word "scheme" (plural, "schemata") to describe the process of storing up concepts or images. A scheme is not just a label or a definition, it is "a cognitive structure which has reference to a class of similar action structures," (Flavell, 1963)[19]. Schemata are not "photographic" records—they are a combination of muscular sensations that go with the actual action. Again, scheme may be partly verbal or abstract. Scheme is used to interpret an event. When we interpret an event or an object we cannot interpret it if it is not "assimilated" first. We take in the object or event and operate on it mentally. Another process which operates in a scheme is "accommodation". When a child forms a mental structure in accordance with reality, he assimilates to form a schema; and when the existing scheme is used to build another new concept, the process of accommodation is being employed. Accommodation is Piaget's term for the process of modifying the existing scheme in order to arrive at a new one. Accommodation helps precise shaping of an object, which the child evolves in forming a correct concept. It is not always that straight experience forms a concept—a concept reaches perfection gradually. Even many basic concepts are acquired through reversible action. As for example, a round disc, when tilted, produces a round image, then elliptical, and then round again. The child experiences hundreds of time this to occur when he plays with various round objects. Hence he forms a

19. Flavell, J. H. "The Developmental Psychology of Jean Piaget". Princeton : Van Nostrand, 1963.

concept of an object independent of the sensory impressions of the present moment. His schema acquires a dynamic element. Thus the schemata (for shapes or direction or movement etc.) make it possible to grasp verbal statement or a visual impression.

Psychologists do not look on schemata as innate properties of the nervous system. They develop out of experience. Accommodation plays a large part in the evolution of ideas—ideas of all sorts. Schema helps forming concepts of any kind from geometric cencepts,. number concepts to any mathematical concept; from physical force to musical harmony, from individual agony to social relations—all are developed in a similar manner according to Piaget's theory. According to the Piagetian view 'reversibility, revisability, flexibility, changeability from egocentric fixed ideas to cooperative and sharing ideas, are all included in schemata, so that the child as he develops now knows how to visualize alternatives'.

The process of developing a scheme then has these elements : (Cronbach : pp 331) (Ibid)

* The person is repeatedly in situations that exemplify or embody the concept.
* The person acts on the objects and observes changes. He often acts in a back-and-forth manner, changing arrangements A to B and back to A again.
* The person begins to anticipate what will happen in such actions and reality confirms (or disconfirms) his expectations.
* The set of confirmed prediction rules is stored as a schema.
* When assimilation fails and some expectation is not confirmed, the person carries out further manipulations or transformations until familiarity generates a new schema.

The child develops innumerable schemata by the time he reaches 6 to 8 years of age by means of the conservation principles with respect to such concepts as number, weight, quantity or volume and shape. The reversing process can be mastered by 8-year olds. Most of his concepts are concretized by now and are less dependent on perception. A mature schema occurs and, with the help of it, he can rectify his wrong acts based on interpretations of the visual impressions. When the child reaches what Piaget calls the stage of "concrete operational thought", knowledge overrules perceptions.

Cognitive Developmental Stages : Piaget

The stages of cognitive development in a child has been best provided by Jean Piaget, a French-Swiss psychologist, who was originally trained as a biologist, but who has more than fifty years observed and analysed the behaviour of children. Piaget observed that children at all ages attempt to solve a wide range of problems they face. We shall discuss Piaget's view in details in the following section.

Born in 1896, Jean Piaget till the 1970s continued his research and published extensively on the intellectual development of children, genetics, logic and epistemology. His early education was in biology, he published his first scientific article at the age of 10. Later he was working in Alfred Binet's laboratory school in Paris, helping to standardize intelligence tests for French children. Piaget became interested in pursuing the reasons for wrong response children made to the test items, rather than in the assessment of intellectual abilities. He left the laboratory school after a short period of time and established a centre for the study of child development and epistemology in Geneva.

In course of his work on child development, his emphasis was mainly on its biological aspect and he described development as organisation, assimilation and accommodation—a process. He formulated some theoretical constructs and propositions to describe child development. Piaget (1970) indicates that individuals being active biological organisms, continuously interacts with their environments. Through this interaction they gain their knowledge about external objects, the self and self/object relationships. The infant inherits the unique capabilities of the human species. These inherited capabilities, not independently, but interacting with the environment, determine the four successive stages in development. In a very real sense developing individuals 'construct' themselves and the world around them. They do not like cameras, merely passively record what they sense. Instead they actively transform and organise sensory impressions into their cognitive structures. This is a central proposition of Piaget's continually emerging theory which he states as follows :

"....Actually, in order to know objects, the subject must set upon them, and therefore, transform them : he must displace, connect, combine, take apart, and reassemble them.

From the most elementary sensory motors actions (such as pushing and pulling) to the most sophisticated intellectual operations, which are interiorized actions, carried out mentally (e.g. joining together, putting in order, putting into one-to-one correspondence) knowledge is constantly linked with action or operations, that is with 'transformation' ....".

Since objective knowledge is not acquired by a mere recording of external information but has its origin in interactions between the subject (person) and the objects, it necessarily implies two types of activity—on the one hand the coordination of actions themselves, and on the other, the introduction of interrelations between the objects. "These two activities are interdependent because it is only through action that these relations originate. It follows that, objective knowledge is always subordinate to certain structures of action. But those structures are result of a 'construction' and are not given in the objects, since they are dependent on action, not on the subject, since the subject must learn how to coordinate his actions (which are not generally hereditarily programmed except in the case of reflexes or instincts)" (Piaget, 1970, p. 704).

The two primary mechanisms of life and growth in every organism are "organization" and "adaptation". The former relates directly to the capability of transforming and combining discrete sensory inputs into structures. As noted this "structurization" involves the organizing of two or more elements into a whole, or totality. These structures are relatively stable and enduring and not transitory. They do change with each successive stage of development of the individual's life process by interacting with the environment he faces at every stage, and he interacts intelligently and rationally. Therefore structurization is, in fact, organization of piecemeal experiences into a rational whole.

"Adaptation" of an organism to its environment requires both 'assimilation' and 'accommodation'. Piaget states : "From a biological point of view, assimilation is the integration of external elements into evolving or completed structures of an organism. In its connotation, the assimilation of food consists of a chemical transformation that incorporates it into the substance of the organism. Chlorophyllian assimilation consists of the integration of radiation energy in the metabolic cycle of a plant" (Piaget, 1970). "Accommodation", correctively, is the outgoing aspect of an operative process and denotes the modification that takes place in the individual's make-up as a consequence of environmental intrusions. For example, a child knows and comprehends the cardinal meaning of 8 and 4 (this is due to assimilation), but he must make an 'accommodation' to deal with different forms while adding or multiplying these two digits.

The fundamental processes of organisation, assimilation, and accommodation are operationally effective throughout the life-span, thus providing the essential continuity across the stage of development. Therefore, they are called 'invariant', their manifestations may change with each successive stages of development. In the Piagetian system, an individual's particular cognitive event is a product of the elements of the environment he experiences at that particular time and it becomes functional invariants of assimilation and accommodation as well as of his cognitive structures. "In turn, cognitive structures are organised and reorganised in systematic fashion from birth to maturity and form the basis for the qualitatively distinctive stages in development and the related "intelligence of the individual" (Klausmeir and Goodwin, 1971[20]).

The continuous interactions between assimilation, accommodation and adaptation are self-regulated. Piaget terms this as the construct of 'equilibration' to designate an "autoregulatory" mechanism. Piaget says : "But on all levels of development actions are coordinated in ways that already involve some properties of order, inclusion, and correspondence.... what is more important, though is that coordination of actions involves correction and self-regulation...." Thus it seems highly probable that the construction of structures is mainly the work of equilibration, defined not by balance between opposite forces but by self-regulation, that is equilibration is a set of active reactions of the subject (person) to external disturbances, which can be

20. Klausmeir, H. J. and Goodwin, William : Learning and Human Abilities : Educational Psychology. 4th ed. Herper International Edition, 1971.

effective or anticipated to varying degrees. (Piaget, 1970, pp 724-725).

Piaget views that development from one stage to another is based on the preceding constructs of one stage gradually merging to the next. This also ensures stability between and within stages. He also takes other classicators like maturation, experience of physical environment and the action of social environment into account, because maturation, according to him, influences the rate of development. The experience of physical environment includes exercise with or on objects, extracting information from the objects by means of the process of abstraction as well as the logico-mathematical experiences. The social environment includes the educational and cultural environmental experiences the individual goes through.

He views cognitive development as a continuous process of unfolding which has the following recognisable stages or levels. Piaget's stages of development followed an invariant order of succession and the structures which characterise each stage are not entirely predetermined by heredity but are also influenced by physical experience and social environment. All children, according to his theory, go through the stages in the same fixed sequential order, but chronological age at which children complete each successive stage varies somewhat.

Piaget's Developmental Stages

Stage 1 : Sensory motor stage (*approximately 0–2 years*) :

In this stage, corresponding roughly to the first two years of life, learning takes place primarily through sensing the environment, manipulating objects and other motor actions. Sensory experiences, such as light, sound, touch and taste become coordinated. By the end of the period young children's motor actions are coordinated, they can even vary their actions. During the sensory motor period, the infant also begins to organise his environment. He learns to discriminate many objects in his environment and to view them as relatively permanent—depending upon his perceptual field and therefore, this phase of development is known as "object permanence".

Though untutored by experience, the newborn infant is not completely helpless, because it is born with inherited reflexes which are the starting points of development gradually organising into sensory-motor stage. This stage is characterised by the child's acquiring sensory motor control. The principal features are : development of extensive trial and error movements; development of bodily control, and eye-hand coordination. The perceptual field is organised as object related. Visual impressions improve when the experiences are repeated. The sensory motor period has been described by Piaget in terms of 6 successive levels of development. These are :

Level I : This level is estimated to occupy approximately the first month of life of the child and involves merely the increasingly smooth and systematic use of natural reflexes. The infant is said to be engaged mostly in "reflex exercise". But even at this stage, only one month after birth, evolution towards greater sophistication can be observed. "Piaget sees evidence suggesting that there also are subtle and limited, but nonetheless genuine, accommodatory modifications in the reflex almost from the first hours of life". (Flavell, 1963)[21].

Level II : During the second stage, from the first to approximately the fourth month of life, the infant begins to display a class of behaviour called "circular reaction". It is a sequence of events consisting "first, of stumbling upon some experience as a consequence of some act, and second, of trying to recapture the experience by re-enacting the original movements again and again in a kind of rhythmic cycle. The importance of circular reactions lies in the fact that it is the sensory-motor device par excellence for making new adaptations and of course new adaptations are the heart and soul of intellectual development at any stage". (Flavell, 1963, ibid). Primary circular reactions are typical of Stage II. They are repetitive acts that center on the infant's own body; thumb-sucking, for example, is frequent in 3-4 months old infant.

Level III : At this level between the fourth to eight months of life appears "secondary circular reactions" of reflexes. The circular reaction needs the environmental events to be repeated and maintained so that coordination of two actions e.g. grasping and hearing can be achieved, supposing a rattle

21. Flavell, J. H. The Developmental Psychology of Jean Piaget N. Y. Van Nostrand, 1963.

suspended above him had been shaken to produce noise. The first coordination of vision and movement also takes place at this period. He repeats the gesture a number of times and each time the interesting result motivates the repetition.

Level IV : This level involves the time between eighth and twelfth months of infant's life when it is on the threshold of performing intelligent behaviour. Truly instrumental behaviour starts occurring at this stage and when an infant pushes the obstacle in its way to reaching an object, it is not accident now, rather an act recognized as necessary for reaching the goal. The secondary circular reactions combine to launch new behaviour which is intentionally goal directed and the first glimmer of real intelligence appears.

Level V : The fifth stage—twelve to eighteenth month—gives rise to "tertiary circular reactions". In the second circular reaction the child tries to recapture an external object by activating the behaviour that is almost a stereotyped and mechanical devise. In the tertiary circular reaction, the child seems to be exploring the relationship between action and object. The child experiments with objects in order to see, understand and pursue the novelty. The infants at this level actively search for new means through trial and error process.

Level VI : During the sixth stage—eighteen to twenty four months of age—the ability to covertly plan without trial and error experimentation emerges. This new process is "insight", the extremely important newly developed process represents the glimpse of intelligence. Therefore, this newly developed process that underlies the emergence of insightful behaviour is called "representation". In operating this process the child's search is for and appropriate solution through the manipulation of internal symbols instead of physical objects.

In summary, the six substages of the sensory-motor period describe an orderly sequence of the different stretches of terrain through which the infant passes on a journey from automatic reflexive reactions to playful behaviour efficiently coordinated with the infant's own goal and desires. It is the fumbling beginnings of the child with subsequent advances to acquire the knowledge of the world.

Now it is to be noted that the point of emergence at each stage varies with the concept, the method of instruction, the cultural group studied and so on. The periods identified by

Piaget are accompanied by the concurrent development of several important mental processes which are required for adaptive and intelligent behaviour.

If a four or five month old baby, playing with a toy ball, rolls it out of sight (say behind a pillow), he will not search for it even it is within his reach. It is as if the object has ceased to exist once it leaves his field of vision. His schema for objects at this age does not include the realisation that they are parmanent. It takes the child to complete more than one and half years to realise the permanence of an object in the field.

Even though all children leaving the sensory motor stage can undertake a series of actions to reach the goal and have attained some order in the environment, their thinking is still limited primarily to immediate sensory experiences and related motor action with minimal amount of symbolic activity.

Stage 2 : Preoperational Stage (*2-to-4 to 7 years of life*) :

This 5 years period can be called the transitional period and is rather haphazard. No clear level of stability is reached in this period. This stage is characterised by the child's learning names of objects, classifying things along a single dimension, and refining his/her sensory motor abilities. Gross relational concepts, such as bigger, older, taller, take form in this period.

A major and noticeable characteristic in the child of this period is the development and quick expansion of language. However, Piaget does not agree that the child's use of the words indicate his perfect conceptualization. The child's labelling of things is different from that of adults e.g. the word "car" is used by a child to indicate any moving vehicle like car, train, bus, truck, bicycle etc. Therefore, Piaget calls this kind of concept a 'preconcept'. Another characteristic of the preoperational child is his 'egocentricism'. He believes the world as he sees it and does not take what the adults say. In a group of children between two to four year old, they are likely to vigorously produce their own thinking in quite unrelated monologues in their own ways. Parallel play is common, yet each will be playing with his own things. The child's world centers round his own ego. Preoperational children fail to decenter i.e. they can think of objects in only one way, rather than multiple ways.

The best-known characteristic of the preoperational child as shown by Piaget with his classical experiments in this regard, is the child's inability to 'conserve'. Since a pre-operational child's thinking is closely tied to his visual perceptions, he does not conserve. He, at this stage, does not think logically (in an adult's eyes), but rather thinks intuitively on the basis of how things appear to them.

At the age from 2-4 the child is extracting concepts from experience. Words heard are associated with objects. Concepts are formed for recurring experiences. Judgements are generally intuitive and direct perceptual comparisons are accurate. Associated concepts are confused for them and, therefore, cannot react to complex situations as the situation is unanalysable for them. They draw conclusions on superficial impressions. But gradually—as he grows older and by the time he reaches 6 to 7 years of age—concrete operations, associated concepts appear and logical thinking through conservation replaces the primitive mode of thinking.

Stage 3 : The Concrete Operational Stage (*7 to 11 years*):

The period of concrete operations is characterized by an orderliness of thinking which gives rise to the ability to decenter and recognize transformation, awareness that some transformations are reversible, and, of course, a grasp of concrete conservation. Concrete operational thoughts appear at this stage. The integrated cognitive system of which Flavell writes (Flavell, 1963) "is an organized network of operations". What kind of mental work is an operation? It is an act of representation, such as adding, subtracting, multiplying or dividing. Piaget has elaborately detailed nine different groupings of logical operations which define the system of concrete operations. Piaget uses the term operations to describe cognitive actions closely organized into a strong network or system. As Flavell says, "the preoperational child operates wholly on a new plane of reality, the plans of representation as opposed to direct action".

The accomplishments of the concrete operational stage are many. Besides the ability to conserve, the child has lost much egocentricism and gains in sensitivity to contradictions inherent in his/her own thought. The child's ability to represent the world symbolically is greatly advanced, but they are unable to produce formal, abstract hypotheses. They cannot understand that possible events are not real events and thus cannot solve abstract problems.

At this stage operations performed by the child are closely connected to concrete objects and actions. Logical thinking does occur, but usually only if concrete objects are available or if actual past experiences can be drawn upon. During this period, as the child's egocentricism wanes, he becomes able to take other's viewpoint, becomes increasingly socialized. Conservation of numerousness, length, area and, ultimately, volume occurs. Additionally decentering becomes possible; he can think of multiple dimensions of a single object. The idea of reversibility is understood. The child at this stage has the ability to classify, form concepts, and to group the same object along different dimensions, for example, chickens as animals and also as cooked food. Therefore, this period in the child's life is characterized by forming concepts, concretization of objects that are perceived and manipulated. Concrete operational thoughts require that information is presented concretely. Operations at this stage can be imagined and results anticipated. Associated concepts like height and width are distinguished, that one can be moving while the other stays fixed—all these operations emerge during the concrete operational stage.

Stage 4 : Formal Operational Period (*11 years through Adulthood*) :

As the child reaches adolescence he/she enters the most advanced stage of cognitive operations. He is now able to deal with more than the concrete, real life situations of the previous stage. Beginning with preadolescence, people begin to display the ability to engage informal reasoning on an abstract level. They can draw hypotheses from their observations, imagine hypothetical as well as real events or deduce or induce principles regarding the world around them. They can think logically about abstract things—things existing only in their own mind. Even without direct experience of an object, a child of this period can construct theories and reach logical conclusions about their consequences, he now can adopt almost adult way of abstracting. Having mastered. decentralization, reversibility and now abstract thinking, the child is able to solve abstract problems, thinks logically as is observed in the fifth or sixth grade children in the elementary schools. Fully concrete operations appear during junior school period. Throughout the adolescent years, intellectual development primarily involves increasing sophistication in the handling of formal operations.

Concrete operational children approach any problem unsystematically and soon fail or give up because their chaotic approach leave them without any real clue to the answer. Formal operational children, on the other hand, handle the problem very systematically and methodically.

The Higher Mental Processes

The course of cognitive development charted by Piaget is accompanied by the concurrent development of several important mental processes which are required for adaptive and intelligent behaviour. Of these processes the important ones are mental representation, concept formation, reasoning, selective attention and memory. The central theme of Piaget's theory is the process of mental representation of the world for the child. According to Piaget, a major advance in the child's ability to represent the events mentally occurs at about two years of age, corresponding closely with the onset of preoperational period. At this time the child begins to distinguish what Piaget calls "signifiers" (internal symbols and signs) from 'significates' (the actual objects, events and actions to which signifiers refer).

Piaget distinguishes between two kinds of signifiers symbols and signs in the development of mental representation. Symbols correspond to the events that they represent and also physically : signs, on the other hand, does not resemble the object or event, but are shared by other members of the environment (e.g. formal language). Piaget argues that representational thoughts does not have its beginning in social language, but rather in private symbols which form the basis for later acquisition of language.

Development of classification skills

Inhelder and Piaget (1958)[22] indicate that children are first able to group two or more things that look alike in the same way. Later they used this in classifying ability in relating one

22. Inhelder, B. and Piaget. J. The Growth of Logical Thinking from Childhood to Adolescence. Basic Books, N. Y. 1958.

class or one member of a class to another class or another member of a class.

Kofsky (1966)[23] summarized Inhelder and Piaget's views regarding eleven "sequenced" classification skills (hierarchical classification) enabling the child to form a construct of classes that stand for an inherent relationship between them. Thus he identified 6 levels of classification skills and the following order of increasing task difficulty (Klausmeir, ibid) :

Level 1 : (a) Resemblance sorting

(b) Consistent sorting as represented by the child, matching and sorting objects on the basis of perceptible attributes.

Level 2 : (a) Exhaustive sorting, as represented by the child, separating from mixed array of all blocks sharing the same attribute.

(b) An understanding of 'someone all' relationships, as represented by the child recognizing some, but not all share the same attribute.

Level 3 : (a) A knowledge of multiple class membership, as evidenced by the child recognizing that the same triangular-shaped blocks may be grouped by size and also by colour.

(b) An understanding that the number of objects in two subclasses equals the number in the Superordinate class.

Level 4 : (a) Conservation of classes, as represented by the child continuing to associate a non-sense-syllable label with a specific geometric form in spite of irrelevant transformations.

(b) Conservation of a class hierarchy and

(c) Horizontal reclassification according to different criteria.

Level 5 : Class inclusion skills, as represented by the child answering questions correctly.

---

23. Kofsky, E. A. Scalogram Study of Classificatory Development. Child Development, 37, 191-204, 1966.

Level 6 : Hierarchical reclassification skills evidenced by the children demonstrating that in a array of four red and three blue triangular-shaped blocks, all the blocks share one attribute (shape), but that any one of the blocks has an additional attribute (colour) shared by only some of the blocks in view.

Kosfky designed 11 experimental tasks to assess the hypothesized classificatory acquisition sequence produced by Piaget and Inhelder and his results showed a general sequence of skills among children of age 4 to 9. By age 4 'resemblance sorting' and consistent sorting were demonstrated by 90% and 81% of the children, respectively. By age 5, 75% of the children demonstrated 'exhaustive sorting'. The most difficult tasks class inclusion and 'hierarchical reclassification' were passed by only 60% and 40%, representatively, of the 9 year old children. It is interesting to note in passing that the sequence of attainments is of more interest in terms of developmental stages than the age at which any skill is attained.

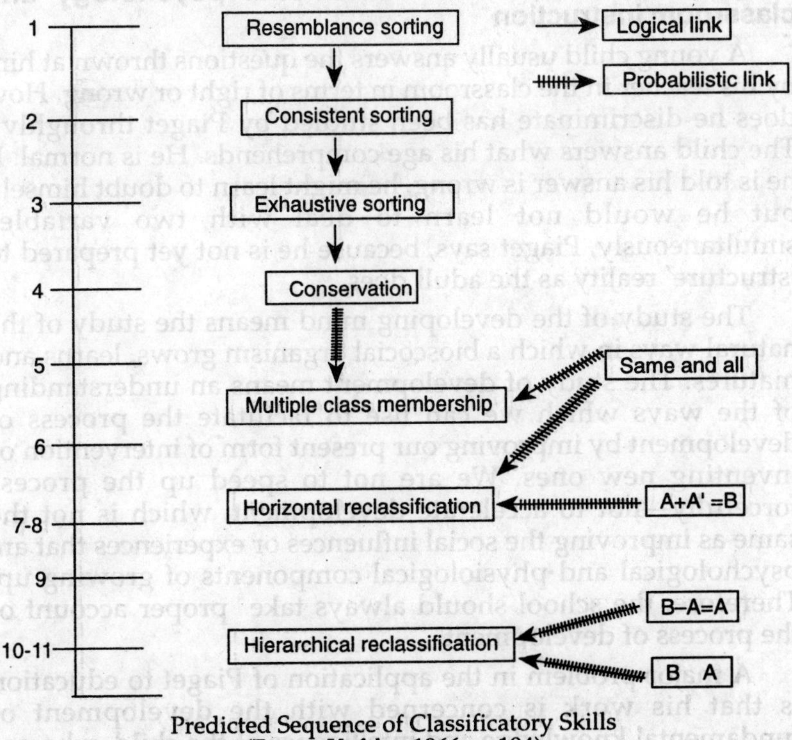

Predicted Sequence of Classificatory Skills
(From : Kofsky, 1966, p. 194)

Here we conclude by mentioning the classification skills laid down by Inhelder and Piaget as : (a) resemblance sorting, (b) consistent sorting, (c) exhaustive sorting, (d) multiple class member-ship (e) horizontal sorting (f) Hierarchical reclassification. These failed to find complete support from Kofsky and others later on, for the order of the emergence of three concrete operational skills : conservation—class inclusion—transitivity, Kofsky found a general correspondance with the squence proposed by Inhelder and Piaget, but there were exceptions too. In summarising Piagiets theory of the child's cognitive developmental stages we note that at the first two years of life the child acquires sensory motor control. At the age of 2 extracts concepts from experiences, at the age of 4 makes intuitive judgements. At the age of 7 he can master concrete operations (control through perceptual anticipation of consequences); and at the age of 11 the child progresses towards formal operations (control through logical deduction of possibilities and consequences).

Piaget's contribution to educational psychology and classroom instruction

A young child usually answers the questions thrown at him by his teacher in the classroom in terms of right or wrong. How does he discriminate has been studied by Piaget throughly : The child answers what his age comprehends. He is normal. If he is told his answer is wrong, he might learn to doubt himself, but he would not learn to deal with two variables simultaneously, Piaget says, because he is not yet prepared to 'structure' reality as the adult does.

The study of the developing mind means the study of the natural ways in which a bioscocial organism grows, learns and matures. The study of development means an understanding of the ways which we can use to facilitate the process of development by improving our present form of intervention or inventing new ones. We are not to speed up the process forcefully—not to accelerate development, which is not the same as improving the social influences or experiences that are psychological and physiological components of growing up. Therefore, the school should always take proper account of the process of development.

A major problem in the application of Piaget to education is that his work is concerned with the development of fundamental knowledge and intelligence of the child, whereas schools are interested in the child's acquisition of skills and information. In spite of the fact that the two are related, the problem lies in the emphasis each places on. Nevertheless, schools concentrating on skills and information has to depend upon the fundamental knowledge as a basic requirement and as acquired through action upon and interaction with the environment. With this realization the current practice in modern education advances propositions to employ the basic pedagogical principles of Piaget in the classrooms:

(1) The first principle drawn from Piaget's theory is the view that learning has to be an active process, because knowledge is a construction from within.

(2) A second principle suggests the importance of social interactions among children in school. Piaget believed strongly that for intellectual development the cooperation among children is as important as the child's cooperation with the adults.

(3) A third principle points to the priority of intellectual activity based on actual experiences rather than on language. Language is important but not at the expense of original thinking. It is necessary to let go the pre-operational child go through one stage after another giving the wrong answers before expecting him to have adult logic and adult language (Sinclair and Kamie, 1970)[24]. Piaget's theory has helped the teachers and teacher trainers to make some progress in recognizing the importance of concrete experiences prior to using words.

Piaget's biological theory of intelligence states that intelligence is a general coherent framework within which all the cognitive parts function. He emphasized the role of action in perception that recognition requires perceptual activities, i.e. the moving of the eyes, hands, or feet to center on various points of the particular special configuration to construct it actively. What is important in perception is active mental construction of the spatial configuration. His theory has been often, however, criticized as a psychology that focusses on sensory information and motor behaviour resulting in the conceptualization of goals and teaching methods involving skills rather than on the child's entire cognitive frame-work.

24. Sinclair, H. and Kamie, C. Some Implications of Piaget's Theory for Teaching Young Children, School Review, 78, 1970, 109-183.

The pedagogical implications of Piagetian theory suggests the kind of reform that makes learning truly active and encourages social interactions among pupils to cultivate the critical spirit. The teacher in a Piagetian school does not present readymade knowledge and morality, but rather provides opportunities for the child to construct his own knowledge and moral standards through his own reasoning. The emphasis of a Piagetian school is on the child's own thinking and judgment rather than the use of correct language and adult logic. But still Piagetian theory clings to the old cliche's of old order of education—educating the "whole child", the individual differences, teaching of children to think, the encouraging of initiative and curiosity and the desirability of intrinsic motivation. Nevertheless, Piagetian theory gives more precise guidelines to translate the old ideals into actual practice.

Bruner's Contribution to Cognitive Developmental Stages

Bruner approached the study of cognitive development from a psychological-experimental frame of reference. He, his colleagues and his students involved much greater number of individuals than used by Piaget, under controlled experiments. Bruner studied the means by which human beings interact with the environment cognitively. He observed the initial emergence of the means of acting on the environment and representing experience, and also the continuity of development (Bruner, Oliver, and Greenfield, 1966)[25]. Bruner agrees with Piaget regarding the description of internal representation of experience. But Bruner emphasized continuity, the importance of language and the importance of education in cognitive development more than Piaget.

Bruner conceived three ways of knowing something : through actualy performing it (through doing it), through sensing it and through a symbolic means such as language. He used three special terms to designate these three actions. Knowing and representing experiences are according to him "enactive", "ikonic" and "symbolic". They denote not only representing internally but also operational on the environment. They follow a sequential course : "acting on the environment—enactive representation; be able to execute the

25. Bruner, J. S., Oliver, R. R. and Greenfield, P. M. Studies in Cognitive Growth N. Y. Wiley, 1966.

act it represents....A picture is a selective analogue of what it stands for and only in a trivial sense is it a "copy" of its referent....yet it is not arbitrary. One cannot fathom the word for something by looking at something. One can learn to recognize the image of something just by looking at something...."

The representation of knot in symbolic terms is not so readily stated, for it involves at the outset a choice of the code in which the knot is to be described. For symbolic representation—whether in natural or mathematical "language"—requires the translation of what is to be represented into discrete terms that may then be formed into "utterances" or "settings" or "sentences", or whatever the medium used to combine the discrete elements by rule. Note too that whatever symbolic code one uses, it is also necessary to specify whether one is describing a process of typing a knot or the knot itself (at some stage being tied). There is, moreover, a choice in the linguistic description of a knot whether to be highly concrete or to describe this knot as one of a general class of knots. However, one settles these choices, what remains is that a symbolic representation has built-in-features that are specialized and distinctive (Bruner et al, 1966).

Bruner's contribution to cognitive development is of interest to the teachers and curriculum workers in planning the classroom programmes. "Bruner's contentions would act as a basis of classifying children at various age levels when they are required to categorize objects sensing the environment—ikonic representation; interacting with the environment through language—symbolic representation." Klausmier, 1971). These three modes of interacting processes start early in the child's life in the order given. Successive emergence of the three modes become interrelated and continue throughout life and never drop out.

We give Bruner's own views regarding three modes and their operational interaction in his own language :

"We can talk of three ways in which somebody 'knows' something : through doing it, through a picture or image of it, and through some such symbolic means as language. A first approach to understanding the distinction between the three can be achieved by viewing each as if it were external—though our eventual object is to view representations as internal. With respect to a particular knot we learn the act of tying it and, when we "know" the knot, we know it by the habitual pattern of action we have mastered. The habit by which the knot is represented is socially organised, governed by some sort of scheme that holds its successive segments together and, in some sense; related to other acts that either facilitate it or interfere with it. There is a fair amount of sensory-motor feedback involved in carrying out the act in question, yet what is crucial is that such a representation is executed in the medium of action.

Representation in imagery is just that : the picture of the knot in question, its final phase or some intermediate phase, or indeed even a motion picture of the knot being formed. It is obvious—yet worth saying—that to have a picture before one (or in one's head) is not necessarily to as belonging to the same class, thereby forming concepts of equivalent. Five modes of responding to the tasks were identified as the bases on which items were classified as equivalent : perceptual, functional, effective, nominal and fiat.

Perceptual : The child renders the items equivalent on the basis of immediate phenomenal qualities such as size, colour, shape, or on the basis of position in time or space, e.g. they are both on the ground.

Functional : The child renders the items equivalence on the use of the items e.g. they make noise – whatever behaviour is functional.

Affective : Equivalence on the basis of the emotion they arouse, e.g. I like both or on the basis of the child's evaluation of them.

Nominal : The child may classify the items by giving a name that exists in the language, e.g. They are all fruits.

Fiat : Sorting out the difference or sameness without giving further information.

Other important characteristic are the developing grouping structures employed with increasing age e.g. the category or concept is formed on the basis of common attributes characterizing the items.

Bruner, more than Piaget, emphasizes the role of the environment and education, in the process of cognitive development. Nelson and Klausmeir (1974)[26] found, following

26. Nelson, G. K. and Klausmeir : Classificatory Behaviors of Low Socio-Economic Status of Children. J of Educational Psychology, 66, 432-438, 1974.

Bruner education not only affects the acceleration or retardation of the conceptual development; it influences the very means of conceptualization employed by the individual.

Flavell's interpretation of Stages :

Flavell (1971)[27] expressed his opinion about the stages of cognitive development as almost like the metamorphosis in the insects if viewed the stages in totality perspective. Four conclusions follow regarding the cognitive items :

(1) The interaction of the individual with the environment during each stage is not isolated and unrelated. The items, while experiencing, interact with one another in specified ways and are utilized by the individual as interrelated items. The items, according to Flavell, form an organized cognitive structure of the individual.

(2) The organized cognitive structures at each successive stages are both qualitatively and quantitatively different from those defining the previous stages of cognitive development. They become entirely new structures at each stage and not an improved version of what had already been achieved.

(3) Each individual cognitive item functions up to the mature level of proficiency irrespective of the stages the child belongs to. For example, the child in the preoperational stage this week, who is not capable of conservation, will be in the concrete operational stage next week and will conserve as is the characteristic of that stage. It seems abrupt or a spurt, but is, in fact, gradual as the child reaches maturity.

(4) All the items that define any particular stage make this abrupt, fully mature transition simultaneously. Therefore, it can be concluded that the child who seems to enter abruptly the stage of concrete operation is in full command of each previous operation, and is immediately capable of all the operations that define the stage.

Flavell emphasizes the importance of the stages in cognitive development. He says that the ongoing stages do not exhibit metamorphic change of cognitive development of the child at each level but that 'stage' is a useful theoretical

27. Flavell, J. H. : Stage Related Properties of Cognitive Development, Cognitive Psychology, 2 : 421-453, 1971.

construct in the study of human cognitive development. Flavell's conception of the 'stages' imply a continuous but qualitative change in the maturing individual's role and behaviour in classification of skills, concepts, principles etc. at the beginning of each stage. But the items that define each stage mature gradually, rather than abruptly. The various items of any particular stage do not achieve their mature level until long after the end of the stage that marked their initial appearance. But for the rate at which various items or dimensions of a particular stage matures, Flavell depicts three possible patterns : (a) some items may emerge at about the same time but matures at different rates; (b) some may emerge at different points of time and reach their final level at the same time; (c) still others may emerge at different points in time, mature at parallel rates and, therefore, also reach maturity at different times.

The overriding educational implication of the theories of cognitive developmental stages rests on the fact that the teacher—with the knowledge of the mental equipment of the child while maturing at each stage—should be concerned with when to start teaching of any particular skill or concept in which he/she is interested, and what is the rate of its maturation. The teacher should also know the extent of gradualness and continuity and where does appear the spurt or abruptness. A teacher can only use the description of stages forwarded by Piaget and others to try to understand a child from the frame of reference of the child and not from the adult point of view. He/She should bear in mind that a growing child perceives himself and the physical world in his own way much different from adult perceptions. The child's conceptions or misconceptions, how they think about themselves and others depend entirely on the constructed image of their own thought process—this very fact had been highlighted by the developmental psychologists. Careful study of Piaget and other stage theorists should enable the adults to understand the child from their point of view and to treat the child as a developing but immature human being.

Social and Emotional Development

The aim of education, as has already been stated in the earlier chapters, is the all round development of personality of a child. Such a child is, in turn, expected to take part in developing the society in which he is born. From the point of view of personality development, the most significant aspect of a child's world is his social environment. It is the demand of the society that individual child is trained in such a way that he/she can contribute to the enrichment of his social environment. All human beings live in a society—an interacting group of people. And each society has a distinctive culture, a body of stored knowledge, characteristic way of thinking, feeling and willing, attitudes, goals and ideals. It is the society which decides, prescribes and limits what a child will be taught and what he will learn. Therefore, acquisition of social behaviour is the essential part of the social development of the child.

As we know, the word development means essentially an "unfolding" of all potentialities and propensities that a child is born with which remain embeded in a single cell. The direction of all growth follows the pattern of gradual unfolding in its general outward movement. Even physically, the arms and legs grow outward from the centre of the body during the embryonic stage and the mouth can perform the intricate motions of eating and speaking long before the fingers have developed an equal degree of dexterity. So it is with social development. Infants are at first completely "self-concerned", but with successive stages of maturation other people in the family become objects of concern and interaction. The child is born in a social environment. In fact, birth of a child is usually a social event, an addition of another member of the family. From then onward a child is continually influenced and shaped by those around him. The infant entirely depends on others to be fed, to be clad, to sleep, to remain clean and comfortable, for security and for mere existence. At the same time, even the newborn infant may also influence and shape the people around him. The alert and responsive child can tame an aggressive mother, appease a tensive and anxious mother and thus better becomes the mother's self-image one month later (Duchowasy, 1974)[28]. Thus from the beginning, humane social and emotional life involves two–way relationships between people.

---

28. Duchowny, M. S., Interactional Influence of infant characteristics and parturient maternal self image, 1974. In Developmental Psychology, 2nd ed. by Robert, M. Liebert, Rita Wicks Poulos and Gloria Strauss Marmor. Prentice Hall, Inc, Indian Print, 1977.

A child's later social and emotional behaviour can only be recognized and accepted when the early roots of such behaviour have been dug out. For this reason, the developmental psychologists have been specially interested in the infant's first social and emotional attachments. It has been observed that each child does appear to take on a "unique" self during the early years. An individual's reacting to them may be utterly confusing without exploration of psychological roots in infancy.

Another important issue is to know the influence of nature and nurture on the development of social behaviour. It will be relevant to know which aspect of the child's personality has an inherent component existing from birth and which aspects are shaped largely or entirely by the social experiences and the interacting environment. A careful examination of the child's early social responses might provide some answers.

The major factors operated and woven into the fabric of the issue of social and emotional development is the question of deprivation and trauma. Early experiences have been examined from many vantage points. The psychologists employed simple observations, case studies observations, complex longitudinal studies spanning many years, and innovative and sometimes daring experimental studies with humans and animals. The crosscultural work of anthropologists is also relevant and, actually, help to understand the true significance of individual differences even within the same culture. The importance of early experiences of childhood in framing social behaviour of an individual was first emphatically pronounced by Sigmund Freud (1856-1939) which alerted both the laymen and professionals at the same time.

The scientific and systematic observation of social behaviour and social interaction of children have been carried on along with the experimental studies. All the observations started with the behavioural expessions of pre-school children. The child's interaction with others—specially with peers of the same age group—forwarded the best examples of his social behaviour and its modification. During the preschool years, children are moderately interested in playmates outside the family. An intense interest in outsiders does not generally appear until children are well into the primary grade. The interaction with peers generate the inherent social traits. For example, a child has been judged as highly "aggressive" if they attack or quarrel with peers frequently, or "domineering" if they try to control or boss others; and "dependent" if they seek a great deal of aid or reassurances in social interactions. General attitude towards parents and toward the world at large are strongly influenced by early parent-child relationship.

Parents are the primary behavioural models for children, but during school years they acquire some new model such as teachers and classmates. At times they assume such importance that they may equal or even exceed that of the parents. But even then, the development of child's social behaviour originates from the social interactions in the family. The child's first social interactional object is his/her mother who gratifies his/her fundamental needs—hunger and sleep and emotional comfort. It is a diad relationship for the first month and then the relationship and interaction extends and includes the father constituting a triad and that relationship mother-child-father engram, constitutes the first social interactional programme. The child's first social interaction appears when the infant is more or less one and half months old and gives its first recognizable smile response at mother's affectionate tender handling. A few months later when the same social responses get attached to the father and other members of the family it may be assumed that the child has stepped into the social-interactional stage of maturity. The observation of such physical and emotional relationship in early months of development led Sigmund Freud to hypothesize the five stages of psychosexual development of the libido. At each stage the libido (the primitive emotional impulse) gets fixated to an external object (releasing social behaviour) leading either to satisfaction and retention of behaviour or to frustration with resultant rejection of (repression, according to Freud) behaviour. Either process elicits new social response which is introjected by the infant as an integral part of self and thus helping the formation of structure of personality. The personality—according to Freud—consists of three components or basic structures—id, ego and superego, as he termed them. Socialization of the ego and formation of an interactive personality is the culmination of the whole developmental process. Freud's theory of psychosexual development and structure of personality will be discussed in detail in the chapter of personality.

Erik Erikson, a neo-Freudian, in explaining social development of the child employed the framework of psychoanalytical theory but with a different emphasis. Erikson accepts the notion that libidinal or emotional energy exists at birth and is at the core of human functioning. He also assumes that development passess through stages, several of which coincide with Freudian one. Nevertheless, he has made some distinct deviations from Freudian theory. First, Erikson places much greater emphasis than Freud on the role of the ego, or rational part of the personality. Because he thinks that the society and the social changes influence the developing child very much. In his theory he transformed the "psychosexual stages" into "psychosocial" stages. Second, he thinks that the growing individual is placed within the larger social setting of the family and its cultural heritage rather than its most restricted triangle of mother-child-father. Erikson's emphasis on social context in formulating his theory is of relevance to the social development of the child. In his theory of child development he thought that humans continue to develop through eight stages throughout the entire life span from infancy to old age. Erikson's stages are composed of fundamental and intimate feelings of men at each successive stages. They are :

Chronological stages	Erikson's stages
Infancy	Basic trust vs Mistrust
$1\frac{1}{2}$ to 3 yrs (approximately)	Autonomy vs Shame and Doubt
3 to $5\frac{1}{2}$ yrs (approximately)	Initiative vs Guilt
$5\frac{1}{2}$ to 12 yrs (approximately)	Industry vs Inferiority
Adolescence	Identity vs Role Confusion
Young Adulthood	Intimacy vs Isolation
Adulthood	Generativity vs Stagnation
Maturity	Ego Identity vs Despair

Erikson's Psychological Developmental Stages (Erikson, 1963, 1972)[29]

29. Erikson E.H. : Eight Ages of Man. In C.S. Luvatelli and F. Stendler, eds. Readings in Child Behavior and Child Development N.Y. Harcourt, Brace, Jovanovich, 1972.

Third, Erikson stresses the opportunity each individual has for resolving developmental crises, whereas Freud focussed on the pathological outcomes of the failure to resolve them adequately. "There is little", Erikson writes, "that cannot be remedied later, there is much that can be prevented from happening at all" (Erikson, 1963, p. 104)[30]. Erik Erikson has given us the model in his conceptualization of an epigenetic sequence of stages of psycho-social-growth, a sequence which leads from the infant's utter dependence on the nurturing care of the mother to the young adult's emotional self-reliance and sense of identity. Erikson's first four stages given above are of relevance to the social development of the child, which we shall discuss for the present purpose.

Basic Trust vs Mistrust

According to Erikson, the very foundation of social development of any child is woven around the theme of trust and hope. At birth, the newborns change their environment, an environment which is alien to them. They are shifted from a cosy and passive environment of total dependence to an interacting independent world. They are coming into the world experiencing a change from the warmth and regularity of the mother's womb to the world of independence requiring his own action and interaction. But, to start with, the independent life the child is not entirely defenseless. Parents, particularly the mother, respond to his bodily needs, and the handling of the child largely determines the establishment of attitudes of trust and mistrust. During the early months the infant's contact with the world is not only through the mouth, but also through the manner in which the parents embrace, talk to or smile at him/her. If a consistence and regular satisfaction of needs is received, certain expectancies about the world are set up. Then the child would trust the environment and in doing so becomes open to new experiences.

Autonomy vs Shame and Doubt

The major conflict that evolves from about $1\frac{1}{2}$ to 3 years of age is self-assertion—thrusting one's own will on others and get his/her wish satisfied. During this time, children rapidly acquire the physical skill to explore the world and begin to see themselves capable of manipulating some parts of it. This

30. Erikson E.B. Childhood and Society N.Y. Nortan, 1963.

gives rise to a sense of autonomy in the children. An autonomous child forces his will on the adults—the adult members of the family on whom they previously were dependent, both physically and emotionally. This sometimes lead to temporary disruption of the previously established relationship. But, according to Erikson, shame and doubt exist alternatively with the thrust for autonomy. Shame and doubt at this stage are based on the feeling of deprivation of the child's remaining dependency and on the fear of going beyond one's own capabilities. The conflict arises between autonomy versus shame and doubt. The latter results from failure to meet parental expectation, whereas autonomy is the outcome of self-control and assertion.

Initiative versus Guilt

Coinciding with Freud's phallic stage of libido development, Erikson postulates a conflict between initiative and guilt. The environment of three to five year olds now invites—or even demands—that they assume some responsibility and master certain tasks e.g. wearing own clothes and shoes by themselves, brushing teeth, washing hands, and feet, receiving phone calls, opening the front door etc. The child must initiate action but fails to see that those actions sometimes conflict with and intrudes upon the autonomy of others. The realization of this fact results in feelings of guilt.

This period is also the period of sex-role playing. Like Freud, Erikson recognizes the increased interest in the sex-role typing displayed by both girls and boys at this stage, when as well the glimpses of self-identity starts taking shape in accordance with the existing social order. The parents also play a decisive role in this matter, but the child's perception of parents operates in this functioning.

Unlike Freud, Erikson sees the child's attraction for the opposite-sexed parent as less incestual and more the result of a reaching out for a dependable opposite-sexed parent who represents his idea of emotional comfort. The sense of rivalry that naturally occurs with the same–sexed parent leads to a gradual identification with him/her and replaces the desired parent. As a result, attachment gets extended also to other love objects as the social field expands. A more realistic view about the same-sexed parent occurs simultaneously through introjection and consequent identification and the rival parent becomes the ideal—socially—toward which to strive. This is the period when the child gradually comes to understand the roles and opportunities presented by the society as well as his role in accomplishment and achievement.

Industry vs Inferiority

As the youngster crosses three to four year of his life, he is now ready to meet the challenges that arise with entrance into the competitive world of formal schooling. This is the time of latency of sexual striving and more of social mixing. With the oedipal and electra complexes settled,* peers become increasingly important and influence strongly the child's social behaviour. The nature of games changes from individual playing with toys (parallel play) to cooperative character of sharing and seeking friendship.

The theme of this stage is the mastery of tasks in the face of feeling of inferiority. As children achieve such mastery they become capable of facing the turbulent adolescent years which lie directly ahead. Infancy and childhood are times of rapid change and growth. The jump from infancy to childhood is not a spurt, but a period of mastering a number of skills and abilities gradually, to become ready for the competitive life ahead, to acquire complex social behaviours. A shift in social relationships is noticeable—the child who was predominantly a member of the family becomes member of both family and peer group. From all conflicts faced from these two social settings the child develops his own identity at adolescent stage when he represents a new generation.

Emotional Development

The educational psychologists nowadays do not study emotional development independent of the development of social behaviour. In fact, both social and emotional developments are integral parts of personality adjustment. Psychologists of early days, however, in their search for different fields of psychology considered emotional development as an independent growth process. But as researches on this line advanced and sophisticated tools came more and more in use, it has been observed that social and emotional developments grow simultaneously in a child and learning plays an important role in developing the child's social and

* See notes on personality development in the Personality Chapter.

emotional behaviour. As a matter of fact, the emotion of a human being from the very beginning results from social interaction in the family in which the child is born.

The experimental psychologists in 1920s and 1930s carried on their experiements on emotion and its development separately considering its immense importance and the range of influence its casts in shaping the human personality. But the invaluable contribution of psychoanalytic theory of Sigmund Freud, and, later psychoanalysts like Adler, Horney and others up to Erik Erikson—, who revised classical psychoanalytic theory and used its observations in explaining human behaviour—found that social and emotional responses are intricately woven and that emotional expression requires a social setting right from childhood. Freud further emphasized the importance of childhood experiences in forming adult social and emotional behaviour contributing to the development of personality and motivation. The theory developed by Sigmund Freud ranks amongst the most far-reaching and influential views in modern history of psychology. He was convinced that the functional aspects of each personality are shaped by experience in the social context. The same message was transmitted by Erik Erikson and other psychoanalytic developmentalists who insisted on the importance of early experience for laying down patterns that will then endure through the entire life span. Freud also perceived and agreed with the biological scientists that the structure of human personality is intrinsic and intrapsychic mechanisms interact to form it. In studying the emotional development in children, Bridges (1932)[31] observed the emotional behaviour of infants from the point of view of development from age to age, and her contention was that 'excitement' was the original emotion. This contention was based on the systematic observation of infants under a month of age, followed by observation of children up to 2 years of their life span. Evidence of emotion was elicited by strong stimuli, the response to which observed to be general in nature. It was thus concluded that emotional reactions of very young infants seemed not to be highly differentiated as fear or anger or love, but could be described as general agitation or excitement. Differentiation of emotional responses must await

31. Bridges, K.M.B. Emotional Development in Early Infancy, Child Development, 3, 324-241, 1932.

maturation and learning. The main characteristics of early emotional response seemed to be alertness, slight tension or restlessness or just crying. The behaviour elicited by emotion increases in complexity as the infant matures.

The first response, Bridges noted, to be distinguishable from general excitement is probably *distress*, which is a disagreeably painful or unsatisfying experience. Responses indicating distress grow out of situations in which pain or discomfort is the stimulus. New or strange objects in addition to physical pain or discomfort, induce distress in children as soon as they can be perceived as strange.

The contrary response to distress is *delight* which differentiate from general responses at later age. Babies under one month old seem to be quiet or excited and respond in a passive way. By the time the infant is 2 to 3 months old, delight or pleasure and joy become distinctly discernible. The child expresses himself by smiling, kicking and waving his arms in such a manner and on such occasions as would seem distinctly to indicate delight. Bright (1932) gives the following chart to describe her observation about the development of emotional behaviour in infants :

Data from Bridges (1932)

Birth	excitement; distress, delight
Months	disgust
6 months	fear, anger
12 months	elation
18 months	affection for adults
24 months	jealousy, joy, affection for children

Emergence of emotional patterns in infancy

By the time the child reaches school age he/she has typically acquired the basic cultural patterns of emotional expression. Gradually the general mass feeling of emotion becomes differentiated into various concrete manifestations. He has learned which responses are appropriate to particular occasion or events. He becomes frightened, angry, fearful, jealous, affectionate, shy and indifferent—as situation demands. These responses bcome recognizable with growth and learning.

The responses like crying and smiling, the manifesting emotion are in the beginning reflex actions in the infant without corresponding feeling of emotion. As the baby grows the young child's responses becomes overtly similar to the emotional responses of older children, that is, they become stimulus-bound. But what portion of these are reflexive and how much learned is not known. With advancing age, emotional response patterns become more differentiated, more varied, complex and recognizable and more and more *conditioned.*

J. B. Watson in 1925 presented the behviouristic theory of emotion and held that there are three independent primary emotions—*anger (rage), fear and love*—and each of them has its own distinctive pattern of behaviour, produced by specific environmental stimuli. This was illustrated by fear reactions which are elicited by loud sound and loss of support, and expressed by reactions like identifiable crying, breath catching and blinking of the eyes. Anger is evoked by restraining of infant's movements, identifiable by stiffening of the body, thrashing of the hands and legs and crying profusely. The third unlearned emotion love is the response to the stroking of sensitive areas of the body and rocking and patting. Response to this being characterized by stretching, cooing, extending arms and smiling.

But later experimental evidences did not support Watson's theory. It has been found that the stimuli that were supposed to produce the various emotional responses reported by Watson did not universally do so. The responses were very individualistic and confusing. Neonates differ from one another in responsiveness to all kinds of emotional stimulation, and the differences could be attributed to the differences in rate of maturation.

Characteristics of Emotional Development

It has already been stated that emotional responses appear from the general excitement of very young infants and that emotional expressions differentiate gradually as the infants grow. It has also been noted that certain responses of children are likely to bring rewards and certain others lead to punishment. The reward and punishment or rather agreement and disagreement on the part of the adults operate which play part in controlling and differentiating emotions in young children. It is due to training that the general excitement of the very young infant develops into rather clearly defined response patterns. Fear and aggression are differentiated in the same manner from general excitement by selective operation of rewards and punishments. The child soon learns to behave in a certain way in order to induce a certain kind of behaviour on the part of others. The child's earliest aggressive responses consist of vigorous crying, kicking, screaming and tense facial expression. When this complex response help getting parental support and thus satisfaction or reduction in tension, they are reinforced and tend to be repeated. Thus emotional expressions may be regarded as learned responses, even though they have a physiological or neurological basis.

As the emotional responses are learned, therefore, they can easily be conditioned. When children have learned to be afraid or to like or to love, they can be considered to have passed through the stage of general excitement. They are now equipped with a response repertoire. They can express themselves emotionally. The number of emotional expressions go on increasing. Variety of emotional responses and their emotional behaviuor become more and more complex because emotional responses get conditioned easily, as an emotionally loaded stimulus occurs consistently with a neutral stimulus without the presence of the perviously emotionally toned one. Once an emotional response gets conditioned to a previously neutral stimulus, this stimulus can be used effectively to condition responses to other neutral situations. These new emotions can be instrumental in conditioning more and more new situations and capable of further conditioning. Such conditioning might go on indefinitely depending upon the habit strength acquired for each response.

The emotional behaviuor is often imitative. It is frequently observed that emotional behaviour of offspring is very much like that of their parents. The emotional behaviour is basically physiological and are considered as inherent tendency. But still they are largely learned responses. The role played by *imitation* is an important one in the acquisition of emotional expression. The mode of emotional expression differs from one culture to another and the difference is due to imitation of the old by the young. The emotional expression sometime differs from family to family within the same culture.

Variation of emotional reactions and forming patterns of emotional responses

Emotional reactions differ from child to child depending upon the intensity of emotion-arousing situation. The same fearful situation may evoke variety of reactions from diffrent children. Some children behave one way in the face of emotion-arousing situation whereas other children behave quite differently. These different reactions to essentially the same stimulus result from a host of previous experiences, some of which may have served to instil in the individual a generalized way of dealing with new situations. Karen Horney (1937)[32] stated that three types of reactions to an emotion-arousing stimulus have been observed. An individual can *approach* the situation, he can *attack* the situation or he can *withdraw* from the situation. Responding to a particular emotional experience mostly depends on learning. The particular reaction to emotion that will be made is probably learned in the same way that other behaviour patterns are acquired. If one behaviour, by some chance, is rewarded by success or diminished anxiety it is repeated. The same behaviour pattern is being used when other similar situations are confronted or it may be generalized to include all or most emotion–arousing situations.

Every child has a great variety of experiences which are accompanied by one effect or another. As the child accumulates a greater variety of experiences, he learns which kinds of behaviour are most rewarding for him in any given circumstance. He, thus, builds up a repertoire of positive emotional responses. He also learns to fear or dislike some other situations and forms negative attitude towards those responses and tries to avoid such situations. Thus a host of experiences produce a cumulative effect and may predispose an individual to a generalized mode of emotional reactions.

Development of Social Behaviour

The development of social behaviour ensues along with the personality development. Any evaluation of personality is based largely on observations of social behaviour—that is, child's interaction with others revealing the inter-personal relationship. This relationship starts in the family and then carried into other communications outside home, especially

32. Horney, Karen : The Neurotic Personalities of Our Times. W. W. Norton and Company, Inc. N.Y. 1937.

with peers and other later associates throughout the life span. Therefore, the nature of social behaviour are best revealed through the behaviours involving friendship and cooperation, attachment and aggression, hostility and dependence and the like. For example (as stated in the earlier section), we judge children to be highly aggressive—if they attack, or quarrel with peers frequently; domineering—if they try to control or boss others; and dependent—if they seek aid or reassurance in their social interactions.

General attitudes towards parents and toward the world at large are strongly influenced by early parent-child relationships. In this section we shall discuss when and how the interpersonal reactions develop—that certain maturational process play a role in this development and that individuals differ in socialization because various factors in the environment play part in shaping it. The process of socialization involves emotional control as well, which takes place through social learning. We shall now discuss the growth and development of some social characteristics, like structure of social groups and friendship patterns in childhood and opinions and attitudes towards others (peers, parents, playgroups, other adult members etc.) and, finally, socially acceptable and unacceptable behaviours.

The shaping process itself is rooted in the child's first relationship with parents and caretakers. As socialization begins other agents of socialization exert their influence. Siblings and peers play central role in the process and soon relevant training and experiences are provided by such institutions as the school, neighbourhood and mass media. Socialization is also a two dimensional process—the child is influenced by the socializing agents changing its behaviour on the one hand, and, on the other, the child shapes its environment by its unique behaviour, thereby making the process more complicated. Some of the children change their environments to a considerable degree rather than being passively shaped by themselves.

Social Behaviour at various age levels

The development of socialization starts as the child reaches a particular maturational level. The first stage can be called as the stage of prosocial behaviour. Most parents, teachers, and the other socializing agents of any culture try to teach children to act in cooperative, helping or giving ways—at least some of the times and in some situations. Such behaviour is usually thought to be in the greater interest of others and society at large, which the psychologists come to call as prosocial behaviours.

In this section we shall consider three such classes of prosocial behaviour which are products of learning and though seem to be overlapped are not identical. We shall also try to get research support on this account and see how such actions are developed, maintained and elicited in childhood.

Cooperation

Generally speaking, 'cooperation' refers to behaviour in which two or more people work together for mutual benefits. The nursery rhymes also help in forming the concept in children as action plays are performed in the classroom—how to clasp each other's hands and sing "zip-zap-zoo. We eat together, drink together, sleep together, dance together, jump together run together etc. etc." This is nothing but a cooperative feeling to be installed. Such action is considered prosocial because society is, to a great extent, built on the foundation of cooperative enterprise. Nevertheless, most developmental psychologists paid little attention to cooperation among children until Azrim and Lindsley (1956)[33] demostrated that children become more cooperative when directly reinforced for acting this way. Cooperative and competetive actions are opposite to each other. In singular play action, the competitive tendency is prominent. As cooperative activities start taking place it will gradually overcome irrational competitive tendencies as children become more cognitively mature and reasonable. This was the belief of Piaget (1962)[34]. But later researches revealed that in some circumstances, practical cooperation declines as a child grows older, and irrational competition in situations when it cannot possibly pay–off comes to be the dominant mode of responding. Another point to be noted is that cooperative work differs from culture to culture. The urban parents who emphasize competitiveness in their children are less enthusiastic about fostering cooperation in them. Cooperation seems to vary in boys and girls also as

33. Azrim, N.H., and Lindsley O.R., The Reinforcement of Cooperation between children. J. of Abnormal and Social Psychology, 52, 100-102, 1856.
34. Piaget, T. The Moral Judgement of the Child N.Y. Collier, 1962.

research work shows but nothing can be generalized on this issue as cross–cultural studies revealed contradictory ideas.

Let us now see what factors tend to stimulate the development of cooperation. Several have been identified. First, verbally, structuring sittuations in terms of mutual gain by creating a "we" rather than "I" orientation, so that children see themselves as working "with" rather than "against" each other. Second, direct experience with positive consequences of cooperation increases the likelihood that such behaviour will occur. In a series of investigations it has been shown that guiding children into a practical cooperative relationship and letting them directly experience its benefits markedly increases cooperation in children of diverse cultural backgrounds. Third and finally, modelled examples of cooperative behaviour by other children can have a powerful influence on elementary school childern.

Like cooperation "helping" also needs two factors, suggests Stanb (1971)[35]. These are : (1) the ability to empathize with the needy other and (2) possession of the knowledge or skills to help effectively. If this reasoning is correct it should be posible to increase children's willgness to help others by training in empathy and relevant skills. With this idea he experimented on the 'role playing' and 'induction' to increase young children helping other children in distress. The variety of possible ways of helping generated spontaneously by the youngsters included direct intervention, verbal consolation to the victim and calling someone else for help. Different situations generated different sorts of responses which were categorized above.

Stanb's induction group closely followed the procedures for the role playing except that the children were asked merely to describe verbally how they could provide help. The consequence showed positive results of other appropriate ways of helping, positive feelings or attempt to reduce pain and suffering. Induction, then, involved pointing out to children the consequences of their behaviour for others. Previous researches already show that children whose parents (revealed in induction process) lend helping hands to others and trained their children in the like manner, tend to show

35. Stanb, E., The Use of Role playing and Induction in Children's Learning of Helping and Sharing Behavior. Child Development, 1971, 421, 805-816, 1971.

somewhat more frequent prosocial acts in nursery schools than children whose parents use other socialization practices.

Stanb categorized the control-group-children's reactions as (a) active help, (b) volunteering information and (c) no-help—if they made no effort to provide direct or indirect assistance. Stanb also measured the willingness to share (discussed in the section below). The behaviour of the children in three situations—assisting a child in distress, assisting an adult in distress and sharing with another child suggested "that specific training procedures, particularly role playing of specific situations, may enhance the subsequent probability of prosocial behaviour" (p. 815).

Sharing is another prosocial behaviour which the children in the middle childhood often express verbally if not behaviourally and support the principle that one should aid the needy. The very idea is prevalent in the society at large where voluntary organizations play a prominent role. In this section we shall discuss how a child's willingness to share with others is acquired and maintained. Before doing so it is, however, important to distinguish between *sharing* and *altruism*. Sharing is actual behaviour, while altruism is a motivation without self interest. Sharing in children are identifiable, as for example by seeing whether he or she shares their food willingly with the peers or share toys while playing with the peers. But whether a child is 'altruistic' in attitude is difficult to determine in as much as altruism implies a feeling, a motivation of unselfishness. It has to be inferred such different situations asking for such revelation.

The developmental trend on this issue shows a positive relationship between age and children's willingness to share. It is less prominent in early childhood and more expressive in the middle childhood—from 8-year-olds to 11+ –years–olds. Several studies show that a child's willingness to share is influenced by his or her immediate emotional state and mood. The feeling and behaviour of immediate sharing can be trained through reward and punishment—rewarding children for acts of generosity and aversive actions or punishment for not sharing: It may increase immediate sharing, but whether it would lead to a positive, and parmanent consequence in future, or not, is not predictive.

But it has been confirmed by White's (1972)[36] expreiment the combination of a modelled example and voluntary rehearsal is a highly effective training technique for sharing. Hoffman (1973)[37] studied that parents' altruistic values are highly correlated with their children's behaviour and was considered to be the single consistent predictor of altruism in the child. It has been observed that exposure to sharing models can increase children's sharing.

Aggression

The most expressed behaviour observed in children from a very early age is aggression of some kind or other ranging from simple protest to bodily attack and assault. The type of aggression that any individual displays and eventually controls do change with increasing age and experience.

The shaping of aggression is generally determined in two ways—'elicitation' and 'cultivation'. Certain kinds of circumstances will draw out aggression more often than others and, hence, can be considered as elicitors of aggression, when, people are attacked they are likely to act in similar way and so attack is the elicitor of aggression. But when there is no provocation and people encourage aggressive behaviour, their actions are considered as cultivators of a general pattern of responding aggressively. The "Frustration-aggression" theorists held frustration as the elicitor aggression—a determinant. They defined frustration as blocking of goal-directed activity, naturally very strong stimulus leading to aggressive responses. Though frustration-aggression theory is not always acceptable—and it has been seen that factors other than frustration can also lead to the occurence of aggression—yet it is an elicitor, no doubt.

Emotional arousal is another consistent determinant of aggression because a child is often noticed to hit the younger brother or sister, for example, when they are upset, agitated or excited. Provoked aggression is also due to social learning. The acquisition of aggressive skills and habits, ways of behaving aggressively may occur through modeling by watching the performance of these acts by others. Continual exposure to

---

36. White, G. M. Immediate and Deferred Effects of Model Observation and Guided and Unguided Rehearsal on donating and stealing. J. of Personality and Social Psychology 21, 139-148 (1972).
37. Hoffman, M. L. Altruistic Behavior and the parent-child relationship—a Report. 36 Developmental Program Dept. of Psychology, Michigan University, August, 1973.

multiple models who act aggressively may induce a general disinhibition so that, beyond imitating particular actions, a widespread tendency to respond aggressively to new situations may develop. It has now been shown that these same principles apply to televized models of aggression and has raised serious questions about violence in children's programmes on television.

Competition is another forceful determinant of aggression. The competitive situations not only produce a sporting spirit, but they can elicit outright hostility as well. High competition also breeds aggression to some extent.

Social behaviour during the Pre-school years

With increased age between 6 and 25 months, interaction proceeds steadily from initial indifference toward the partner (for social interest) cooperative play situations. Infants between 6 and 8 months of age are generally observed to ignore each other. Babies between 9 and 13 months of age show some interest in partners. The social contacts are limited to looking, smiling and grasping the partner. Between 14 and 18 months, attention to the partner increases considerably and, gradually, the social contacts and cooperative play become far more personal and friendly.

Social development is markedly accelerated during the nursery school period when a child's contact with peers become more frequent and intense. The study with nursery school children show that as pre-school children grow older they spend less time in relatively non-social activities and more advanced types of social behaviour become increasingly frequent. The most rudimentary from of social interaction, parallel play (each individual child playing with his/her toys only), is characteristic of two-year olds, but relatively uncommon among children of four or five years of age, who indulge in more associative or cooperative play.

Many factors account for these modifications in social behaviour. With greater maturity, a child's greater physical and intellectual abilities enable him to participate in more complex and cooperative activities. Moreover, older children have been rewarded more frequently for outgoing and friendly responses and at nursery schools and on playgrounds, cooperative socially oriented responses bring further satisfaction; hence, these responses become stronger and are more apt to be repeated. At the same time, spending time without activity and merely observing are discouraged by parents and teachers, so they become weaker responses and tend to drop away.

In the pre-school stage the number of social conflicts and quarrels decrease and friendly contacts become more pronounced as age increases. During first two to five years children form their first friendships—generally, but not exclusively—with others of their own sex. Friendship partners change characteristically and markedly with age, and the number of friendship increases. A socially-oriented and responsive preschool child seeks out companions and has variety of contacts with them. In the course of learning the modes of social interaction, such a child has both satisfying and frustrating experiences and, consequently, show contradictory behaviour at times. For example, the boy who grabs a toy from a playmate and shows aggressive behaviour at one moment may run to comfort a crying unhappy child the next moment.

Popular children and leaders can be distinguished as early as the nursery school period. Some children are continually being sought out as playmates, others are consistently shunned and avoided by their nursery playmates or classmates. Some youngsters ordinarily assume a dominant role in their relationships with peers, while others are passive followers.

There are great individual differences in responses to social conflicts, but the average nursery school child between two and four years of age is involved in some sort of conflict every five minutes. In general, boys tend to fight, make more attacks, whereas girls tend to argue more. These sex differences are more pronounced among older nursery school children, reflecting more firmly their sex-tying behaviour. In general the interactiveness of preschool youngsters are more characteristically cooperative and friendly than unfriendly, hostile or competitive. Aggressiveness tends to be a fairly stable characteristic, the frequency of a child's conflict is carried to the next higher stage.

Competitiveness appears as early as the age of three or four. Those between the ages of four and six compete with considerable intensity, grabbing things from each other, disregarding other child's feelings and intentions and refusing to give help or materials. By this age competitive motives are strong enough to produce improvement in performance when the child is competing with some other. As children advance in age, they become acutely aware of the prevalent attitudes of culture, and consistent reward for competition—hence they adopt competitive values and motivations.

Boys are more competitive than girls, and lower middle class children are noticed to be more competitive than the upper middle class ones. Aggressiveness and competiveness are not usually connected with each other in nursery school children but are associated in older children and adults.

In middle childhood

Social relationships of the school years are more extensive, more influential and more enduring than those of earlier years. The major social developments of this period reflect children's increased socialization, more firmly established sex-typing and stronger social pressure for conformity to group standards.

Preschool friendship, being casual, unstable and transient, probably have relatively few important or enduring effects on child's personality. In middle childhood, the situation is different Besides his/her parents and teachers, the child's close friends are probably their most important "socializers" and they have direct and powerful impacts on his/her personality and social development.

From roughly ages 7 to 12 the youngsters are strongly concerned with their gangs, an informal group with rapid turnover in membership. Later on, with age, the group becomes more structured and sometimes highly organized. The social relationship of these years (from 10 to 14) may have far-reacting influence. The child's choice of extracurricular games, reading, choice of books, movies, radio, television programmes can be swayed by his/her peers' opinions and suggestions. This media, in turn may provide new identification models and new evaluation of certain types of values, attitudes, characteristics and behaviours.

The elementary school children, in choosing their friends, prefer members of their own sex, particularly at the sixth, seventh and eighth grades. Most boys between the age of 6 and 8, however, ignore sex and girls are included in the group, and vice versa. The boys choose girls as freely as they choose boys, and it is same with the girl's choice. In eastern culture the cutting age is lower than the other advanced countries. But by and large, everywhere, at the age of eight, approximately, attitude seems to change and associations with members of the opposite sex decrease sharply. By 11 or 12 boys and girls are completely segregated from each other in play groups and social gathering. In 1939 Compbells observed: "This stage of segregation began with haughty aloofness, became apparent contempt, and active hostility, and then changed to shy withdrawal which seemed to mark the end of this period and the beginning of adolescent heterosexuality and puberty".

The segregation of the sexes is probably related to the cultural pressures on children for sex-appropriate behaviour to be adopted. The nature of play is also sex-typical—boys interested in playing vigorous, competitive games involving muscular skills and dexterity, whereas girls are generally engaged in more quiet, sedentary activities. With increasing age, reading interests also differ. Boys prefer adventure, exploration, travel, biography, mystery and science stories and fictions, whereas the girls prefer fairly tales and romances. Friendship in middle childhood is fairly unstable. Since interest fluctuate rapidly at this time, there occurs additional new friendships, sometime along with the old friends and sometimes old friendship is terminated with new substitutions. With advancing age interests become more and more stable and enduring.

Adolescent Social Patterns

Adolescent social relationships are more complicated than young-age friendship patterns. Adolescent's social situation is a particularly difficult one, since he/she lives simultaneously in the two worlds of children and adults, in a kind of marginal or overlapping status, not knowing where he or she belongs. All at once he/she has many new urgent conflicting demands put on him/her. For a boy, for example, at this stage, is expected to choose a professional line of education, making himself fit for a vocation and to achieve some independence from his family. In addition, his sex-drive increases as a result of hormonal changes, and he must cope with strong, forbidden impulses. Finally, since he has greater mobility, his social world broadens and he can maintain friendships over a wider

<u>Note</u> : Campbell, E. H. The Social sex Development of Children, Genet. Psychol. Monogr. Vol. 21, No. 4, p. 465, 1939.

geographical area. Earlier, most of his peers and friends are from his own neighbourhood and social class group but, in high school, he is likely to meet boys and girls from other parts of his community and from other ethnic and cultural groups. From them he may learn new attitudes, customs and value system.

Among his peers, the most noteworthy influence on the development of social behaviour comes from the immediate groups of peers or cliques. They generally are the members of his own small, select group and come from the same socio–economic class background, tend to be alike in personality and interests and share common purpose and values. Cliques are generally based on personal compatibility, congeniality and close ties of affection and mutual admiration. Mutual interests tend to bring people together. In early adolescence shared preferences and the ability to do exciting things together are central in the formation of friendship, but, in later adolescence, acceptability to members of the opposite sex—particularly among girls—becomes a more important criterion. Friendships are also related to similarities on social maturity, in mental age, sociability, criticalness of self and others, extroversion, degree of conformity or rebellion, social skills and knowledge.

The function of the peer group is very important in shaping an adolescent's social behaviour. This is the period when the adolescent seeks independence from his family and seek more and more dependence on his peer group. Acceptance by peers become an ardent necessity and, therefore the adolescents put premium in getting along with others, on being popular and friendly. Their company and suggestions become surpassingly important to him. His peer group actually serves the purpose of a teacher to an adolescent by helping him to learn social skills and attitudes and assisting him in adopting the adult standards. He is likely to adopt the fashions, values, beliefs, and fads, style of life of the peer group in conformity with their standard and status—thus giving rise to generation gaps. Some adolescents are swayed by the peer group's value systems—accepting them without examination, uncertain about how to achieve it—he feels reassured if he behaves as others do. In fact, he worries if he feels that he is different from others.

The social behaviours that give rise to moral behaviour and value system that individual adolescent member adopts are greatly influenced by his peer group at the adolescent period. An adolescent peer group ordinarily reinforces and strengthens the values that members have acquired from parents, approved by the social class and community. Generally, the group rewards what it regards as positive social and moral values and severely punishes antisocial and disapproved values and behaviours. The peer group appears to be less an originator than a reinforcer of moral values and behaviour patterns developed in the family. "Adolescents as a whole, prone to admire, respect and reward very much the same moral behaviour as do the respectable members of the adult community : their parents, their teachers etc." (Peck and Havinghurst, 1960)[38]. This is hów the external value systems of any society perpetuates with a few exceptions at times or sometimes roll on in cyclic order. Barring very few socially deviant adolescents, the development of social behaviour among adolescents assume the normal adult pattern of the society and culture.

Emotional control and Re-education

The emotion and emotional expressions are inherent in human being. We have discussed how frustrations and other factors lead to aggressive behaviour. But it is necessary to control primal behaviour so that socialized behaviour can emerge. Learning from experience is the major process by which uninhibited responses can be channelized. Childhood behaviour is channeled to a large extent by numerous immediate external constrains : the expectations of others, parental reward and punishment, and peer pressures, self-imposed standards, to name few. Thus they learn self-control. Self control is a term that refers to behaviour in which the child monitors his or her own actions in some way in the absence of pressures in the immediate situation. There are related aspects of self-control, the ability to resist temptation, the ability to tolerate delayed gratification and imposing a standard of achievement upon oneself.

In its broadest definition, a resistance to temptation refers to refraining from the opportunity to engage in a socially prohibited but otherwise tempting act, such as cheating,

38. Peck, R.F. and Havinghurst, R.J. The Psychology of Character Development, Wiley, N.Y. 1960 .

stealing etc. The self-control, in this case depends upon the disciplinary measures taken at home or at school. The disciplinary measures may involve physical punishment for breaking the social standard or psychological techniques like reasoning, withdrawal of love, portrayal of suffering by the parents or teachers and so on. The physical punishment may be effective in very young age, when children are not amenable to reasoning, but with intellectual sophistication and development in age psychological techniques become more effective. The studies on child-rearing practices (cross-cultural) show that reasoning and explanation play a very important role in the development of self-control among children who are older and with the youngers punishment and reasoning combined was considered to be effective.

The second aspect of control is to learn the delay of gratification, which means that the children learn to postpone immediate gratification for the sake of more valued outcomes that will come with patience and effort. Now we shall see how a child learns the delayed gratification and also we shall consider the underlying psychological processes. It is an important aspect of socialization. The self-control, in this case, takes places after a series of trainings undertaken. Such trainings suppose that delaying gratification involves two steps : an initial decision that one wishes to wait and then an effort to maintain one's resolution and bridge the waiting time. Walter Mischel, who has done pioneering experimental work on delay of gratification, has also conceptualized the underlying psychological process involving these two steps and showed that the steps are influenced by somewhat different factors (Mischel, 1974)[39] of which the decision-process needs attention. In situations where the child must make a choice between accepting or not accepting the frustration of delay for the sake of earning a superior outcome, he or she probably considers the subjective values of both the immediate and delayed rewards and the probability of obtaining them. In most life-situations, attaining delayed rewards involves not only simply waiting but also engaging successfully in some required activity. Therefore, decision-making depends on the child's confidence in being able to perform the activity. The child's decision also depends on this

39. Mischel, W. : Processes in Delay of Gratification. In L. Berkowitz, ed. Advances in Experiemental Psychology, Vol. 7, N.Y. Academic Press, 1974.

consideration of the degree or extent or intensity of difference between immediate and delayed reward or risk involved. The rational choice would be to take immediate reward if the risk involved is considered to be great, on the other hand when the subjective value is considered to be substantial and when obtaining delayed reward is not too risky the rational choice would be delayed reward. Nevertheless, waiting cultivates tolerating the frustrating time-span.

The third aspect, achievement standard and striving states that the self-control is learned easily if the set achievement standard is easy to attain. All people come to set standards for themselves. In general, higher the standard more effort must be expended to attain it, otherwise the situation becomes quite frustrating, children's self-imposed standards or personal standards differ from person to person depending on the stringency of the standard and amount of effort put to achieve it. Self-imposed standards of achievement and self-reward are largely products of socialization. Effective socialization can be considered to be prime factor in self-control, particularly when the self-imposed standard is based on intrinsic motivation i.e. when where is no external socializing agent is present. Now setting the self-imposed standard depends to a great extent on modelling of an adult in life situations, children are exposed to many models, including mother, father, teachers and playmates, and thus they may observe discrepant standards of achievement. This may cause problem for the child to set self-imposed standard for him. But in spite of it the achievement standards set by children for themselves are strongly influenced by the kind of behaviour they observe around them reinforcing self-control. The children learn to develop during their early years, a set of values or principles regarding correct, appropriate or good behaviour. They are either taught by the socializing agents to self-control or they teach themselves from experience. Self-control is a trait to be cultivated, to be learned throughout the life-span.

CHAPTER IV

Human Abilities

A human ability is a union of a native process (or processes) in humans and a content (or contents) inferred from relatively permanent changes in behaviour (Klausmeier, 1975, P. 12)[1]. Abilities are of two kinds : Cognitive and Psychomotor. When a child understands the meaning of a statement in acquiring language or comprehending a word, his understanding means a process or operation and also certain content i.e. words or their meaning. A psychomotor ability, on the other hand, helps a human being to acquire specific skill for a specific work, e.g. manual dexterity needs acquisition of skill as well as well-guided arm-hand movement while manipulating an object. Persons high in this ability are able to perform any specific task involving manual dexterity.

Both cognitive and psychomotor abilities are the products of maturation and learning. In turn, possessing a particular ability facilitates further learning. Extensive researches conducted on human abilities have yielded beneficial results, so that it is now possible to easily identify and classify different human abilities. As a consequence, important advances have been made in this research area and a series of new formations about the intellectual and learning abilities have been obtained. Substantial knowledge about human abilities are in store following hard work of different researchers in this field.

It has been established that abilities develop quite slowly across the years, but once developed they enable the individual to deal with his physical and social world more effectively.

Nature of abilities

The identification of abilities by scientific methods is a complex process. An ability is, in fact, a configuration of abilities, identified through correlational and experimental research. Any single ability needs consistency among separate

1. Klausmeier, H. and William, G. Educational Psychology. Harper International-ed. Harper and Row. N.Y. 1975.

performances involving that ability. In that sense an ability is a mediator which helps the individual to interpret the ideas and actions of others as well as to take action all by himself.

Fleishman and Bartlett (1969)[2] in a comprehensive work on human abilities identified five important attributes of abilities :

1. Abilities are a product of maturation and learning. Much practice and learning are required to comprehend the concepts and principles of any subject. The maturational level of an individual child limits what he can learn. Thus abilities develop and mature at different rates from birth through adolescence. For example, verbal comprehension develops more rapidly than arithmetic reasoning in early childhood.
2. Abilities developed during the formative years permeates into adulthood and persists throughout the period.
3. The present abilities of the individual affect the rate at which he learns related new tasks. Thus, the student high in spatial ability and arithmetic reasoning achieves higher in physics than the one low in both, motivations and other factors being equal. Equally important is that the study of physics will probably contribute to further development of both abilities. They complement each other.
4. Abilities vary from specific to general, and the more general the ability the greater is its transfer. Arithmetic computation e.g., is an ability which facilitates only the learning of new tasks involving computation, whereas spatial ability facilitates the learning of broad classes of tasks in mathematics, science, engineering and other technical areas.
5. Abilities are more fundamental than skills. The term 'skill' refers to the level of proficiency on a unitary task or a configuration of tasks. Basic abilities are basically involved in performing each skill. To summarize, an ability is :

   (a) a product of maturation and learning;

---

2. Fleishman, E. A. and Bartlett, C. J., "Human Abilities", In Mussen P. H. & Rosenzweig, M. R. eds., Annual Review of Psychology, Palo Alto California; Annual Review, 1969, pp. 349-380.

(b) developed during the formative years persists in adulthood;

(c) that the present abilities of the individual influence the rate at which he learns related new tasks;

(d) that one ability may underlie performance on more specific tasks than another;

(e) more fundamental than a skill.

On the contrary, Cronbach (1970)[3] shows that there is very little distinction between abilities, skills and achievements—one is the complement to the other. People develop the skills and achieve with an underlying ability through practice. Now, as they develop their skills and consequent achievements, the underlying abilities are also being improved—skills and achievements are, hence, considered synonymous.

Cognitive abilities and their organization

Cognitive ability (as research reveals) is mainly represented by intellectual ability. In order to deal with this part, it is essential to identify first the cognitive abilities in human being. The identification is done mainly through systematically carried out experimental researches with the help of factor analysis method. Factor analysis mainly involves the study of test results by correlational methods in order to assess the amount of relationship among the variables employed in the test. Here, tests are specially developed to identify hypothesized abilities in different sets of consecutive subtests. They are continued one leading to another until the system is completed. As a result many small scale studies are to be conducted in order to achieve a related large scale model of this kind. Following this method Guilford (1967)[4] hypothesized a structure of human intellect, comprised of 120 separate abilities. Twenty-five of these abilities are classified as divergent—production abilities. He and his associates worked for 15 years on identifying and describing these 24 abilities only—others remained to be examined by later researchers.

Another way of identifying human abilities is through large-scale programmatic research in school settings, using achievement as well as ability tests. In this method a direct

3. Cronbach, E. J., Essentials of Psychological Testing, 3rd ed., Harper & Row., N.Y., 1970.
4. Guilford, J. P., The Nature of Human Intelligence., N.Y., McGraw-Hill, 1967.

relationship between human abilities and school tasks can be demonstrated. This method can be utilized with a broader perspective.

There are five different viewpoints, regarding the nature of cognitive abilities :

1. that there is a single unitary ability
2. that there is a set of primary abilities
3. that there are larger number of specific abilities
4. that there are indefinite number of specific abilities related to learning hierarchies
5. that there is a hierarchical structure involving both general and specific abilities.

These viewpoints have been incorporated in various research areas of intellectual ability. The cognitive ability involves and is also manifested through thinking, reasoning, memory, imagination, language and intellectual and other similar cognitive functioning of the human mind. The cognitive ability—as expressed from the researches on learning of the later behaviourists (who came away from the radicals)—revealed that it contains the concept of mediation, which assumes that influential internal processes intervene between children's exposure to external events and their reaction to them. The child's potential ability to build internal models of the world and external environments, and to manipulate those models so as to explain the past as also to draw conclusions about future is, in essence, known as 'cognition' and the ability to perform the various cognitive activities is known as cognitive ability. Intellectual ability is one such cognitive ability which ranges from simple concept formation at primary stage to higher mental processes—like mental representation, higher concept formation, reasoning and information processing in later years of life.

General Intellectual Ability (Cognitive)

The presence of general intellectual ability has been concretely established as testing of intelligence began in 1911*, introduced and performed by Alfred Binet. The 1916 Terman adaptation of Binet-Simon Scale declared (by Terman)[5] intelligence as the ability to carry on abstract thinking. A similar

---

* Revised form, after 1905 scale of Binet.

5. Terman, L. M. : The Measurement of Intelligence,. Houghton Miffin, Boston, 1916.

concept of intelligence was proposed by Thorndike (1926)[6] as the ability to make good responses from the point of view of the truth or fact. Still later Wechsler (1958)[7] developed an intelligence test to measure intellectual ability "as the aggregate or global capacity of the individual to act purposefully, to think rationally and to deal effectively with his environment". These psychologists were neutral with respect to the role of genetic and environmental determinant of intelligence. However, Burt et al (1934)[8] conceived of intelligence as an all-round intellectual ability that is inborn. Similar to the Indian concept of 'Buddhi'. Hunt (1961)[9] viewed intelligence as totally determined by environmental conditions. All these confirmed intelligence to be defined as unitary ability. For decades until 1950s, the concept of intelligence as a unitary ability was not seriously questioned and the hereditarian idea of an 'unchanging rate of intellectual growth' was, more or less, widely accepted. Students were put in one or another curriculum or in one or another track early in their school-life on the assumption that they were properly placed and would remain in that particular track till the end of their school years.

The researchers from 1960 onward started doubting intelligence as a single unitary ability. In fact, as early as in 1938, Thurstone[10] administered a large number of separate tests that tapped various mental functions. He factor-analysed the test scores and arrived at what he identified as "Primary Mental Abilities", which are separate in kind but parallel in structure. Each ability comprised of two or more discrete abilities and each of these primary abilities is assumed to underlie a set of related achievements or skills. Because the abilities are separate in kind, individuals who are high in one ability may not be high in the others. These five most prominent abilities are : verbal meaning, number facility, reasoning, perceptual speed and spatial relations. These abilities are assumed to be most critical in school work, though they are not equally important at all ages. A brief description

---

6. Thorndike, E. L. : The Measurement of Intelligence. Bureau of Publications, Teachers College, Columbia University., N.Y., 1926.
7. Wechsler, D : The Measurement and Appraisal of Adult Intelligence (4th ed). Williams and Wilkins. Baltimore. 1958.
8. Burt, C., Jones. E. Miller, E. and Moodie, W : How The Mind Works. Appleton-Century-Crofts-1934.
9. Hunt. J. M. : Intelligence and Experience. Ronald. N.Y. 1961.
10. Thurstone, L. L. : Primary Mental Abilities. Psychometric Monographs. no. 1, 1938.

of each ability (there is also a related test for each ability at several age levels) follows : (Thurstone, 1963)[11] :

V– Verbal meaning : The ability to understand ideas expressed in words. In the later school years this is the most important single index of a child's potential for handling academic tasks. In the lower levels it is tested by a vocabulary test in picture form; at the upper levels, by a vocabulary test.

N– Number facility : The ability to work with numbers, to handle simple quantitative problems rapidly and accurately, and to understand and recognize qualitative differences. At the lower grade levels the N. scores are determined by a pictorial test that requires no reading. Addition problems are also used. At the upper levels arithmetical reasoning problems are included.

R– Reasoning : The ability to solve logical problems. Separate measures of this ability are not provided in the batteries designed for grade K through 4. (lower levels) In the 4-6 battery it is measured by word grouping, letter series and number series tests.

P– Perceptual speed : The ability to recognize likeness and differences between objects and symbols quickly and accurately. This ability is important in acquiring reading skills but tends to plateau at a relatively early age. For this reason it is included only with the three batteries designed for the lower grades.

S– Spatial relations : The ability to visualize objects and figures rotated in space and the relations between them. The test measuring this ability appears in every level of the PMA test battery (Thurstone, 1963).

The work of Thurstone and his associates generated immense interest in identifying more specific abilities because their work was considered to be a mark of sharp turn from the accepted notion of intelligence as a general mental ability. Now we shall consider the structure of intellect as comprising of 120 specific abilities.

Specific Abilities

J. P. Guilford (1966) does not accept the concept of a unitary general intellectual ability or of a few primary mental

11. Thurstone, T. G. : Examiner's Manual IBM, 805 edition, PMA Primary Mental Abilities for Grades 6-9, Chicago : Science Research Associates, 1963.

abilities. His model (1966) is a foremost illustration of the systematic identification of specific intellectual abilities. Figure 4.1 diagram 120 possible human abilities in the cognitive domain, most of which have been identified (Guilford and Hoepfner, 1966)[12] . Guilford (1967)[13] defines an ability as a union of an operation, a content, and a product. In Guilford's structure of intellect, there are five operations, four types of contents, and six products; therefore, there are $5 \times 4 \times 6 = 120$ abilities. A brief overview of the operations, contents and products follows :

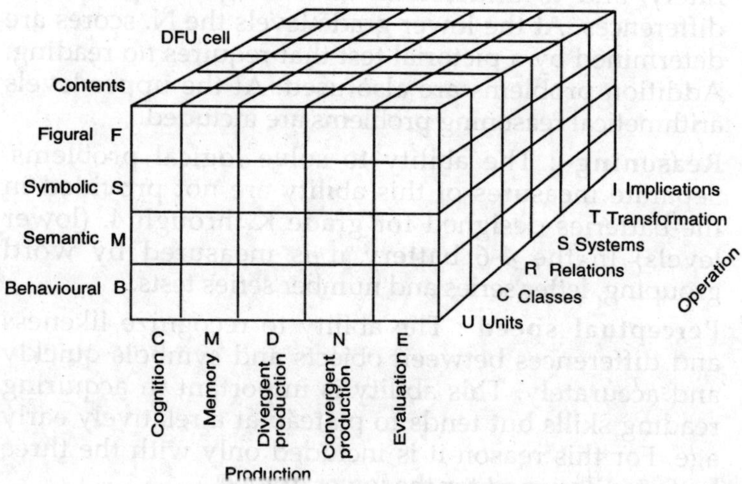

Fig. 4.1 : Model of the Structure of Intellect (Adapted for Guilford and Hoepfner, 1966)

Operations

Major kinds of intellectual activities or processes; things that the organism does with the raw materials of information, information being defined as "that which the organism discriminates".

C– Cognition, immediate discovery, awareness, rediscovery, or recognition of information in various forms, comprehension or understanding.

M– Memory, retention or storage. With some degree of availability of information in the same form it was

12. Guilford, J. P. and Hoepfner, R. The Analysis of Intelligence McGraw Hill, N.Y., 1966.
13. Guilford J. P. : The Nature of Human Intelligence. N.Y. McGraw-Hill, 1967.

committed to storage and in response to the same cues in connection with which it was learned.

D– Divergent production. Generation of information from given information, where the emphasis is upon variety and quantity of output from the same source. Likely to involve what has been called transfer. This operation is most clearly involved in aptitudes of creative potential.

N– Convergent production. Generation of information from given information, where the emphasis is upon achieving unique or conventionally accepted best outcomes. It is likely the given (cue) information fully determines the response.

E– Evaluation. Reaching decisions or making judgements concerning criterion satisfaction (correctness, suitability, adequacy, desirability, etc.) of information.

Contents

Broad classes or types of information discriminable by the organism.

F– Figural. Information in concrete form, as perceived or as recalled possibly in the form of images. The term 'figural' minimally implies figure-ground perceptual organization. Visual spatial information is figural. Different sense modalities may be involved, e.g. visual, kinesthetic.

S– Symbolic. Information in the form of denotative signs, having no significance in and or themselves, such as letters, numbers, musical notations, codes, and words — when meanings and form are not considered.

M– Semantic. Information in the form of meaning to which words commonly become attached, hence most notable in verbal thinking and in verbal communication but not identical with words. Meaningful pictures also often convey semantic information.

B– Behavioural. Information, essentially nonverbal, involved in human interactions where the attitude, needs, desires, moods, intentions, perceptions, thoughts etc. of other people and of ourselves are involved.

Products

Forms that information takes in the organism's processing of it :

U– Units. Relatively segregated or circumscribed items of information having 'thing' character. May be close to Gestalt psychology's figure on a ground.

C– Classes. Conceptions underlying sets of items of information grouped by virtue of their common properties.

R– Relations. Connections between items of information based upon variables or points of contact that apply to them. Relational connections are more meaningful and definable than implications.

S– Systems. Organized or structured aggregates of items of information; complexes of interrelated or interacting parts.

T– Transformations. Changes of various kinds (redefinition, shifts, or modification or existing information or in its function).

I– Implications. Extrapolations of information, in the form of expectancies, predictions, known or suspected antecedents, concomitants, or consequences. The connection between the given information and that extrapolated is more general and less definable than a relational connection (Guilford & Hoepfner, 1966)[14].

Three types of intelligene are associated by Guilford with the four types of contents : Concrete intelligence pertains to abilities involving figural content. Mechanics, operators of machines, artists, and musicians depend heavily on these abilities. Abstract intelligence pertains to abililities involving symbolic and semantic content. Learning to recognize words, to spell, and to operate with numbers involves abilities with symbolic content. Abilities with semantic content are required for understanding verbal concepts and ideas of all types. Present-day intelligence tests are heavily loaded with test items requiring the use of abstract abilities. Social intelligence pertains to behavioural content, understanding the behaviour of others and oneself. Teachers, lawyers, social workers, politicians and leaders are higher in social intelligence than other professional groups.

The concept of abilities is most meaningful when considered in connection with outcomes of learning and broad subject matter fields. In Figure 4.2, the abilities connected with

14. Guilford; J. P. and Hoepfner, R. : The Analysis of Intelligence, N. Y. McGraw Hill, 1966.

each types of content are related to outcomes and curriculum areas. For example, the ability to think productively with figural material is associated with performance in art and music and with certain aspects of the applied arts, such as home economics, agriculture and industrial arts. As noted earlier, mathematicians and physicists also demonstrate high-level spatial abilities, which, in Guilford's system, involve figural content. An example of abilities involving symbolic and semantic content is productive thinking that leads to learning factual information, concepts, and problem-solving skills and to developing creativity in the language, arts, social studies, science, mathematics and other subject fields. Abilities with behavioural content are less clearly defined, but as noted in Figure 4.2, include understanding oneself and others and interacting in a group.

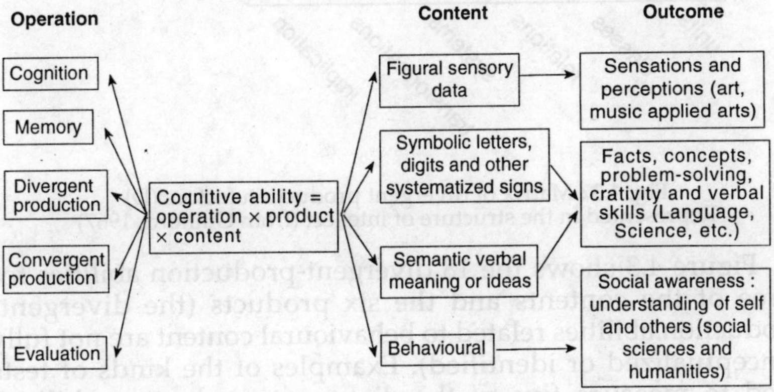

Fig. 4.2 : Schematic arrangement of cognitive abilities and learning outcomes (Adapted from Guilford and Hopfner, 1966)

Divergent-production abilities

The most important contribution of the structure of intellect (SI) is a new way of thinking about the nature of intelligence. The fact that many relatively distinct abilities have been identified poses a direct challenge to the notion that all human beings can be placed from high to low on a single continuum of general intellectual ability and should be treated accordingly in educational and vocational settings. There are many intellectual abilities, and the same individual may be at quite different points on the various continua. Some students are much stronger in divergent—than in convergent—production abilities, and vice versa. In this connection, the identification of the divergent-production, or creative ability has already made some impact on educational practices and should produce many more changes in the future.

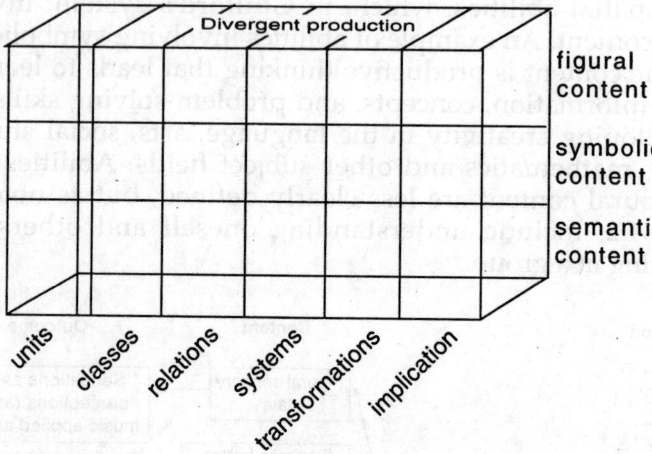

Fig. 4.3 : Matrix of divergent production factors (D) Represented in the structure of intellect (from Guilford, 1967)

Figure 4.3 shows the 18 divergent-production abilities for three of the contents and the six products (the divergent-production abilities related to behavioural content are not fully conceptualized or identified). Examples of the kinds of tests used to measure five of the divergent-production abilities follow (Guilford, 1967)[15]. Three of them are tests for classes and two are tests of transformation. Study them carefully with two purposes in mind. First note that the items do not call for responses to be scored as correct and, second, relate the content of the test items to kinds of assignments and activities that may be relevant for students as part of their regular instruction in schools.

Divergent production of figural classes (DFC) is measured by several tests.

(1) One of them called "Alternate Letter Group", e.g. AHVTC to form subgroups, each of which makes a class according to the figural properties of the letter.

15. Guilford, J. P. : The Nature of Human Intelligence. N.Y. McGraw Hill, 1967.

Illustrative responses are AHT (all having horizontal lines), AHVT (all having straight lines) or HVC (all open sides) etc.

(2) Figural similarities

(3) Divergent production of Symbolic classes (DSC)

(4) Divergent Production of Semantic classes—where meanings are always involved in semantic content and not in figural or symbolic content. A sample item may be quoted :

From the seven words below, make some small classes of objects. 1. Arrow 2. Bee, 3. Crocodile, 4. Fish, 5. Kite, 6. Sail boat 7. Sparrow.

Sample answers : 1, 2, 5, 7 (found in air); 3, 4, 6 (found in water); 2, 3, 4, 7 (animals); 3, 4, 5, 7 (have tails) etc.

These are the examples of three divergent production test items, one each for figural, symbolic and semantic classes. Detailed information about other divergent operation × content × production abilities is given by Guilford (1967). Similarly, he gives examples of divergent-production tests that deal with "transformation" like Divergent Production of Figural Transformation (DFT) and Divergent Production of Semantic Transformtion (DMT).

DFT is measured by match problems, in which, given figures in the form are transformed or changed in a specified way by the removal of some of the matches intended to search for 'novelty' in a person. The DMT, on the other hand, is a search for 'originality' in a person. As such, tests were designed to measure any of these three :

(1) ability to produce responses that are statistically rare in the population,.

(2) ability to produce remotely related response and

(3) ability to produce clever responses.

Guilford is convinced that writers, planners and scientists are strong in divergent production in the semantic area; that inventors and those in the visual arts are strong in the visual figural content; that mathematicians and mathematical scientists and cryptographers are strong in the symbolic content; and that musicians are strong in auditory abilities paralleling those of the visual. Guilford points out that any of the preceding might be strong in more than one area. As noted before, however, he states that a combination of specific abilities, rather than a general verbal ability, or several primary abilities, underlies success in all these areas.

Learning hierarchies

The next viewpoint regarding the nature of cognitive abilities to consider is that of Gagne (1970)[16], who has identified what he calls "learning hierarchies." The functional unit of a learning hierarchy is the relationship of one higher intellectual skill to the prior mastery of the subordinate skills essential to attaining it. Gagne illustrates the concept of a learning hierarchy by relating many intellectual skills that are required in complex achievements associated with various curriculum areas of the school. For example, Figure 4.4 shows a learning hierarchy for a prekindergarten mathematical skill. As may be noted in Figure 4.4, the highest performance in this

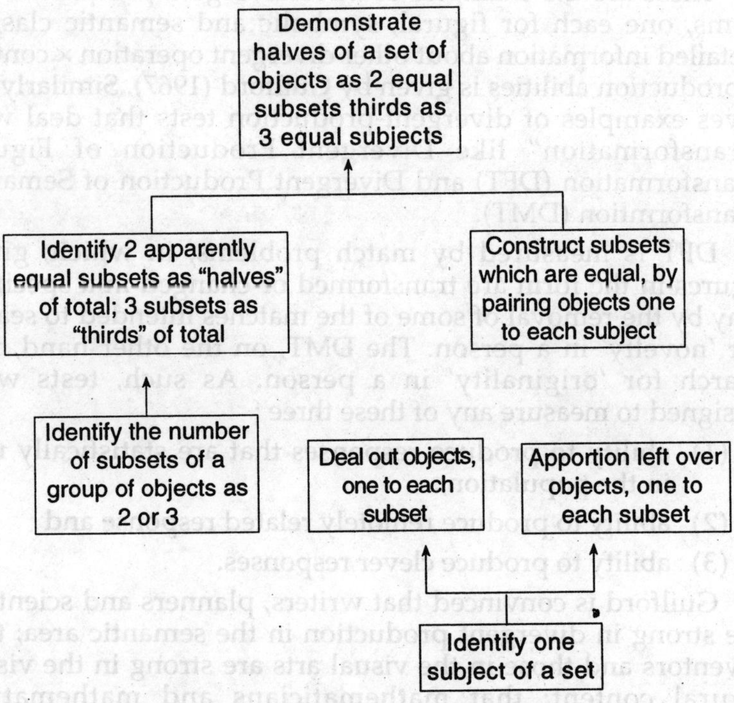

Fig. 4.4 : A learning hierarchy for a prekindergarten mathematical skill (Source Gagne, 1970)

16. Gagne, R. M. : The Conditions of Learning. 2nd ed. N.Y. Holt, Rinehart and Winston, 1970.

hierarchy is to demonstrate the "halves" of a set of objects as two equal subsets and the "thirds" as three equal subsets. In analyzing what is required of the child to be able to do this, one arrives at the subskills as indicated in Figure 4.4.

Gagne indicates that any set of related learning activities which cumulate into successively higher levels of achievement can be analyzed into their constituents and prerequisite intellectual skills. Thus, an indefinite but a very large number of specific intellectual abilities or skills, is implied by the concept of learning hierarchies. One's intelligence is composed of the skills he has mastered.

A hierarchical structure of abilities

Figure 4.5 outlines a hierarchical structure of factors in human abilities : a general factor, two major group factors, seven minor group factors, and an indeterminate number of possible but unidentified specific factors. Vernon (1950)[17], a

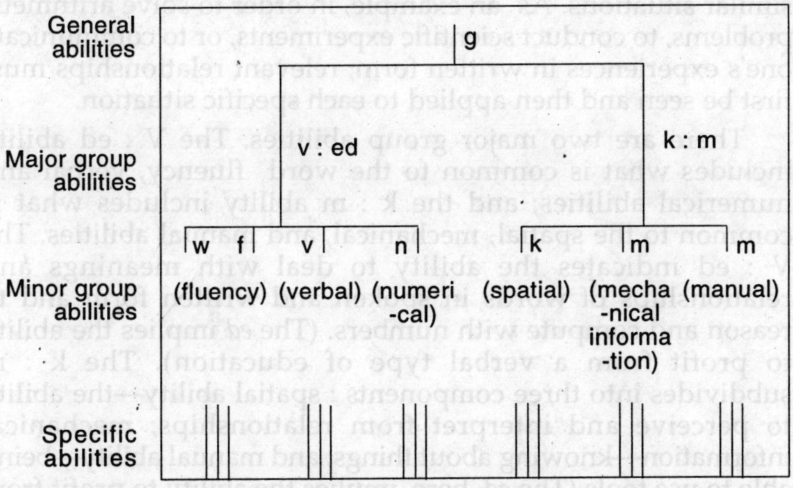

Fig. 4.5 : Hierarchical structure of human abilities (Klausmeir etal, 1975)

British psychologist pioneered in the formulation of this model. Smith (1964)[18] and Lovell (1965)[19], both Englishmen, indicate

17. Vernor; P. E. The Structure of Human Abilities. N.Y. Wiley, 1950.
18. Smith, I. M. Spatial Ability. Its Educational and Social Significance. London University of London Press, 1964.
19. Lovell, K. Educational Psychology and Children, 8th ed. London University of London Press, 1965.

that the general and group factors are widely accepted by British psychologists. Until recently, British psychologists had not given the specific factors serious consideration.

At this point we are considering the structure, not the nature of the abilities outlined in Figure 4.6. Furthermore, this discussion is not meant to imply that the abilities as stated at any level in the hierarchy are themselves fully understood. There are unresolved differences of opinion about how these and other abilities are manifested in the performance of individuals, therefore, the structure should be considered hypothetical.

According to Lovell (1965), the ability, referred to also as general intellectual ability or intelligence, is considered the basic ability underlying all activities in the cognitive domain; it accounts for a part of what is common to many specific tasks. It involves the ability to see relevant relationships between objects or ideas and to apply these relationships to new but similar situations. As an example, in order to solve arithmetic problems, to conduct scientific experiments, or to communicate one's experiences in written form, relevant relationships must first be seen and then applied to each specific situation.

There are two major group abilities. The V : ed ability includes what is common to the word fluency, verbal and numerical abilities; and the k : m ability includes what is common to thc spatial, mechanical, and manual abilities. The V : ed indicates the ability to deal with meanings and relationships of words in spoken and written form and to reason and compute with numbers. (The *ed* implies the ability to profit from a verbal type of education). The k : m subdivides into three components : spatial ability—the ability to perceive and interpret from relationships; mechanical information—knowing about things; and manual ability—being able to use tools (The *ed* here, implies the ability to profit from technical education). The six minor group abilities can be subdivided further if a sufficiently large number of more specific tests is given and the analysis is continued.

The preceding hierarchy, just as Guilford's structure of intellect, is hypothetical rather than a reality. Persons working in this field do not agree as to the precise nature of the hierarchy. For example, Cronbach (1970)[20] has outlined a

20. Cronbach, L. J. : Essentials of Psychological Testing 3rd ed. N.Y. Harper and Row, 1970.

hierarchical structure of abilities that is shown in Figure 4.6 includes six rather than four levels. The two top levels in Figure 4.5 are divided by Cronbach, as shown in Figure 4.6. Cronbach's hierarchy at the lowest level can be related to areas of instructions quite directly. The model does not imply two kinds of schooling—verbal university oriented and technical work oriented as is the case of the hierarchy in Figure 4.5.

A hypothetical structure of human abilities is shown in Figure 4.6. Relate each of the four sets of ideas about human intelligence—Terman, Thurstone, Guilford, and Gagne–to one or two of the levels or lines of Figure. 4.6.

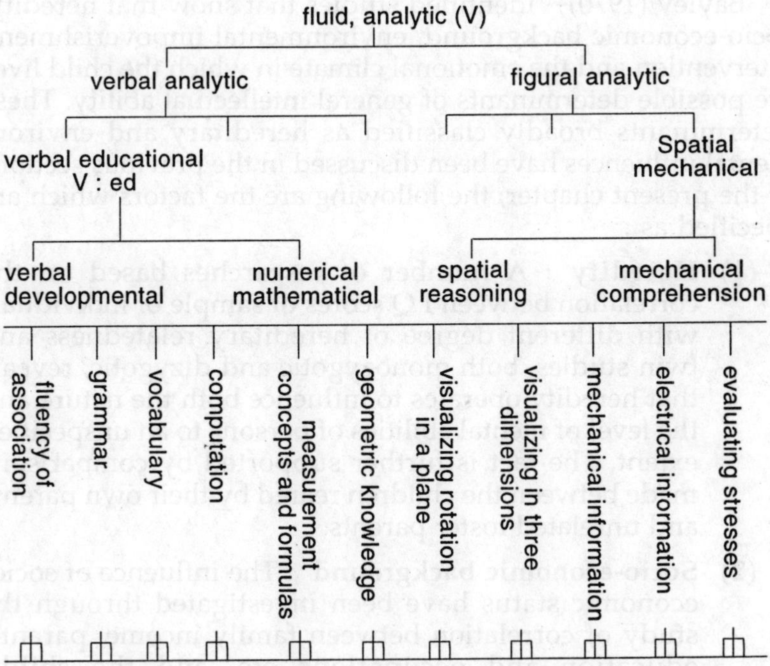

Fig. 4.6 : A possible hierarchical structure of abilities (Cronblach, 1970)

Organization and determinants of intellectual ability

In all abilities one general factor, several group factors, and many specific factors were identified. Each general or group factor which is common to the achievement of several tests, may be considered as the ability which underlies the particular achievement. A general factor accounted for only part of what is common to many tests and that each of the group abilities accounts for what is common to the classes of performances.

The application of the tests on school children noted that there were differences in the pattern of gains on the various tests of achievement and aptitude and that differences were related to the students, sex, socio-economic status, and possibly to the characteristics of the schools they attended and the communities in which they lived. Therefore, it can be conclu-ded that the differences of cognitive ability among individuals is determined by the biological and environmental factors.

Bayley (1970)[21] identified studies that show that heredity, socio-economic background, environmental impoverishment, intervention and the emotional climate in which the child lives are possible determinants of general intellectual ability. These determinants broadly classified as hereditary and environmental influences have been discussed in the previous sections of the present chapter; the following are the factors which are specified as :

(1) **Heredity** : A number of researches based on the correlation between I Q scores of sample of individuals with different degree of hereditary relatedness and twin studies, both monozygotic and dizygotic, reveals that heredity operates to influence both the nature and the level of mental abilities of persons to an unspecified extent. The fact is further supported by comparisons made between the children reared by their own parents and unrelated foster parents.

(2) **Socio-economic background** : The influence of socio-economic status have been investigated through the study of correlation between family income, parents, education and occupations etc. and the child's intelligence using various kinds of composite ratings. Until about 2 years of age, the correlation between these socio-economic variables and the child's tested intelligence is low and often negative. From 3 years of age on through the adolescent years, the size of the correlation increase, is generally positive and is often as

21. Bayley, N : Development of Mental Abilities; in Mussen, P.H. ed. Carmichael's manual of Child Psychology. Vol. I N.Y. Wiley, 1970.

high as 40 (Klausmeier and Goodwin, 1966, 1975)[22]. This is interpreted as evidence that socio–economic status is also a partial determinant of intelligence.

(3) **Environmental impoverishment** : The orphanages and other foster homes and institutions in which infants and young children are placed early in life and brought up there for a long period of life tend to secure low score in intelligence tests. This may be due to the impoverished environment of those institutions but the result cannot be taken to be perfectly conclusive because the number of researches of the cross-cultures have not been widely compared by the authors. Apparently, impoverished environments contribute generally to low intelligence and the greater the impoverishment, greater is the deleterious effect. The impoverished environment is perhaps itself detremental to normal growth of abilities in human being.

(4) **Physical Impoverishment** : Closely associated with socio-economic factors and environmental impoverishment is the factor of physical impoverishment which, in addition, includes poor nutrition, a high incidence of disease, slow physical growth and poor health all equally contribute to lowered mental abilities.

(5) **Intervention** : During the many decades that psychologists and educators were unaware of, or did not accept the idea that children's IQs do in fact change across time, intervention studies were not carried out by earlier researchers. Several intervention studies in the meantime carried, suggests that intervention may improve motivational conditions. Intervention may create better opportunities for children to learn and reduce anxiety. Debilitating diseases can be avoided and malnutrition can be dealt with so that IQ can be raised. Several studies also confirm that increase in IQ cannot only raise temporarily over a short period of time, but also can be maintained so over a long period to come.

(6) **Emotional claimate** : The child at the early stage expresses rapid and instantaneous emotional reactions

22. Klausmeier, H.J and Goodwin, W : Learning and Human Abilities : Educational Psychology, 4th Edition. Harper and International Ed. Harper and Row. N.Y. 1966, 1975.

to stimuli which evoke emotion and they are mainly of primary type. The emotional climate in which the child is reared has a long standing influence in his cognitive life as well. Emotions affect his mental development. For example, IQ fluctuations have been found to parallel the fluctuations in the emotional climate at home. Acceptance and rejection of parental love have been observed correlated positively or negatively with intelligence, later achievements and acquiring higher mental ability of children in school years.

Psychomotor Abilities

The growing child, along with his development of mental abilities, needs growing physically strong in order to enable himself/herself to become an effective individual. To grow means the development of his psychomotor potential to reach to the fullest extent of his hereditary dispositions and beyond, if possible. The emotional climate of the family rests in the interaction between children and parents and other family members. It reflects the general attitudes and feelings that prevail at home in the family group. The underlying thinking and outlook of life and general behaviour of each individual family influence the child's rearing processes. The child rearing process is again dependent on the emotional climate prevailing in a home atmosphere. If children get a sense of security from their homes, that helps them cope more adequately with the tasks of classroom bearing in future and other problems they will encounter at school. On the contrary, lack of affection and love in the family climate or punitive and disorganized attitudes of the adults in the family will lead to problem behaviour in the children. That will again hamper with successful school adjustment and learning ability.

Guilford (1958)[23] identified six psychomotor processes which he believed to be involved in many kinds of motor performances. These processes combined with specific parts of the body, may be called psychomotor abilities. they are :

1 — strength,

2 — coordination,

3 — Impulsion, pertaining to the rate at which movements are initiated from stationery position.

23. Guilford J. P. A System of the Psychomotor Abilities, American Journal of Psychology. 71 : 161-174, 1958.

4 — Speed—pertaining to the rate of movements after they have started.

5 — Precision—dealing with the accuracy with which bodily positions can be held and with the accuracy of directed movements once started.

6 — Flexibility—referring to the extent to which the part of the body is free to bend or to the scope of movement pertaining to a particular joint.

Psychomotor abilities are thought to be basic to later activities of the children activities such as singing, speaking, learning, writing, typing, manipulating various objects and to attain dexterity. Further, certain perceptual motor tasks—such as taking shorthand or playing an instrument—require not only physical movements, but also the perception of words, their meaning and understanding instructions that direct the physical movement. Hence the underlying abilities are called psychomotor.

We have already seen that cognitive abilities are improved through learning how to read, to solve problems, to think and the like. So also the psychomotor abilities are brought to higher levels through engaging in appropriate physical activities. The consistent progress in identifying and classifying psychomotor abilities and corresponding motor sets and activities, cataloging of human abilities for later improved performance by the individual have become possible through researches carried in this line, which may help the educators to organize and restructure the educational programmes and practices.

MENTAL ABILITIES AND INDIVIDUAL DIFFERENCE

Problem for teachers

Mental ability is not a single ability, but is cumulative and active—a combination of physical, thinking, intellectual and other potent mental activities. It is a determinant of individual differences. Mental abilities are influenced both by heredity and environment. They undergo developmental processes and are shaped in their own way. As the child grows first in the family, different homes have different effects by providing different kinds of stimulation and feedback. All the abilities function together to help the child to gain new knowledge, to assimilate them and to become aware of himself and of his surroundings. The evidence of the inheritance of ability and the influence of home environment will help to explain why children differ.

Stability and change in behaviour determine the nature of individual differences. Many teachers and psychologists have assumed that standing in mental ability do not change. Standings remain fairly stable over the years, but IQ is not 'constant' and other indices of ability are also not constant (most reports of stability come from correlational studies). But evidently individual differences in basic skills are highly stable. The student who is ill-prepared for Grade III has a high probability of being ill-prepared for Grade IV or V. Schools can develop the skills the weak student lacks to some extent but a strong student will, meanwhile, advance to higher levels on the basis of his native equipment. The school can only build on what the student has so far been furnished with.

Despite statistical stability indicated by correlation in test situations over time, important changes may occur in some indiviuals. Initially, the students who show unstability in test scores may improve their positions gradually. Early growth may be characterized by spurts and lags, but early tests have almost no relation to school age tests. Test in infancy generally measure motor coordination and some glimpses of intelligence and attention pattern. But they are not comparable to the intellectual and analytic abilities of later years. So it is with language abilities. The school records show that after grade I, the person usually retains his or her relative place in the group. But important changes in rank do occur. Stability can never be measured by test scores only—it depends much on maturity and learning experiences. Individual differences in scholastic ability, though, tend to be stable over the years. Some individuals, however, make upward or downward changes in the standing.

Influences of Heredity

That heredity plays important role in identifying ability gains ground from the fact that some families produce eminent persons generation after generation. This is an uncertain evidence, however, since distinguished families can provide many advantages for their children which are not possible for ordinary families to provide. Best evidence comes from twin studies, especially the one-egg-monozygotic (MZ)-twins who receive precisely the same genes. When they are reared in the same home their experiences have also much in common. Whereas the two-egg-dizygotic (DZ) twins are—like brothers and sisters—sharing 50% of the genes in common.

The correlation of test scores for MZ twins reared together is about as high as the correlation of two tests on the same person. The correlation for DZ twins is generally around 0.50—a fifty-fifty chance. Whatever the chances, "there is a consistent indication that heredity has an influence and that anatomical and biochemical differences can surely be expected to have behavioral consequences" (Cronbach, 1977)[24]. Most of the authors working on the same line give different values for the coefficient of heritability for human ability—which may be due to their treatment of genetic dominance or the correlational share of either heredity or environment.

Heritability of mental ability

The heritability of test performance was actually a belief, but not based on facts or findings. The essential concepts, facts and conclusions about heritability are worth attention chiefly because of the controversy about them. It is the view of many authors dealing with the subject that the facts on inheritance have little or no bearing on present day educational policies. Abilities develop out of experience and the exposures they receive, and are strongly influenced by the conditions of development. But the native factor cannot be ignored totally. Abilities are strongly influenced by the genes. These two statements are not inconsistent, but complementary to each other.

Heritability defined

Heritability is a statistical concept, comes from genetics—more specifically from animal breeders. Research on the heritability of human traits does shed light on development. When a disease is shown to be heritable, genetic counselling and engineering can reduce the number of children born with that disease. It has also been discovered that certain abnormalities are not heritable. The fact is that research on human heritability is hard to conduct because conditions are beyond control and convincing results are difficult to secure. But a new trend in child development issue is distinctly visible that mental ability, in general, has indeed been going up not only in the developed countries, but the world over, i.e. in the

24. Cronbach, L. J. Educational Psychology, 3rd ed. Harcourt Brace Jovanvich, Inc. N.Y. 1977.

less developed and the developing countries as well. Technological advancement has generated a spirit of keen competition which has again influenced the going up of mental abilities. The new generation has definitely gained on this more than the generation of the past. It has become evident that today's children perform much better in the intelligence tests during the pre-school period and in adolescence than the children of early forties. It is also true that recent cultural opportunities are easily available these days and have accelerated the development of young children in this generation (Thorndike, 1975)[25].

Developmental Influences : The Role of Home

How does environment affect ability of a child ? An achiever is generally recognized as possessing higher mental ability. But then, achievement of a child is very much influenced by the home environment, the child gets. Mental ability does not grow independent of physical ability. Therefore, the factors related to the physique and health are strongly connected with mental ability. The food the child gets, the type of care he or she is used to, the conversations addressed to him/her in the home and the emotional support that follows his/her early trials and failure or successes, all leave a mark on the intellectual development in a child. The above influences—to begin with—are also responsible for the individual differences in mental ability among children. Later, the child's peer group and associates, his teachers and guides, friends and relatives—all accumulate to enrich his expriences and strengthen mental ability. The cumulative experiences of each child from his surroundings and from his own perceptions make the difference. Consistent opportunities to use a type of reasoning, frequent occurence of intelligence evoking situations, presence of many discriminating incidences with appropriate reward and reinforcement enhance the richer development of mental ability. Any difference in these sequences elicits individual difference.

Conversely, restricted experience retards development. Researches and surveys reveal that rural children or children from remote regions, children less exposed to advanced modes and methods, earn on the average lower scores than the more advantageous group of urban and metropolitan children. But

25. Thorndike, R. L. Mr Binets Test 70 Years Later. Educational Researcher 4 (5), 1975, 3-7.

what is important for us to know is not so much the difference between the groups, which is much smaller than the difference within the group. Sometimes children belonging to the disadvantageous group may show tremendous capability given the opportunity and that is not very infrequent. Many of them even earn high scores on mental tests. But the effect of restricted environment becomes progressively deteriorating and harmful for the children if they are to remain in the same environment for longer period.

Nevertheless, it oversimplifies to predict that good environment or poor environment account for differences in ability. Not all the children from good environment score high in mental tests, there exist poor achievers as well. The sharp distinction between the good and poor environment responsible for enhancing or lowering mental ability would imply a steady rise in standing for some children (coming from good environment) and steady decline for others. But individual retest records available are of many shape. The different growth curves available show steep declines. Some up-and-down patterns, some records that they proceed in the same level for many years and then either march upward or show a downward decline. Perhaps hereditary patterns of physiological development control this timing of mental growth to some degree (Cronbach, P. 321 ibid). Some increases or declines are again strongly related with emotional condition of the child. Radical changes in mental ability may be due to the emotional upsets.

Other very influential developmental factors are parental attitude, child rearing practices and home climate which affect intellectual development (as discussed in earlier section). Parental attitude and techniques affect the growth of mental ability. Researches on achievement motivation reveal that some homes directly train ability to learn and motivation to learn. Emphasis on intellectual achievement has a powerful effect. The parents who foster achievement motivation create learning situations for the child and help him extend his competence. Children from democratic homes tend to be more curious and competitive when they enter school. It has also been found that exceptional increases in ability from age 6 to age 10 are strongly associated with child's personality at age 6. The one who will gain tends to be aggressive and competitive and is more likely to initiate his own activities. The independent child is emotionally free to gain more from his environment (Op cit. p 323).

The effect of home atmosphere is traced by observing the parent-child interaction and then testing the child at successive ages. The longitudinal studies available agree in finding autonomy, and democracy in the home, and a positive emotional tone beneficial, but each study adds important details. What the mother does in the first three years has a strong relation to the boy's midadolescent IQ. Maternal style seems to have less effect on the girl's characteristics on the other hand. It has been observed that the boys who developed intellectual strength had been subjected in early years to encouragement and strong pressures. The boy reared by a hostile mother typically showed inferior intellectual performance from age 4 onward. It is the nagging, over-attentive mother who seems to damage the child's long run intellectual development. It should be kept in view that intelligence is not a thing, it is a style of work—a mental ability put to use. Individuals differ in its utilization. To say that one person is more intelligent than another means that he acts more intelligently, more of time.

Role of School in organizing developmental differences

The individual difference of mental abilities has urged the schools to reorganize learners and lessons. Traditionally, the schools are age-graded irrespective of individual capacity. The school entrance age has become the norm and each branch of learning been introduced according to age norm. The awareness of individual differences in abilities has led the schools to reorganize their methods of management and teaching instruction so that the ability is reflected in the student's performance. The schools have later come to realize that organisational plans that violate the facts of development and individual difference of ability are continually under challenge.

The studies about some distinctive demands of pre-adolescent children paved the way for the establishment of junior high schools. These schools offered a varied programme in which the pre-adolescents could explore their interests, abilities and talents. The same practice continues till the children reach adolescent stage and are set in the secondary and then at higher secondary set ups. The schools in organizing their set up at this stage take the physical and psychological features typical of adolescence as their concern and forward richer programmes so that explorations of varied interests can continue through various courses of the curriculum. But even in this organization, the schools are age graded. As a result of the influence of some psychologists for the last fifty years on educational practices, there appeared some educational innovations regarding reshuffle of age placement. Some other psychologists are totally against this idea of age grading. This is most evident in the "open universities" programme in the country. Such universities require an untraditional organization so that adult can enter the programme without giving up their occupational and family responsibilities.

All these show that it makes little sense to assign children to learning experiences solely on the basis of age. The abilities range widely among the school-going population. Hence there remains a scope for the school to organize classes on the basis of ability grouping along with test score and age. But this kind of grouping at the elementary level is not always uniform. Students homogeneous in one or two respects differ in other dimensions and as the dimensions are increased, the group loses its homogeneous character and reveal uniqueness. Furthermore, the teacher is in a difficult position to select his method of teaching both from the academic and affective point of view. The personality difference that requires the teacher to restrain one or encourage a second and to give emotional support to the third will face a confusion, though the students are select in ability. Grouping does function at higher levels of schooling. This has guided the higher secondary education to be divided into streams.

Average and below average students are likely to achieve somewhat less in ability-grouped classes. It is commonly believed that forming a section of low ability students of adolescent age make them feel inferior and eventually may create more complicated problems. There remains a chance of the individual's self-concept being wounded. But the evidence does not support this. It is a simple logic that, one weak student may find higher selfconcept in a low-ability group where the pressure of competition is lower than in the group where abler classmates are in the array of competition. Therefore, looking from both the viewpoints the option should rest on the school administration as to how to make the ability grouping so that weaker student can profit from it. The next choice is to regroup students within a class for each school day. This is known as "Flexible Grouping" (Cronbach, op cit). Whatever the type of grouping the psychologists today are opposed to the idea of keeping the child for the entire school day confined to a special kind of programme inside the general set up. The special kind of programme includes grouping according to interests, talents, abilities, skills, as well as for the handicaps.

All these are concern of the school and, therefore, schools always try to plan some innovative programmes continually in order to make management able to change the organization according to the changing demands of the society. But the difficulty is that a school has to manage a large group of homogeneous students with average abilities and has to remain within a set curriculum. Therefore, to fit the students with diverse abilities and talents into the general schedule is not always practically possible. So, a change in the reorganization of curriculum is necessary for the planners of education.

Recent curriculum movements have brought ideas and related learning materials into the elementary curriculum that were formerly reserved for high schools and have brought the college materials into the high school studies. Once it was thought that the elementary schools should teach just information, plus technical skills in primary abilities like reading, writing and elementary calculations. Contemporary think tanks later assumed, instead, that critical thinking, creative expressions and skills of independent investigation should be fostered from the early years. Most of the psychologists have come to believe that readiness is created through experience and not something that simply unfolds according to 'Nature's time–table'. The programme mentioned above, the planners thought, would minimize diversification of ability training and bring students into a homogeneous group where differential abilities will also be considered to a certain extent. Because, readiness is not readiness for a subject or topic, it is readiness for a certain learning experience. Current attempts to place intellectual content earlier in the curriculum assume that methods can be adapted to the concepts, thought processes and attention span of the younger child.

In order to cope with the individual differences in ability another method has come into practice—to prepare large group projects. In this programme, the teacher can devise a group activity within which every student works at his own level. The student then has the self-respect and interest that come from contributing to a group project, develop self-reliance, cooperativeness and individual worth. Each student then would work according to his own ability and improve spontaneously without the frustration of a too difficult task or the tedium of work that is too easy. Within the main unit each one can work on a subdivision that arouses his interest. If he has a special weakness, he can be directed into a task that will remedy it; and if a talent, into a task that will develop it.

This system is a synthesis of the age–old problem of generalized versus specialized instruction in schools, and is at present in operation. But it should be kept in mind that diversified activities require ingenuity. The teacher cannot use the same plan (once prepared) year after year, because each year different students of different abilities, interests and with differing talents will come. Even if next year's class takes up the same topic, the unique social structure and interests of that group call for somewhat different emphasis, organization and source materials. However, the present programme seems to be a workable one in the present social organization where work and school education ought to be complementary to each other.

Characteristics in which Students in Schools vary Individual Differences

Students vary in the age at which they enter any stage of cognitive development or any facet of any stage of other developments that simultaneously take place as the child grows. The major important variations of concern to education shows five categories of characteristics that affect an individual's readiness to start a particular learning task, his progress in learning task and the upper limits he may reach. The five categories are cognitive abilities and related characteristics, psychomotor abilities and related characteristics, affective characteristics, family and socio-economic status and sex (Klausmier 1971, p. 156). The variables associated with cognitive abilities and psychomotor abilities, their determinants regarding individual difference have already been discussed in earlier sections.

As regards affective variables—such as level of motivation and values—variability among students are pronounced.

Atkinson (1965)[26] identified one pervasive motive as the need to achieve success and related need to avoid failure. Individuals vary in these needs—one with a high need of achieving success and low need of avoiding failure act with vigor. Others with high degree of fear of failure puts off the task or even does not participate at all. Individuals in the affective domain vary widely in other motives such as for love and belongingness, for self–esteem and for selfactualization and also in attitudes and values.

As regards sex, differences in the intellectual and psychomotor domains are very small on an average, except in physical strength, height and weight. In language and in handwriting speed the average achievements have been noticed to be higher for girls than boys. In more or less all measures, it has been found that the differences between members of the same sex are far greater than the differences between the averages of the two sexes.

The differences in achievement and cognitive abilities are sometimes regarded as due to the variances in socio-economic status and social class distinctions. These two factors are closely related. The lower the income, the lower is the social class, although other factors also contribute to this classification. The evidences available declares that the opportunities and records in life are unequally distributed creating social class difference and more good things and ample opportunities go to the children belonging to the upper class strata, higher status families. The child who is either low in academic ability or is from a low socio-economic status face barriers to hurdle in order to achieve happiness, success and progress in school.

Two very prominent factors play in initiating and perpetuating varying socioeconomic status and make it more complicated. They are impoverished home (discussed earlier) and hostile neighbourhood conditions and unresponsive schools (ibid). These are social aberrations and has far fetched implication in deciding individual difference. Thus, we see that students at any age or any stage of development vary widely in intellectual or cognitive ability, academic and nonacademic achievements, psychomotor abilities, affective characteristics

26. Atkinson, J. W. The Mainsprings of Achievement Oriented Activity. In Krumboltz, J. D. ed. Learning and Educational Process. Skokie, Ill. Rand McNally, 1965.

and socioeconomic status. Also, their home and neighbourhood conditions differ. "All of these conditions are related to what students are ready to learn (a state of readiness) at a point in time, to the progress they make over a period of time and to the highest level of achievements they eventually attain" (ibid). It is essential for an educationist to know each student's current level of achievement in current curricula so that individual difference levels could be identified. With this knowledge he can advance to set educational programmes using the fruitful information about the student's amount of the store of knowledge in the cognitive domain, for predicting what the student is ready to learn, where to start afresh, and how to progress.

IQ scores or specific ability scores, in fact, have limited value in working out the instructional programme for an individual—they are not always very accurate too. They sometimes are misused because too much reliance is placed on their accuracy, stability and usefulness. Therefore, more comprehensive systems had been suggested. Some have been adopted by various institutions in many advanced countries (where they are still at the experimental level) and also in various other countries and cultures—both who are advanced technologically and those who are on the way to advancement.

Thinking

"Critical thinking displaces rote & drill". (Newsweek 27th June 1986, p. 59.) The story takes a note of distressing evidence concerning reasoning ability—reveals the fact that the movement to teach thinking in schools has gathered considerable momentum—exciting breakthrough of cognitive research. (Schrag, 1988)[27]

Thinking has been defined by Dewey (1933)[28] with the underlying idea that 'thinking is exploration'. He defines thinking as :

A reflective thinking, in distinction from other operations to which we apply the name of thought involves (1) a state of doubt, hesitation, perplexity, mental difficulty, in which thinking originates and (2) an act of searching, hunting, inquiring to find material that will resolve the doubt, settle and dispose the perplexity.

27. Frencis Schrag. Thinking in School and Society. Modison Routledge. N.Y. 1988.
28. Dewey, J. How We Think. Lexington, MA : DC. Health, 1933.

Thinking has various forms which are used by the thinkers as is required by the situation. Thinking may be reflective, intuitive or as simple as day-dreaming. But effective thinking is a mental activity which is a cognitive equivalent of territorial exploration. Thinking would be 'purposeful' if it is experienced as directed to a problem or task one has set oneself. Therefore, thinking may be 'descriptive'—when the mental process involved is set loose, and it may also be 'normative'—when it involves certain purpose. It is an awareness of wrestling with a problem which is experienced in relation to some difficulty one has been worrying about. Thinking, in such cases, can be equated with problem–solving—problem in the sense that thinking is evoked in these situations where one is not quite, sure how to go on. Thinking, from the educational point of view is a mental ability which is used to solve a problem. It can be tailored or pinpointed according to the nature of the problem to be solved. But it does not follow a single mental process or a set of processes as is employed in problem–solving and learning. Thinking is qualitatively as well as quantitatively different from just problem-solving.

As thinking is an ability, it can be analysed into components and they can be developed. A good thinker is a person who is both intelligent and thoughtful. In the first sense, thinking is something skill-like and in the second sense, it can be commended something more like a virtue, a trait, a character. It is the skill-model of thinking ability which seems to be attractive to the educational community since it leads to development and improvement—it can be broken down into subcategories which can be demostrated, practiced and corrected independently. If we could identify the separate components of thinking, then learning to think could be made much more efficient. Then thinking as a process could be gradually 'built up' out of components. The missing and weak components could be identified as well and they can be practiced in isolation and can be improved upon. Dewey identified five stages comprising a complete act of thought. Bransford and Stein (1984)[29] have forwarded very similar list of what they call parts or components of problem-solving process : "Identify the problem .... Define and represent the problem .... Explore possible strategies .... Act on the strategies .... Look back and evaluate the effects of your activities'. None

29. Bransford, J. and Stein, B. "The Ideal Problem Solver". N.Y. W.H. Freeman, 1984.

of these sub-skills can be practiced independently of others, but shift is made from one to the other gradually. When the five phases are completed, a thought process would evolve.

Like problem-solving method of Bransford and Stein, the "information—processing" components given by Sternberg (1985)[30] identified a set of sub-skills of thinking. Sternberg's project is an attempt to analyze intelligent performance into its elementary components. He assumes that when an individual performs an intellectual task he is engaged in the processing of information. Sternberg has identified a number of different species and different specific individual component processes according to their function in the completion of task.

Two of the related components can be mentioned here : (1) "inference" and (2) "mapping" (Sternberg).

"In inference, a person detects one or more relations between two objects, both of which may be either concrete or abstract".

"In mapping, a person relates aspects of a previous situation to aspects of a present one".

These components were first postulated on the basis of introspection of what was involved in solving a practicular kind of problem. The problems were then "broken down" into a series of sub-problems so that subjects could perform each problem in its entirety or as a series of sub-problems of increasing magnitude. In this way the time needed for each "step" could be measured. It was then easy to reach the conclusion that what might appear to the subject as a single instantaneous performance, is actually comprised of several separate operations.

But some psychologists argue from the pedagogic point of view—that there are two further bases for arguing that thinking is unitary. One has been derived from psychometric studies of intelligence which reveal a general factor (g) underlying component performance across all domains. Spearman was the first to postulate the construct (g) to account for the positive correlation among tests of mental ability. The second view is based on the existence of people's capacity to think in a very general way. Whatever way we take to look at thinking—unitary or piecemeal (operational)—all thinking is creative in

30. Sternberg. R. Beyond IQ : A Triarchic Theory of Human Intelligence". Cambridge University Press, 1985.

essence. In the present view, "creative" does not necessarily mean original, but that there is some element of novelty in all effective thinking; it requires some degree of exploratory behaviour. Thinking as an ability is important for the educationists because it tries to make up for a gap in one's education.

Thinking and Cognitive Psychology

What is a thinking ability? In order to understand the effective thinking as an ability and its utilization in education we should assess, first, the significance of contemporary cognitive psychology and the cognitive domains of mind. R. Glaser (1984)[31], one of the leading contemporary educational psychologists, thinks that the vast amount of knowledge that is accumulating in cognitive psychology concerning ability of the people to reason and solve problems "should have lasting effects on improving and increasing the general use of these abilities".

The cognitive approach started from the Behaviourist and Gestalt tradition. The contemporary Cognitive Psychology takes the computer approach; as Lachman, Lackman and Butterfield (1979)[32] puts :

"Computers take symbolic input, record it, make decisions about the recorded input, make new expressions from it, store some or all of the input, and give back symbolic output. By analogy that is most of what cognitive psychology is about. It is about how people take in information, how they record and remember it, how they make decisions, how they transform their internal knowledge states and how they translate these states into behavioural outputs".

In spite of this simile in the above quotation, this does not imply that the cognitive psychology presumes that computers are mind or human brains. Neither their operations, nor their capacities are identical with those of humans. The cognitive processes in humans are not simply coding or recording but includes long range of interests, and concepts of cognitive psychology are extremely large and constantly evolving. One aspect is that the cognitive approach discovers "problem solving"—like processes implicated in the tasks which would

31. Glaser, R. "Education and Thinking : the role of knowledge". American Psychologist, 39, 93-104, 1984.
32. Lachman, R.; Lackman, J. L.; and Butterfield, E. E. "Cognitive Psychology and Information Processing." Hillsdale, N. J. Lawrence Erlbaum.

ordinarily be considered as quite unproblematic. The other important aspect of thinking from the cognitive psychology point of view is that the underlying mental processses in thinking are of the kind of mental "representation". For example, many of us are familiar with the fact that the same number, say 'five' can be "represented' in a variety of ways, as V in Roman notation, 5 in decimal notation of 100 in binary notation. They are all mental representations. In the same way in order to perform a task, the mind must have a way of storing and using an immense amount of information. The cognitive psychologist would want to know what kind of information is coded, how is it organized and how has the organization been affected by learning and maturation.

Again, it is not essential that the representation employed always be a propositional one, we can solve problems by manipulating quasi-pictorial images which "depict information in a spatial medium" (Cohen, 1983)[33]. Such evidence supports the contention that the manipulation of visual and verbal information may legitimately be considered distinct modes of thinking, whereas underlying mental processes to be investigated are not observable but are inferred from the "input and output".

Thinking and Learning

The history of psychology says that early Behaviourism had eliminated the concept of thinking entirely from its vocabulary. Learning, according to them, follows the principle of conditioning and could account for the most complex form of performance. The cognitive psychologists, on the other hand, emphasize the role of our native endowment and have forwarded a theory of learning of their own. The need for formulating a theory of learning has been derived from their interest in the problem of how knowledge is represented. Long before the ascendancy of the information processing paradigm, psychologists interested in verbal recall noticed that such recall reflected subject's tendency to organize words in particular ways. Working on this premise, they gradually came to notice that not only words, but also meaning was organized in memory and that became the dominant interest of the cognitive psychologists. Therefore, it was just a natural step onward to inquire into the evolution of this organization (Gestalt

33. Cohen, G. The Psychology of Cognition, 2nd ed. London, Academic Press, 1983.

viewpoint) and role of learning in that evolution until Piaget offered a concrete theory of thinking and learning. Piaget began studying this question.

Piaget's ideas were followed up by the experimental cognitive psychologists. They were then engaged in finding out the learning processes and arrived at a contention that learning is not a unitary process but a complex of many processes. The search of learning processes within the cognitive tradition resulted in distinguishing three types of learning—"accretion", "restructuring" and "tuning" (Rumelhart and Norman, 1978)[34]. "Accretion" involves adding new data to the existing database of knowledge. When existing memory structures or "schemata" are not adequate to account for new knowledge, either old structures must be modified, i.e. "tuning', or new structures to be generated, i.e. "restructuring". Of these three, "restructuring" is most important, according to the authors (ibid) and the other two are significant as well. "Restructuring takes place after a considerable time and effort. This mechanism may be linked with the subjective experience like "understanding". There are two ways of restructuring : (i) "pattern generation" and (ii) "scheme induction." Restructuring calls for divergent thinking. It plays a fundamental role in creative work. Cognitive restructuring, when applied in learning, involves the processes of attention, coding and transformation. While learning, a person may overlook a crucial fact or misunderstands a rule and sometimes tries to take irrelevant elements into account. It is not easy to distinguish the relevant from the irrelevant. It is only through restructuring that mistakes are eliminated. It helps to know about the problem because restructuring is based on flexible experiences. But even experiences can misdirect, then again restructuring through pattern generation and scheme induction the problem becomes clearer and specific. A logical reasoning is necessary in the restructuring process and the process involves not only images and meaning, but also should concentrate on symbols. As restructuring process is used in problem–solving situation, thinking ought to be organized, transform symbols to derive implication, record the reasoning process and proceed on eliminating errors. A good problem-

34. Rumelhart, D.E., and Norman, D.A. "Accretion, Tuning and Restructuring : Three modes of Learning." In J.W. Cotton and R. L. Klatsky (cols) "Semantic Factors in Cognition", Hillsdale, N. J. Lawrence Earlbaum, 1978.

solver does not have to be taught to structure, he locates intermediate goals or tasks employing divergent thinking all by himself. Rumelhart and Norman (1978; ibid) further distinguished four ways in which a basic structure or scheme can be 'tuned'—(1) improving the accuracy, (2) generalizing the applicability, (3) specializing the applicability and (4) determining the default values. Without going into the details of these processes individually, we are interested in this context to state that all these are stages of problem-solving and requires some kind of inferential process—a going beyond the information given. That state can be equated with thinking and that is how thinking and learning are related.

Creative Ability

What is creative ability ? Creative ability, known as creativity, is integrally related with cognition. In fact all creativity tests are like intelligence tests of a special type with a divergent stance. Interest in it can be traced to Galton's pioneer studies of intellectual genius. Galton observed that some people are distinguished by the orginality of ideas and the fluency freedom of their mental associations. Creativity is the function of both the affective and cognitive domain of human behaviour. Mackinnon (1982)[35] defined creativity as (1) an idea or response that is novel or at least statistically infrequent, (2) an adaptive response that will solve a problem, fit a situation or aid in goal attainment, or (3) a sustained original insight, elaborated upon to the maximum possible degree and evaluated. He says that the task of psychologists and educators is "to discover talent when it is still potential and to provide that kind of social climate and intellectual environment which will facilitate its development and expression" (p 484). Creativity should not be viewed as limited to aesthetic pursuits only, rather it exists in many forms and in many people. A child's creativity may be expressed through various ways and in countless settings.

Another way of defining creativity, proposed by Jackson and Messick (1968)[36] involves judging a person's products in terms of four criteria : Novelty, Appropriateness, Transcendence of Constraints, and Coalescence of Meaning.

35. Mackinnon, D. W. The nurture and Nature of Creative Thinking, Amer. Psychologist, 1962, 17(7).
36. Jackson, P.W. and Messick, D. Creativity. In P. London and D. Rosenhan. eds. Foundations of Abnormal Psychology. N.Y. Holt, Rinehart and Winston, 1968.

It is perhaps obvious that a creative product must be novel in the sense of being unusual, but more is also required. If we ask a nine-year old boy : "How much is 2+2" and he replied "17", we would be obliged to call the response unusual, but hardly creative. Thus the addition of the critetion of appropriateness sets in. In practice, though, appropriateness is not always easy to agree on. An artist dismissed as merely unusual and vulgar by one generation may be hailed for true creativity by the next. The third criterion, transcendence of constraints, refers to combining elements in a way that at once defies tradition and yields a new perspective. The production of innovative scientific theories illustrates this quality. The fourth criterion, coalescence of meaning, suggests that creative products do not divulge themselves fully at first glance, it needs repitition and clarification. The implications of a scientific innovation and the subtleties of great art both require careful and repeated inspection.

Jackson and Messick's model helps us to understand further what we are trying to get at as creativity but we still need a definition sufficiently precise to suggest measurement techniques. Search was begun in the works of J. P. Guilford and his associates which we have already referred in earlier sections. Their distinction between convergent and divergent cognitive operations has direct implication for measuring and understanding creativity. Guilford himself has described it this way :

> "In view of the active nature of creative performances, the production aspects or steps are most conspicuous and probably more crucial.... with some productive-thinking factors and the tests, that measure them, thinking must at sometime converge toward one right answer.... With other productive-thinking factors and their tests thinking need not come out with a unique answer; in fact, going off in different directions contribute to a better score in such tests. This type of thinking and these factors come under the heading of "divergent" thinking. It is in divergent thinking that we find the most obvious indications of creativity" (Guilford 1957)[37].

37. Guildford, J. P. Creative Abilities In The Arts. Psychological Review 1957, 64, 110-118.

The Guilford group has researched quite extensively various dimensions of divergent thinking in children, adolescents and adults, in search of measures that can be discriminated from convergent thinking and from general intelligence as usually reflected in IQ. The principal research technique was factor analysis in spite of the technical disputes regarding some interpretations of the work involved in it. Yet Wallach (1970)[38] was on firm ground in stating that the significant outcome has been to identify "ideational fluency"—a person's ability to generate a plentiful number of ideas that are appropriate to a task—as a measurable characteristic that is cohesive but readily distinguishable from measures of convergent thinking.

The work of Michael Wallach and his associates stands at the fore determining (1) whether children differ from one another in a consistent way in ideational fluency that can be readily measured; and (2) Whether such measures can be used to predict later creative accomplishments. The Wallach-Kogan findings (Wallach 1971)[39] show clearly that the various procedures are internally reliable and consistent :

> "Children who tended to generate larger number of ideas or larger number of original ideas—in response to one of these procedures tended also to do this for the rest of the tasks. It did not matter for example, whether the request for ideas were framed in visual or verbal terms. On the other hand, children who generated smaller numbers of ideas—or smaller numbers of unique ideas—for one of the tasks were comparably low in their standing for each of the remaining tasks." (Wallach, 1971)

The next question was to determine whether these individual differences among children reflected anything more than difference in intelligence. By using WISC, IQ scores for each child were obtained and it was found that IQ was not related to the creativity measures. Whether a child produced a large number of ideas simply was not predictable from the traditional measure of intelligence. The second question is whether creativity measures are related to, or will predict, real-

---

38. Wallach. M.A. : Creativity. In P.M. Mussen, ed. Carmichael's Manul of Child Psychology, 3rd ed. N.Y. Wiley 1970.
39. Wallach, M.A. The Intelligence/Creativity Distinction. General Learning Press, 1971.

life accomplishment. The answer, on the basis of a growing body of evidence, appears to be positive.

The creative ability has four key expressions : Fluency, Flexibility, Originality and Elaboration. These abilities are accepted by every one working in the field as being associated with creativity. A fluent individual comes up with many alternatives of the same expression easily and not limited to few spontaneous flexibility implies that, without instructions the individual produces responses that indicate a readiness to modify and change things and ideas from the manner in whch they were earlier or are commonly experienced. Originality involves the production of products that are judged clever or remote, and Elaboration involves the expanding of products in greater detail and at a higher level of analysis and arriving at an imagination as well.

Creativity requires a person not only to recognize something as being correct and appropriate response, but also to 'produce' something meaningful. The scoring of the student's responses on creativity, therefore, is not done on the usual right or wrong basis but in terms of response for fluency, cleverness and remotenes of the ideas which are rated to evaluate originality. The number of different responses is identified in scoring flexibility. This we will corroborate while discussing the measurement of creativity.

Cognitive Variables and Creativity

We have indicated in the previous section that the concept of general intellectual ability in terms of (IQ) is not in harmony with the concept of many specific intellectual abilities. Although this is the case, tests of intellectual ability do sample a composite of abilities that underlie broad classes of performance. Therefore, a low or moderate correlation may be possible between IQ and measures of specific divergent thinking abilities influencing creativity. In that case, intelligence tests cannot be used to identify high creativity in children. It has been noticed (Torrance, 1965)[40] that students of high IQ vary markedly in creativity and highly creative students vary markedly in IQ. "The best conclusion at present is that intelligence, as measured, accounts for only a minor portion of the variation in creative performance and by itself is by no

40. Torrance, E. P. Rewarding Creative Behaviour. Experiments in classroom creativity. Englewood Cliffs N. J. Prentice-Hall, 1965.

means an adequate measure of creativity". (Taylor and Holland, 1962)[41].

Personality Variables and Creativity

Barron (1969)[42] studied creativity in adults over a period of several years. He believed creative thinking to be of different nature. According to him, the making of thoughts is the most common instance of psychic creation and is typical of mankind generally. Any new thought produced by an individual cannot be considered as creative because it is though new for him may not be so novel for others. These are parts of convergent thinking, but, instead, creative thinking implies, as Barron puts :

"......... All of us are both creatures and creators, but we vary both in our quality as a creation and in our power to create.

Great original thoughts or ideas are those which are not only new to the person who thinks them but new to almost everyone. These rare contributions are creative in perhaps a stronger sense of the term; they not only are the results of creative act, but they themselves in turn create new conditions of human existence.

Creative power of an outstanding order is marked by the voluminous production of acts which can claim a notable degree of originality and occasional productions of acts of radical originality (Barron, 1969, p.19)."

The adult personalities Barron (1969) studied were living writers, mathematicians, architects and scientists. Large differences in personality variables were found among the more creative individuals within the same group and few differences were found between the general creative groups. The personality characteristics which describe creative individuals by Barron (1969) is given below :

"Appears to have a high degree of intellectual capacity

Genuinely values intellectual and cognitive matters.

Values own independence and autonomy.

41. Taylor, C. W. and Holland, J. N. Development and Application of tests of creativity review of educational research, 325 : 91-102, 1962.
42. Barron, F. creative person and creative process. New York : Helt, Rinehart and Winston, 1969.

Is verbally fluent; can express ideas well.

Enjoys esthetic impressions; is esthetically reactive.

Is productive; gets things done.

Is concerned with philosophical problems; for example, religion, values, the meaning of life and so forth.

Has high aspiration level of self.

Has wide range of interests.

Thinks and associates to ideas in unusual ways; has unconventional thought processes

Is an interesting, arresting person

Appears straightforward, forthright, candid in dealings with others.

Behaves in an ethically consistent manner; is consistent with own personal standard (Ibid. P. 70)."

But the above adult version of the relation of personality variables and creativity is certainly different from the point of view of children's creative ability. What is expected of the school age children is to produce ideas and things novel to them. If properly instructed they will gradually develop the abilities and personality traits essential for more mature level of creativity.

Family Variables and Creativity

The discovery that creativity can be identified as a characteristic that predicts accomplishment leads us to the practical question of whether it is possible to train for creativity. The important variable in this respect is the background from which the child comes. The retrospective accounts of creative persons furnish the background, base, homelife and pressure or lack of pressure that are associated with later accomplishment. Using this strategy, Mackinnon (1962)[43] has reported that his sample of creative architects often received extraordinary respect from their parents, who expressed confidence in their ability to do what was appropriate. The same parents gave much freedom of exploration, granted and supported the decisions taken believing that their children would act independently, reasonably, efficiently and

43. Mackinon, D. W. : The Nature and Nurture of Creative Talent. American Psychologist. 17, 484-495, 1962.

responsibly. Strong emotional parental ties might have been frequently absent. It was not only that closeness was lacking but the over-dependency and fear of rejection which often characterize parental behaviour or parent-child relationship was also not experienced. Fathers were models of effective behaviour and mothers caring, active women with autonomous career and interests. Furthermore, if one or both parents frequently are of artistic skill and temperament becomes an additional help.

This shows that reward and incentive can play vital role in developing many aspects of creative behavior in a child. But in some cases it has been noticed that reward remained only a minor facilitator of creative performance. It can thus be concluded that, if not concrete reward, intrinsic motivation and stimulating environment does help a creative child to be fostered. The performance on measures of creativity reflect substantial individual difference in individual's capacity for creative thinking and that this capacity is more important than the motivational variable in accounting for wide differences that exist between people.

A creative child will easily grasp new relationships, give new interpretation to problems or improve existing standards. But even before showing creative ability the learner must discover the nature of the environment—he must realize his surroundings. He moves from discovery to creative reaction.

Factors influencing creativity

Various factors in the child's physical and social environment affect his creative expressions. The general principles of growth and learning also apply to creativity. The child's creative expressions will be limited by the extent of his discovery of his physical and social world. Other factors involved in creativity are the ideas—original and acquired. Since creativity involves new interpretations and recognization of experiences, the wider the child's experiences the greater will be his wealth of ideas and greater will be his potential for creativity. Again, a person, to be creative, must be flexible in his response style. He must be dynamic, must know how to modify his course of action while solving a problem. A creative child will be less rigid and less influenced by a rigid environment. Therefore, the environment which the creative child faces should be challenging and stimulating to enhance creative expression. Another factor influencing creativity is social climate. The climate should be free and uninhibited—where criticism does not lead to loss of interest on the part of the child. Criticism should not be that severe that can damage the confidence of the child. It can be said that nothing is more detrimental to creativity than the feeling of inadequacy. That is why it is necessary for a creative child to have an understanding teacher.

A healthy personality is also important for a creative child. Garfield, Cohen and Roth (1969)[44] report that psychological studies of creative individuals usually described them as mentally healthy, alert, ·generally independent–minded, dynamic, flexible and possessing a definite self-concept.

These factors are actually discovered from the tests applied—hence are more specific than general. Therefore, they do vary from individual to individual. Even researchers with disabled persons show amazing creativity. Investigations with deaf persons reveal that onometopoeic words (i.e. ouch, groan, jingle, zoon, fizzy etc) in deaf subjects tend to produce "nonsound images" in response to sound stimuli (Khatena and Torrance, 1973)[45]. The meaning and sound are supposed to help these subjects break away from established mental sets and produce novel and creative responses. Perceptual sets are sometimes restructured by them to produce new ideas, new thoughts. It is their own feelings that establish novel and meaningful associative bonds as in the case of "verbal originality". This fact suggests that creativity can transcend the boundaries of set perceptions of normal people and generate creative responses by both meaning and imagination.

There seems to be no definite peak period in the growth curve of creativity. As a cognitive ability a child is able to think creatively at ages 2-3, but will probably be insecure and immature, but perfect to his own thinking. The fact to be emphasized is that this ability in children follow a growth curve and can be peaked at any point of life time, which varies from individual to individual. The fact remains that the creative children did not suddenly become creative and reached their peak in the growth curve, but that their maturity

44. Garfield, S. J. Cohen, H.A. & Roth, R.M. "Creativity and Mutual Health". The Journal of Educational Research, 1969, 63, 127-49.
45. Khatena, J, and Torrance, E.P. "Thinking creatively with sounds and words : Norms-technical manual". Both Lexington, Mass. Personal Press, 1973.

is a gradual process. It is the duty of the parents and educators to recognize the importance of enhancing creativity in a child through training and practice from childhood onwards until the stage of readiness has been arrived at.

Now, in order to enhance creativity in a child, it is first necessary to identify a creative child through test results. Cognitively considered, the creativity tests include both divergent and convergent intelligence. Divergent thinking, according to Guilford (1950)[46], is a general ability that can be applied to a great variety of tasks. The convergent thinking, on the other hand, is stimulus-oriented i.e. induced by the stimulus and more specific than the divergent ones. Creativity is essentially a product of divergent intelligence. The divergent mind usually expresses such behaviours which are flexible, full of inquisitiveness, shows healthy self-concept and free from inhibition. Consequently, most of the creativity tests typify such behaviours and offers stimuli which would elicit these kinds of divergent responses manifesting creative ability of the tests. From various test results it can be surmised that the creativity in a child would reveal his originality, imagination, invention, flexibility and fluency through divergent intelligence tests. But later researches show that creativity is much more than divergent thinking only. Convergent thinking behaviour is as important as the divergent one in identifying creative talent. Many qualities which make up a talented divergent thinker—such as purposiveness, inquisitiveness, autocriticism and ability to think critically—are also present in a convergent thinker. Thus a creative mind has the strength of convergent thinking plus something more as shown by divergent thinkers. There is no clear–cut dichotomy between convergent and divergent behaviour in reality. A creative person is both divergent and convergent as well in using his thinking and imagination.

Creativity Tests

It has been well-accepted that IQ scores are relatively good predictors of a variety of behaviours labelled intelligent and adaptive. But creativity—which can be estimated as beyond measured intellectual skills—produces great ideas and significant accomplishments. The creative persons even with average IQ scores may be highly successful in various fields like art, scientific research, mathematics, literature, writing and

46. Guilford, J. P. Creativity. American Psychologist, 1950. 5. 444-54.

performing arts. Though creativity testing movement started with intelligence tests for classifying individuals, continued researches evidenced that intelligence was unrelated to creativity (Helson and Crutchfield, 1970)[47]. But it is essential to note that though creativity and IQ are unrelated, it is only among individuals with a relatively high level of intellectual ability creativity is expressed. We do not usually find exceptionally creative individuals below the average IQ range, because creativity is entirely a cognitive ability.

As intelligence tests could not identify a creative person scientifically, the need for the creativity tests was obvious and, as a result, a number of solely creativity tests appeared from various researchers on the line.

Tests of Creativity

In recent years a large number of tests that purport to measure creative abilities have been developed. One illustration follows :

The Torrance Tests of Creative Thinking (Torrance, 1966), intended for use from kindergarten through graduate school are tests of divergent thinking that include verbal and figural activities. Activities are scored for fluency, flexibility, originality and elaboration. These are some of the tasks in the Torrance tests :

1. Ask-and-Guess. Given a sketch, the pupil is told to (1) ask all the questions needed to know exactly what is happening in the drawing (2) to guess as many causes as possible for the action in the picture, and also (3) to guess possible consequences of what is taking place in the picture.
2. Product Improvement. This task presents a picture of a stuffed animal and allows the pupils 10 minutes to list the cleverest, most interesting and unusual ways they can think of for changing the toy to make it more fun to play with as a toy, regardless of cost.
3. Unusual Uses. The respondent is given 10 minutes to list "interesting and unusual uses" for a common object, such as a tin can or a cardboard box.

47. Helson, R. and Crutchfield R.S. : Mathematicians : The Creative Researcher And The Average Ph.D. Journal of Consulting and Clinical Psychology, 34, 250-257, 1970.

4. Just Suppose. Here the respondent is asked to guess what would happen if a certain situation occurred. This is an example : "Just suppose clouds had strings attached to them which hang to earth. What would happen ?" Five minutes are allowed for the test.

5. Picture Construction. Here the respondent uses a shaped piece of coloured paper as the nucleus for a drawing. He has 10 minutes to draw a picture or object "that no one else will think of", incorporating the piece of colored paper and to title his drawing.

6. Incomplete Figure. Ten incomplete figures are completed by the subject, and each is given a title.

7. Repeated Figures. The subject is given 30 parallel lines or 40 circles and instructed to draw a picture, using the given elements as the main part of the picture.

Creativity tests usually show lower reliability than educational achievement tests. Because multiple responses are given in many instances and because judgements of quality of response must be made, scorer reliability (the correlation between scores assigned to the same test by two judges) may also be lower than desirable. In accordance with these possible limiting conditions, we feel that tests of creativity should be used experimentally in arranging for instruction dealing with creativity not to evaluate students' characteristics or to make decisions affecting students' teaching-learning activities, choice of courses, or careers.

CHAPTER V

Learning

Learning as a topic is as old as the history of psychology itself. As psychology can be defined in a number of different ways—'a study of soul', with an easy transition, became 'the study of mind' and with the rise of Watsonian behaviourism, the word mind became first unfashionable and then positively taboo, and most psychologists switched to describing their field as 'the study of behaviour'—the definition of learning also follows a similar trend. The definition of learning stems from the philosophical branch known as epistemology or the theory of knowledge and is, therefore, defined as 'acquisition of knowledge.' It presupposes some mental construction and operations.

Hence learning and knowing are closely related which together forms an experience, and thus the first definition of learning emerged as "To learn means to gain knowledge through experience" (Hilgard and Bower, 1977)[1]. Learning in this way is acquiring knowledge. Because it is acquired knowledge, therefore, learning is also memorization, presupposing a storage of information gained through experience retained and recalled when necessary. Learning is also an ability to remember and reproduce.

These contentions clearly form an interconnected cluster of concepts which are compiled in the dictionary meaning of learning, (Evans, 1978)[2]. "The acquisition and subsequent storage of information by an animal is a way that allows it to modify its behaviour in the future. Learning needs to be distinguished from MEMORY, which is the act of storage or the storage mechanism itself, and REMEMBERING, which is the process of learned information out of store. All animals with any degree of complexity in their nervous system are

1. Hilgard, E.R. and Bower, G.H. Theories of Learning, 4th ed. Prentice Hall of India Private Ltd. New Delhi, 1977.
2. Evans, Iris, Psychology, A Dictionary of the Mind, Brain and Behaviour. Arrow Books Ltd., 1978.

capable of learning, and in the case of mammals, and primates in particular, the learning powers are sufficiently developed to allow enormous flexibility and adaptability of behaviour ...."

From the above broad meaning of Learning we can derive a second definition of learning—as 'modification of behaviour', from the point of view of behavioural psychology. Learning does not refer to all of the relatively parmanent modifications of behaviour. Some changes in response patterns are the results of inherent growth processes or maturation. Some changes do occur due to temporary organic impairment and people learn to live with it. Still others arise from temporary biochemical conditions, such as fatigue, hyperthyroidism or a low basal metabolism which induce changes in activity level or produce specific ways of acting, but we cannot consider them learning —they may exert experiential influences that are responsible for learning.

Learned behaviour is not always permanent—either because human being is never static, he is always changing or an inherent decay process is operative in him. These changes within the person brought about by experiences that constitute learning are themselves constantly undergoing modification. But learning behaviourally brings about some changes, some modifications in behaviour, which become relatively permanent and form habits—the responses acquire almost reflexive character. Thus, learning may be defined as a process or operation inferred from relatively permanent changes in behaviour that result from practice.

On the other hand, relatively permanent changes that result from maturation and the temporary changes in behaviour that result from drugs, fatigue and the like are not considered to be learning. When babies about 6 months old grasp for the first time a small object between the thumb and the forefinger (prehensile grasping), they are manifesting behaviour that emerges with maturation and that requires little or no learning. When the child first walks upright, runs rather than walks, or does any of the similar things that all children do with little practice or instruction, it is more a product of maturation than learning, although the latter is certainly involved (Klausmeier & Goodwin, 1975) [3].

3. Klausmeier, H.J. and William Goodwin. Learning and Human Abilities, Haren International, N.Y. 1975, 4th ed.

But normally a 3 year old child cannot recognize the letters and words, but when he receives little formal training and instruction and the experience being repeated by practice, six months or one year later he recognizes the letters and words to a great extent. Gradually his fields of learning and experience broadens and within 6 years of age he can read all the words in the book prescribed for him. That means learning takes place when an external push has been provided to involve the learner's active effort.

The psychologists use the term "learning" more broadly than it is used in popular speech. While it is almost impossible to give an exact definition of learning that will be generally acceptable to all psychologists, we can at least note certain phenomena to which the term is or is not applied as illustrated by Hill (1977). He states, "In psychological usage, what is learned need not be correct or adaptive (we learn bad habits as well as good), need not be conscious or deliberate, need not involve any overt act (attitudes and emotions can be learned as well as knowledge and skills). Reactions are as diverse as driving a car, remembering a pleasant vacation, believing in democracy, and disliking one's boss, all represent the result of learning".

The interest in the phenomenon of learning arises from the very fundamental fact that "man has always been curious about themselves, have always wanted to know more about what makes them "tick" (Hill, 1977)[4], i.e. learning about themselves". The psychologists went a step further and inquired how does learning take place. What factors determine what we will learn and how rapidly can we learn it? How people are motivated to study learning and became curious about themselves and how did they come to be as they are at present. Learning plays an important part in identifying what we are and what we do—and this would increase self-knowledge.

There are innumerable people in innumerable situations when and where they learn. The outstanding field of learning in operation is the sphere of formal education—a deliberate action taken by the students and teachers. We think at once of students looking for better methods of study (study the

4. Hill, Winfred, E. Learning : A Survey of Psychological Interpretations 3rd ed. Thomas Y. Crowell Co. Inc. 1977.

strategies) of teachers wanting to improve their, say, classroom techniques, and of people in industries seeking better ways of training new workers. We may also consider the mothers looking for the best ways of raising their children, the counsellors trying to improve a client's emotional and social adjustment, the animal trainer preparing seeing eyedogs for their work and an advertiser attempting to develop a conscious preference for a client's product. In all of these cases, knowledge about the learning process represents power.

In this way again, in characterizing learning, experimenters working with animals or non-verbal humans need some kind of working definition of learning which does not require verbal instructions, verbal questions and verbal answers. They obviously have to observe some kind of overt behaviour of the animal, presumably one indexing the specific learning for him. Therefore, framing such an operational definition of learning turns out to be rather difficult business. Hilgard (1977)5, forwarded a more or less serviceable and provisional definition of learning.

"Learning refers to the change in a subject's behaviour to a given situation brought about by his repeated experiences in that situation, provided that the behaviour change cannot be explained on the basis of native response tendencies, maturation, or temporary states of the subjects (e.g. fatigue, drugs etc.)."

According to Hilgard, the above definition has the import of allowing an inference regarding "learning" only when a case cannot be made for another explanation. It does not state sufficient conditions for learning, since some cases of repeated experience with a situation do not produce much in the way of observable changes in responses. These facts have already been explained in the earlier paragraphs. We are now in a position to consider some of the behavioural changes that are excluded by the provisional definition above. They have been compiled by Hilgard as follows : (a close review reveals that they are not exclusively different from learning).

(1) Native Response Tendencies versus Learning

The native responses are those responses which are characteristically unlearned activities and do not need outside

5. Hilgard, Ernest R. and Bower, Gorden H. Theories of Learning, Prentice-Hall of India, New Delhi, 1977.

help for acquisition of such behaviour. They are innate behaviours of organisms included in reflexes (physiological responses to stimulus), the tropism (the innate movement operation for performing an act) and the biological instincts (such as birds's nest building). These behaviours are innate and unlearned. These behaviours are characteristics of various species and those more nearly idiosyncratic to one species are called "species-specific" by Hilgard. The concept of instinct has been the most controversial of these terms, partly because of a vagueness of connotation, partly because of a tendency to use the word as explanatory.

Such species-specific behaviours are called innate, because their forms are believed to be set down in the nervous system of all the members of the species independent of learning or experience of some sort. But gradually it turned out to be very difficult to classify behaviours as altogether innate or altogether learned. Later animal psychologists like Hinde (1966)[6] and others found that expression of some so-called instinctive behaviour depends very much upon variations in experience and learning. The research on imprinting by Professor Lorenz (1952)[7] also illustrates the in-between nature of behaviour with large instinctive components. Hess (1958)[8] also provided support to the above contention. Similarly, the ethologists who study natural behaviour of species in their natural habitats have discarded the "innate" versus "learned" standpoint of behaviour because they are not seen to be so exclusively either—or affair.

(2) Maturation versus Learning

Maturation is the natural growth process independent of training. Learning cannot take place until maturation reaches respective stages. Relatively pure cases such as swimming of tadpoles and flying of birds can be attributed primarily to maturation. Maturation refers to the general processes of development which occur in the normal individual from birth—rather—from conception to the point of psychological and physiological maturity. These processes which include the development of body organs and the cerebral cortex, follow near-identical lines in all members of a particular species and

6. Hinde, R. A. Animal Behaviour : A Synthesis of Ethology and Comparative Psychology, McGraw Hill. N.Y. 1966.
7. Lorenz, K. Z. King Solomon's Ring. Crowell–18, N.Y. 1952.
8. Hess. E. H. "Imprinting" in Animals, Sc. Amer, 198, 81-90-18, 1958.

they proceed more or less independently of external influences of learning. Maturation also brings in changes in behaviour as a result of physiological or anatomical changes but they occur irrespective of learning and is more systematic and methodical than the changes of behaviour as an effect of learning. Maturational changes occur apart from any specific stimulation from the environment, whereas the changes or modifications of behaviour that are associated with specific stimulation are said to be learned.

Depending on a specific situation, the above distinction is not clear-cut always, but develop through a complex interplay of maturation and learning. This is illustrated aptly in the development of language in a child. The child does not learn to talk until old enough, but that development depends upon appropriate stimulation from his verbal community at the critical time. The language the child picks up when he is able to talk is obviously the language of a specific environment and thus, a specific language is learned. Therefore, maturation and learning are not exclusively independent of each other. Even while maturing normally, the factors in the embryonic stage, needs proper and nourishing environment inside the mother's womb. Normal growth and behavioural changes can only occur under a specific environmental influence to bring in permanent change at each stage of development, and to be recognized as the effect of learning.

(3) Fatigue and Habituation versus Learning

Similarly, motor fatigue and sensory habituation are distinguished from learning proper. The motor fatigue occurs when a motor act is repeated in rapid success and for a relatively long period resulting in loss of efficiency—it becomes slower and weaker in amplitude until eventually the subject may refuse to perform it. The response in this case is said to be suffered "fatigue" or that its performance shows "work decrement". The fatigue occurs faster the greater the effort of the response. Recovery from fatigue occurs mainly as a simple function of "rest time". When interpreted in the form of performance curve, the fatigue and recovery curves look very much like curves of experimental extinction and spontaneous recovery giving it an appearance of learning experience. However, common practice has been to apply the "learning' label to the spontaneous recovery and not to experimental extinction. Because fatigue, unlike extinction of a conditioned reflex, is presumed not to induce enduring and relatively "permanent" changes in the behaviour. But this is not correct, because extinction effects can also be reversed, an extinguished response can be trained. Therefore, we can say that there is no crucial difference between fatigue and learning or rather fatigue can be a product of learning when considered solely at the behavioural level of measuring the elicited response.

The second kind of change is called "sensory habituation" which means that "presentation of a stimulus produces a certain perceptual reaction (what Pavlov called the orienting reflex or OR). This reaction can be recorded electrically throughout the nervous system. If the stimulus is repeated over and over in a monotonous series, the OR aroused by each presentation becomes less and less, eventually declining to an almost undetectable level %". (Hilgard, p. 20). Habituation is not sensory adaptation. In habituation the reduced or altered responsiveness can be traced directly to 'changes' at the receptor surface. The subject becomes habituated with the stimulus, i.e. he gets used to it. It is not a reflex like adaptation but exhibits many of the same functional properties we ascribe to learning or (to extinction). It dissipates with time—like forgetting it is easily disrupted or dishabituated by interpolation of a novel or interfering event. It can be rehabituated again and again like relearning and even generalize to other similar stimuli, displaying all the trends of learning and follow the principles of dynamic laws of learning. This can lead us to assume habituation as learning. Habituation in reality depends on the complexity of the stimulus to which the habituation occurs, requiring higher brain centers for its discrimination, and consequently, is similar to learning. It takes place from some kind of development of an internal representation of the stimulus event or of its general class (or some kind of 'stimulus recognition'). This had either been learned by the organism or stored a replica or model of the habituated stimulus. Stimulus recognition in cortical habituation is the result of learning.

(4) Performance versus Learning Factors

Learning is always inferred from performance, but performance is not identical with learning. It is like the difference between knowledge and action, where action takes place from knowledge. "The concept of learning versus actualization, of knowing to do something versus actually doing it" (Hilgard, p. 21).

Performance does presume learning, but performance in many cases fail (in spite of learning) due to some other intervening factors, like lack of motivation or drive or effect of drugs etc. All these will be discussed comprehensively in later sections.

All the above factors are documented briefly to ascertain the fact that learning is involved integrally in such a large range of activities, it is very difficult to include some in defining learning and eliminate all those we wish to exclude from the perview of learning. Taking for granted the all inclusive nature of learning, different learning theorists had put forward their own points of view not disregarding the definition of learning but emphasizing certain factors and eliminating others. The controversy between the theorists is not over definition, but over 'fact and interpretation'.

Factors associated with Learning

The general nature of learning can be compared with the general nature of psychology as a science of behaviour, as already been mentioned in the beginning. Learning is a kind of psychological and physiological behaviour, different from maturation or growth and development. Learning is a behaviour because it corresponds with responses. Responding is generally described physiologically in terms of the contraction of muscles or the secretion of glands or conduction of electrical impulses through sensory nerves. These are all activity behaviours—the function of the body. All behaviours are not overt or observable. When we read or listen to something, we are behaving—the behaviours are known as covert. It is this kind of behaviour which is the concern of the learning psychologists. They are interested specifically in those changes of behaviour which are the effect of learning. Therefore, behaviour or, rather, the changes of behaviour—a learned response to an unfamiliar stimulus is the first factor associated with learning.

The changes in behaviour can occur as a result of physiological or anatomical changes. It can also occur as a result of accident or drugs and disease and deterioration of the body. Over-work of the body may result in the setting in of fatigue, which is again a change in behaviour. But these are not the behavioural changes caused by learning. They are accidental factors causing changes in bodily responses.

Learning is modification of behaviour : when new responses appear in the organism as a consequence of external stimulation and changes are noticed in the normal performance of the body and mind of the same organism. In human learning, one learns as he grows. Both normal maturation and learning take place in this process of growth and development.

The major factors involved in learning have been enumerated by Skinner (1964)[9].

Ability or Capacity

Learning is described as an ability or capacity to learn and consequently assumes difference among species as well as individual difference among the same species, especially among human beings, because learning advances stage by stage from very simple elementary type to very complex and abstract form. The various species in animals have different capacities to learn. This is obvious on the highest stratum in the organismic ladder who have greater capacity to learn than other living things. But within the species, the learning ability differs among individual learners. We shall discuss the significance and the process of identifying individual differences in learning in details later on. In fact, when we classify child learners as feeble-minded, or normal or exceptional, we classify them in part in terms of their ability to learn.

Motivation

Motivation directs and initiates one's behaviour. It is a state under which an individual attends to certain aspects of his environment. Motivation comes from motives. A motive is an internal state which leads to behaviour being directed in a particular direction or towards a known goal. It is similar to drive, which, basically speaking, is anything which pushes an animal or human into action. Drive is physiological and tends to refer to instinctive forces which have great significance to an organism, e.g. sex, hunger, thrist etc.—which, when consummated, give a sense of relief or pleasure. It is said that motives have energizing function and directive tendency. Motivation also involves such directing function and is sometimes equated with "need", "want" and "interest" and indicates certain aspects and conditions. Skinner's view is that the term motivation is a general term and does not have

9. Skinner, Charles E. Educational Psychology (4th ed.). Prentice-Hall of India (Private) Ltd. New Delhi, 1964.

precise definition. The motivation in an individual has been inferred from the reaction of the individual in a particular situation. We infer hunger when we eat, or thirst when we drink. We also infer needs for affection, or interest in science as a result of individual behaviour, because all human beings tend to display certain behaviour under certain environmental conditions. We ascribe certain motives to all persons because they are members of the human race(Skinner, p. 396, ibid). The above motives are called primary, because we are born with them like animal instincts. Other behaviours are more specific and are assumed to be derived from these primary motives. Nonetheless, they are very important so far as learning is concerned, because these secondary motives, (or the derived motives) as they are called, are learned and acquired. These motives are important in accounting for learning. Most of the learning theorists believe that learning cannot occur without motivation—that all learning is motivated. Though there are some learning theorists who think that learning does take place even when there is no motivation.

Purposes or goals

Just as motivation in learning is being inferred from the behaviour of the individual, an end-state or goal can also be inferred from the same behaviour. As the individual responds, he responds with a purpose. He has a purpose in attainment of a goal. As for example, just as hunger is inferred as a motive, getting and eating food is a goal. Goals, according to Skinner, can be immediate or long-ranged. They can be objects or states or conditions, can be simple and complex. The term 'incentive' can be compared and equated with goal although they are not synonymous. The term incentive is used to specify a goal-object or state which is more or less explicit and not inferred like goal or motivation.

Besides the above factors which are associated with learning, below are given certain other factors presented by Skinner (1964 ibid), which are connected with learning responses and establish a relationship between the concepts of motivation, goal and learning process.

Rewards or effect

Reward means something which is pleasant and satisfying to an organism, but in particular anything which, when presented after a particular pattern of behaviour has been performed (effect), increases the likelihood that behaviour will be performed again. Learning theories are intimately concerned with the term reward and ask such questions as : "what are the effects of rewarding or punishing responses. Whether that sheer repetition of a response can cause it to become learned; or that some sort of reward is essential if a response is to become established". A special term—*reinforcement*—has been used as equivalent to reward in learning. Reinforcement literally means strengthening something. In learning psychology, it refers to the strengthening of a behavioural response by one means or other—normally a reward. The word "reinforcement" has been used first by Pavlov in describing his theory of classical conditioning in learning—a purely physiological motive, as cautioned by Pavlov himself, but gradually and frequently used in contemporary discussion in learning in psychology. "It refers to the effect of attaining an object or state (goal) that satisfies a motive (need or want) on the establishment of a response".

Practice

"Practice", "exercise", "repetition" or "drill" are terms used commonly as integrally related with learning process. The associated questions are : what is the role of practice in learning ? Does practice alone results in learning or it takes practice plus something else to produce learning ? Is learning possible without repetition ? These are relevant questions that are to be answered while discussing the learning process.

Forgetting

We learn, but we also forget. Forgetting starts functioning after learning has taken place. It is a loss of the ability to recall data from the memory store. Early theories of forgetting assumed that the information become destroyed or faded away through disuse or with passage of time. Current views tend to the theory that information placed in store is never totally lost (except through brain damage) and that forgetting is more a matter of breakdown in the mechanism of extraction or information retrieval[10]. Forgetting follows learning and that is how it is related with learning process.

10. Psychology, A Dictionary of the Mind Brain and Behaviour, by Dr. Chris Evans, 1978. opcit.

Transfer of training

It is generally accepted in learning that responses learned in one situation may be elicited and can be appropriate in a new situation. This is the phenomenon of transfer, which assumes that new learning may be accomplished with greater efficiency and ease when it is influenced by previous learning. This condition is called transfer of training. Transfer of training means learning one particular task and by doing so passing of information or habits which affect the learning or performance of a subsequent task. Learning theory needs to account for the transfer effect.

Some Basic Considerations of Learning

The principal concern of education is with the learning of children. The management, direction, and facilitation of learning in the classroom is central in importance for formal education. Modification of behaviour is deliberately planned for and directed in the school. The academic accomplishments of students, to a degree, are reflective of the learning that is planned for and directed in the school. Such learning is broad in scope and of great significance to culture. But the changes in behaviour that are evidenced by academic accomplishment represent only a small portion of learning that actually takes place. Much is learned in informal way—the incidental learning that occurs both inside and outside the classroom is very extensive and is of great social significance.

The learning that occurs both formally and informally among human beings is characterized by extremely complex patterns of stimuli and responses, both in life situations and sometimes in controlled conditions. Learning under life situations is incidental, imitative and, on some occasions, deliberate and compulsive. Formal learning takes place under controlled conditions either in the institutions or in the laboratory. Our discussion began by looking at a setting in which learning is the primary focus in school. Children in the school face a bewilderingly complex learning situation. It is complex from their point of view and, at the same time, from the point of view of the educational psychologists and the teachers who attempt to analyze child learning.

In the laboratory learning situations, the experimenter, teacher or the psychologists have much more control over the conditions presented. They can manipulate certain variables, held others constant and measure precisely the resultant changes in behaviour, and laboratory results can be used and transformed into real life situations. Man is a complex organism and this complexity makes him difficult to study in the laboratory. But still laboratory learning helps evolving certain fundamental principles to be applied successfully in formal education. Here, two points mainly need to be considered are (1) what psychological gain is achieved by studying learning under the somewhat artificial conditions of the laboratory, and (2) what difficulties are involved in applying the results to other, non-laboratory situations (Hill, 1977)[11].

There are two main ways in which the psychologists gain by taking questions about learning into the laboratory. One of these pertains to measurement. The laboratory situation permits experimenters to measure the subject's behaviour more adquately than is possible outside the laboratory. They can keep accurate record, of how and what kind of errors a subject makes and successive stages by which mastery is reached. This improved measurement is valuable for three reasons : first it gives a more complete picture of the learning process—details are recorded. Second, it protects researchers from the mistakes of noticing and remembering only what they expect —success as well as failures are equally noticed and objectively evaluated. Third, apart from systematic biases, careful measurement also protects against all unsystematic errors when the research is carried on as part of everyday work. Thus, measurement in the laboratory will be more thorough, more precise and more objective than measurement in comparable situations elsewhere.

The other gain from studying learning in the laboratory is in 'control'. Essentially, this gain is associated with our ability to study one thing at a time. When we control a variable we hold it constant so that it will not interfere with our studying another variable.

During recent years, research workers have been concerned with the need for making their findings in the school conditions themselves, making the class rooms their laboratories. They conduct their studies in school conditions, school settings using typical courses and subject matter. Techniques for measuring

11. Hill, Winfred, E. Learning : A Survey of Psychological Interpretations 3rd ed. Thomas, Y. Crowell Comp. Inc. 1977.

gain in these situations may be classified as those that measure "indeterminate gain" and those that measure "determinate gain" (Davis, Robers, A.)[12].

The "indeterminate gain" has been used as a technique to study the individual's performance at a given time. The researchers, with this technique, conducted wide surveys of school achievement e.g. cross–sectional study of recognizing concepts. The technique provides a measure of the status of the different age or grade levels under exciting conditions and affords a means of comparing the performance of individuals and groups. In one survey an investigator calculated the percentage of pupils in grades four to twelve who were familiar with the meaning of five as a concept in social science.

A more refined technique is the "determinate gain" where the measurement of different individuals or groups can be repeated over a period of time. For example, changes in scores of pupils in 'reading', 'arithmetic', and 'spelling' during a five-year period. They showed marked improvement in achievement in these subjects as pupils advanced from the lower to the higher educational levels, measurement being taken of the same pupils at the end of each year (longitudinal study).

One of the striking features of this study was to show increments over an extended period of time and repeated measurements made it possible to gain insight into the rate of progress from one testing period to another. It was a "moving treatment" as contrasted with the technique of "indeterminate gain" which represent static kind of situation.

Learning in school is a continuous process. It extends through periods of instruction and study followed by testing, after which further instruction and study occur. The results of learning are confirmed in a regular manner by some kind of evaluation, which may be followed by a consideration of difficulties and the elimination of errors.

In spite of the advantages in measurement and control, we must not suppose that they provide easy answers to questions about the practical management of learning. Because they typically study single variable out of their usual context. For example, it has been established in a number of experiments that larger reinforcers lead to better performance in a learning

12. Davis, Robers, A., In Educational Psychology, edited by Skinner, Charles, E. opcit.

situation. Does it follow that more lavishly a teacher praises students for their success, the better the student will do their work ? The student may become so used to this effusive praise that it would soon be no more reinforcing to them. It is necesary, therefore, that we have to be cautious not to be rash to generalize directly and confidently from the laboratory studies to classroom application. However, the laboratory studies, in addition to providing basic knowledge about the process of learning, suggests many possible applications to the classroom and to other applied settings.

Researchers in the field of learning, or for that matter in any branch of science, are concerned with discovering scientific 'laws'. All the experimental procedures are directed toward such discovery. A law is a statement about the conditions under which certain things occur. Some laws are highly precise and accurate and some are less so. But in both cases we know that certain things occur under certain conditions and, given those conditions, we can predict the occurrence of the event, though it may not be always correct. It is, therefore, surmised that, in general, the experimental procedures have some sort of predictive value which are often useful.

All laws state a relationship between a dependent variable and one or more independent variables. A variable is any measurable characteristic—a person, a situation or anything else. A dependent variable is one about which we make prediction and independent variable is one we use to make predictions. In a study of learning, the dependent variable is some aspect of the learner's performance, while the independent variable may be any characteristic of the learner, task or situation. In all experimental cases, a relationship exists between an independent and dependent variable (however high or low) in such a way as to make possible prediction from the independent to the dependent variable. These laws are primary focus of science, in general, and, hence, of psychology of learning as well.

Scientific laws are statements about the way the world operates and consequently they involve abstractions. Abstraction is a simplification of reality (Hill, 1977, ibid) as it is presented to our senses. Every intellectual activity involves organization and simplification of reality—whether we consider simple perceptions or complex thoughts and whether we look at science, art, sports, business or any other area of human effort. Our scientific pursuit is only rediscovery of reality as described and interpreted or reacted to by some one. There is no such thing as pure reality, some descriptions are more accurate and more detailed than others, but no description is complete. These are the weaknesses of experimental investigations which occasionally lead to errors. But nevertheless, the scientific laws serve two main purposes one is practical—to provide means of predicting and controlling events; the other to gain knowledge, helping science to make scientific inquiry about reality.

Nature of theory of Learning

The above discussion leads us to understand the nature of learning theories. The researcher's work is dedicated towards establishing general principles or interpretations. This effort takes us into the realm of scientific theory. "A theory is a higher level of abstraction, i.e. an organization and simplication of the events being described. In broadest sense, a theory is a systematic interpretation of an area of knowledge (ibid)." In the psychology of learning, "system" or "systematic interpretation" is preferred by the modern learning psychologists as they think this to be better term than theory. Theory sometimes is used to refer to a kind of formal logical system—a narrow concept. However, theory, system and systematic interpretation, all convey the same idea and can be considered as synonymous.

The theoretical systems for the interpretation of learning have grown up along with the experimental study of learning. Although the experimental study of learning to a large extent grew out of everyday problems in education, it soon became involved with theoretical issues and with experiments appropriate for dealing with them.

Winfred Hill enumerated three functions of theory :

(i) It is an approach to the area of knowledge, a way of analyzing and talking about the doing research on learning—a researcher's guide so to say.

(ii) A theory of learning is an attempt to summarize a large amount of knowledge of the laws of learning in a fairly small space. In this process of summarization, some exactness or detail are likely to be lost.

(iii) The theory of learning is a creative attempt to explain what learning is and why it works as it does. The laws give us the "how" of learning, the theories attempt to answer the "why" question of the same "why". They seek to provide the basic understanding which is one of the goals, not alone of science, but of all forms of scholarship (Hill,1997, ibid).

Kinds of theories

The important theories of learning can be primarily classified as 'Connectionists' and the 'Cognitive' theorists. Though they differ much among themselves but agree in treating learning as a matter of connection between stimuli and responses. A response may be any item of behaviour, while a stimulus may be any input of energy that tends to affect behaviour. Connective theories typically assume that all responses are elicited by stimuli. These connections are called by variety of names, such as habits, stimulus—response bonds, and conditioned responses. Their attention is on the responses that occur, on the stimuli and associated conditions that elicit them and the ways that experience changes these relations between stimuli and responses.

Now what exactly are stimuli and responses ? Every student of psychology, from the very beginning, is supposed to understand the paradigm S—R, which is assumed under connectionist theories of learning. The symbols S—R means that the stimulus is connected with or leads to response. The environment provides the sources of energy it contains that impinges on the sense organs of living creature. We call these impingements of energy (impulse or the electrical waves coming from the object) stimuli. For example, light waves impinge upon the eye and we see, sound waves impinges upon the ear and we hear, chemicals upon the taste buds and we taste and so on. As the stimuli stimulate our sense organs under standard circumstances, all organisms react or respond in their characteristic ways. Certain responses seem automatically to follow certain stimulation and are typically called "unlearned responses". But in learning, some responses or reactions do not naturally or automatically follow certain stimulation but they do become connected (after repetitions) with these stimuli and become acquired responses, and are consequently, called "learned responses" (conditioned responses). The major principle operating here is that learning occurs through contiguous association of events or ideas and a bond or connection is being established between the stimulus and response constituting an associationistic frame work.

In the S-R paradigm, the 'S' represents stimulus, 'R' represents response or reaction and the arrow (–) represents the associative connection. The psychologists who are pioneers on learning experiments, conducting their work in their laboratories, belonging to this associative framework group, are renowned learning psychologists like Pavlov, Watson, Guthrie, Thorndike, Hull, Skinner and Tolman who forwarded their own theories. But Tolman, being influenced by Gestalt psychology, deviated from other connectionists learning psychologists and was the first systematist of cognitive theory.

Cognitive System

Cognitive interpretations are concerned with cognition (perception, attitudes, knowledge, intelligence and beliefs) that individuals have about their environment and the ways that cognitions determine their behaviour. In these interpretations, learning is the study of the ways in which cognitions are modified by experience. The cognitive theories involve more thinking, more complex approach of the problem given and interplay of reasoning and intellectual exercise of the mental processes. Learning in cognitive way is not only acquisition of knowledge by association but acquiring such knowledge through systematic and continuous reasoning requiring application of logical insight into the learning material.

Cognitive theories, also known as Field theories or Gestalt Theories, focus in their concepts "the processes which intervene"[13] between stimuli on the one hand and responses on the other. The cognitive theorists are more concerned with the processes of human learning than the connectionists and, therefore, they emphasize on the mental processes involved in eliciting responses to a given stimulus. The mental processes, according to the cognitive theorists are the intervening variables which are important in producing the type of responses to a particular stimulus. Cognitive theorists maintain that a human learner has an organization in his perceptions, that they are meaningful items of knowledge—stimuli from the environment are not discrete and independent,

13. Hilgard, E.R. Theories of Learning. New York, Appleton-Century-Crofts. Inc. 1956.

each, from the other. As the stimuli impinge on our sense organs we are aware of the fact of seeing or hearing or tasting and so on. This awareness is a reminiscence of the previous awareness. Likewise, the human beings can also anticipate what may follow after. We relate experiences and events (stimuli and reactions) in time and our reactions are meaningful not just a mechanical connection of S and R. The word "cognitive" connotes a type of activity in the mind or brain that correlates with these concepts.

"The cognitive theorists or field theorists look upon the learner as a dynamic energy system set into an environment that is in turn a complex of other dynamic energy systems."[14] 'Dynamic Systems' mean the learner is in constant interaction with other systems which produce change in him. This change in behaviour is a product of learning. The word dynamic is further important because it emphasizes the fact that the learner is not passive. The change in him—which is a product of learning—is constant and continuous as he is constantly interacting with various environments—it is a natural process of life. The environment is also 'dynamic' in the sense that it is essentially changing and is never static. So the learner as one dynamic system is a part of the larger system-environment, constantly interacting, hence adjusting, adapting, modifying, changing, or, in short, learning. The changes of behaviour of the learner is not erratic, but lawful and is capable of accounting for in terms of generalizations or principles.

Common sense makes use of both kinds of interpretations. The simple reactions—or even more complex physical skills such as habits or practice (repetition)—can be explained very simply by connectionistic interpretation whereas, while discussing matters that involve meaningful words or deliberate decisions or thoughtful remarks, the interpretation is cognitive. Connectionist theories often lend themselves to greater precision and fit in better in scientific approach in which human learning is one part of the natural world, simpler in connotation and same response-bound. Cognitive theories commonly make more allowance for the power and flexibility of human intellectual processes and the ways in which people deal with complex problems. However, this has not been at all a clear cut distinction and over the years the gap is becoming

14. Anderson, 1964, Anderson, G.L. in Educational Psychology, ed. Charles, E. Skinner. Prentice-Hall of India, New Delhi, 1964.

narrower allowing numerous middle positions and combinations. Hilgard (1975, op cit) says, "The cleavages between the theorists of opposing camps are difficult to understand because some of the distinctions which at first seem to contrast sharply later are found to be blurred in the light of subsequent experimental knowledge.... The differences between two theorists are primarily differences of interpretation". Hilgard found three so-called differences between the connectionist and cognitive interpretation of learning behaviour in laboratory experiments and thinks that the differences observed remained so as they were rather inferred than verified.

1. Peripheral vs. central intermediaries

The stimulus-response theorists tend to believe that some sort of chained muscular responses, linked perhaps by fractional anticipatory goal responses, serve to keep a rat running to a distant food-box. The cognitive theorists, on the other hand, more freely inferred central brain processes, such as memories or expectations as integrators of goal-seeking behaviour. Both group relied on their inferences and logic and could not verify them physically.

2. Acquisition of habits vs. acquisition of cognitive structures

When the question is, 'What is learned' in learning psychology, the answer for the stimulus-response theorists is "habits", and for the cognitive theorists is "cognitive structures". Though they are, apparently, different in kind but same in form. It is true that what we learn is the skills by practicing them, but unless we know the fact about the object —that is, the cognitive structure of the object—it is difficult to acquire the skill. "A smooth running skill illustrate the learned habit, knowing alternative routes illustrates cognitive structure".

3. Trial and error vs. insight in problem solving

When the question is 'how a problem is solved' in learning psychology, the stimulus-response psychologists finds the learner assembling his habits from the past appropriate to new situations. Either the learner finds out the elements which are common with familiar ones or tries to find out the aspects of the new problem which are similar to the aspects already known to him, which he met before. If these two methods fail, he resorts to trial and error using his learnt behaviour repertory one after another until the problem is solved. The cognitive psychologists have grave doubts about this method. They think that the learner may be successful sometimes to reach a sudden solution by applying trial and error method but may not be successful in all the situations. If the familiar situation is changed, there is no guarantee that the learner would be able to bring the requisite past experiences to bear upon the solution in this novel situation. According to the cognitive theorists, the preferred method of presentation permits a perceptual structuring leading to "insight", that is, to the understanding of the essential relationships involved. The stimulus-response psychologists try to emphasize the past experience of the learner in solving the new problem, whereas the cognitive psychologists prefer the study of the contemporary structuring of the problem leading to solution. But the difference of the two groups of psychologists methodologically is not very sharp as neither the S-R group totally neglects the present facts, nor the cognitive group ignores the past experience entirely.

The above three issues, more or less, point out an apparent difference between the two major families of theorists which has helped the emergence of two groups of theories in the history of learning psychology. A few psychologists have attempted to resolve the dilemmas presented by these apparent conflicts by postulating more than one kind of learnfing; e.g., Mowrer proposed two kinds of learning—one dependent upon contiguity (association) alone and the other requiring reinforcement or effect. Tolman suggested a number of different kinds of learning".[15] But some issues lie outside this conflict between the two groups of theorists. For example, there may be intra-difference regarding the role of reinforcement or interpretation of extinction between two particular psychologists belonging to the same group, stimulus-response theorists or cognitive learning psychologists.

Four of the learning issues mentioned by Hilgard (op cit, pp. 25) are given below :

1. Contiguity versus Reinforcement

The term contiguity comes from the law of association. The oldest law of association is that ideas expressed together tend to become associated. The stimulus response theorists describe

15. Tolman, E. C. "There is more than one kind of learning". Psychological Review LVI, 1949, 144-155; reprinted in L.M. Stolurow (ed). Readings in Learning. Englewood Cliffs. N.J. Prentice-Hall Inc. 1953, pp. 62-77.

the association as between stimulus and response than as between ideas. Some theorists have used the term contiguous association producing learning. Guthrie and Tolman belong to this school. Others, such as Thorndike, Skinner and Hull think learning does not take place without reinforcement and that contiguity alone cannot produce learning.

2. Extinction of learned responses

A well-rewarded learned response may be extinguished if the stimulus is repeatedly presented without reinforcement. The extinction of learned response may occur either due to the fact that the animal or the subject simply learns to expect no reward and stops responding because of that expectancy. According to the aversive theory, the animal or the subject gets actually aversive or frustrated. It is so frustrating for the learner that it sets up active inhibitory processes which compete with performance of the formerly learned response.

3. Learning as jumpwise or by small increments

According to some psychologists, as for example Guthrie,, learning occurs completely in one trial, that which was last done in the presence of a stimulus combination will be done when the stimulus combination next occurs—because it refers to the last response of a succession than to recency in time. This means that learning takes place at its most basic level in all-or-none fashion. Whereas Hull, belonging to the same camp of learning psychology as Guthrie's, maintains that learning takes place gradually, modifications taking place even below threshold, so that several trials may be necessary before the results of learning reach threshold and begin to be revealed in performance. The difference of opinion of this kind is not the inter-difference between two theories but it is a difference between two theorists on one issue of learning.

4. One or more kinds of Learning

The contiguity-reinforcement dilemma led the psychologists like Thorndike, Skinner and Mowrer to accept various kinds of learning. One or two basic laws cannot provide a method to cover the acquisition of motor skills to abstraction of ideas. Tolman at one time pointed to the possibility of seven kinds of learning. Gagne (1970)[16] has argued for similar distinctions.

---

16. Gagne, R.M. The Conditions of Learning (Rev. ed) N.Y., Holt, Rinehart and Winston, 1970.

These four issues help us to make it clear that the theories of learning are not opposed and exclusive to each other. The difference lies not in point of view but in preference. This revealation induced the later learning psychologists to take a "functional" outlook of learning principles.

Principles of Learning Theories : SIMPLE LEARNING

The main purpose of a learning theory is to explain learning operations and to a lesser extent to predict and control the course of learning. Earlier theories of learning advanced a few principles that purported to explain all operations and all outcomes of learning in all living organisms. The modern theories are less ambitious. We shall start with the main principles underlying the earlier theories briefly and pass on to the views of modern learning psychologists who insist on the functional approach in order to describe learning and reinterpret its principles. The theories of learning largely depend on the research work done by different researchers on the basis of one basic principle and their work is dedicated toward establishing general principles for interpretations. This effort takes one into the realm of scientific theory of learning.

1. ASSOCIATION

(a) Contiguity

The earliest experiments in the history of learning psychology that advanced the basic data on which our knowledge and theory of learning rests, were conducted by Ebbinghaus in Germany, emphasizing the principle of association (contiguity)—a product of the School of Associationism, originating early in the days of Aristotle (384-322 B.C.).

Aristotle laid down the basic principles of memory—similarity, contrast and contiguity—which have not yet ceased to dominate theoretical thinking about learning. Alexander Bain (1818–1903)[17] was through and through a psychologist in the days of philosophy. Bain's discussion of intellect was nothing more than his discussion of association. He held to two fundamental laws of association : contiguity and similarity. Bain held the law of contiguity to be a matter of the previous concurrences of actions or sensations. He explained learning and memory in the following terms : "they tend to

17. Alexander Bain : The Senses and Intellect, 1855.—later published in his book Mind and Body in 1872.

grow together, or where, in such a way that, when one of them is afterwards presented to the mind, the others are apt to be brought up to idea". Thus these laws seemed to Bain to explain retentiveness. It depends, he noted, upon the 'repetition' of contiguities and also, upon attention. It depends further upon the general retentiveness of the individual, for there are "individual differences" in "the aptitude of acquirement". These principles are still regarded basic in learning and memorization more than hundred years later.

Next important contribution on associationism came from Withhelm Wundt. Association, for Wundt, was one of the most important cases of the operation of the law of "psychic resultants". To him, association was the fundamental principle of connection and in its primitive form it is 'simultaneous' although it readily becomes successive. It occurs passively, for active association is 'apperception'. Wundt's concept of apperception focuses on three aspects of the doctrine : apperception as phenomenon, as cognition and as activity. First, Wundt, by declaring apperception as phenomenon postulates that it belongs within the range of attention—a conscious process, and can come under experimentation. Secondly, Wundt further distinguished apperception from association by saying that the former occurs in logical connections between mental contents, whereas associative connections are not logical. Apperception had been held by Wundt to have a "congnitive" function and apperception synthesis leads to concept formation and thus connected with learning. Thirdly, according to Wundt, apperception is active, a constant current in the stream of consciousness. Apperception means flux and change and hence related with learning.

The importance of apperception had earlier appeared in Johann Friedrich Herbart (1776-1841), a philosopher, but best known as the "father of scientific pedagogy" which he founded upon psychology. The importance of his theory lies in the fact that his work had a definite influence upon the later experimental psychology—the work later done by Wundt in his laboratory at Leipzig. Herbart's idea of apperception involved no free selection of the mind—to him, everything depended upon the mechanics of resultant, based on a sort of connectionism. It is in connection with this picture of the mind that the word 'apperception' appeared in Herbart's exposition. According to him, the apperceiving of an idea is, therefore, not only the making of it conscious, but also its assimilation to a totality of conscious ideas—which Herbart called the "apperceiving mass". The phrase "apperceptive mass" contributed importantly to base psychology for the process of education and learning.

The new psychology of content of associationistic psychology of Wundt (Wundt's psychology was fundamentally introspective, sensationistic, elementistic and associationistic) had been put to test through series of experiments. It was Hermann Ebbinghaus (1850-1909) who was primarily a psychologist of content, because he accepted the psychology that had proved itself amenable to experimentation. Ebbinghaus, with his sole reliance on Fechner's book and his own interest, set about adapting Fechner's method to the problem of the measurement of memory, picking up frequency of repetition as the essential condition of association. He showed how repetitions could be used as a measure of memory. It was Ebbinghaus who fixed the outcome of British associationism by seizing upon repetition and making it the basis of experimental measurement of memory. His work was highly original in this research. The learning material used by Ebbinghaus were his own invention. He invented the nonsense syllables, it would seem, out of nothing at all in the way of ancestry. The logic was that if he was to measure the formation of association, he had to have a material, uniformly unassociated with which to begin. He framed 2,300 such syllables (two consonants with one vowel in between) more homogeneous than list of words, which could be associated in lists for learning. He was his own subject of the learning experiment, and drew the first curve of forgetting and learning as well, on the basis of his own performance on learning.

(b) Connectionism : Trial-and-error learning

The next exponent of associationism in learning was Edward, Lee Thorndike (1874-1949). His theory goes by the name "connectionism", he reexplained the principle of contiguity in the connectionist tradition. The basic principle of learning accepted by Thorndike in his earliest writings was association between sense impression and impulses to action (responses). Such an association came to be known as a "bond" or a "connection". Thorndike conducted series of researches in animal learning and his experimental conclusions led to the establishment of a "bond" or "connection" between stimulus and response which is either strengthened or weakened in the making and breaking of habits of the animals in the laboratory condition. The "bond" psychology—or simply "connectionism", as Thorndike's system is called—is the same stimulus-response psychology of learning, originally introduced by Watson in his psychology of behaviourism as a protest against the prevalent psychology of mentalism in Structural and Functional Psychology of Wundt and his followers who accepted psychology of conscious experiences only as subject matter.

The characteristic form of learning, according to Thorndike, was identified as trial-and-error learning—a process of learning by selecting and connecting. In this paradigmatic situation, the learner is confronted by a problem situation in which he has to reach a goal, such as, escape from a problem box or attainment of food. He does this by selecting the appropriate response from a number of possible responses and connecting his behaviour with correct response. A trial is defined by the length of time (or number of errors) involved in a single reaching of the goal. Thorndike, like a true mechanist of his day, sought to provide a mechanistic account of animal learning, confined to elementary events and operations. His theory will be discussed later on.

CONDITIONING

(a) Classical Conditioning

Russian physiologist, Ivan P. Pavlov (1849-1936) introduced a process of learning, known as conditioning, that gave the major impetus to theory building in learning. The essential elements of the classical conditioned-response is a reaction that normally follows a specified stimulus selected. It is assumed that the stimulus-reaction is unlearned. A new stimulus is now presented in association with the original stimulus. After a time the original stimulus is withdrawn and it is found that the new stimulus now elicits the original response. The response has now become 'conditioned' to the new stimulus.

In Pavlov's classic experiment he conditioned the flow of saliva in a dog to the ringing of a bell. It has been found that the time relationship between the unconditioned and conditioned stimulus is a critical factor. Ordinarily the conditioned stimulus should precede the unconditioned stimulus. A second important factor is that of reinforcement. After a conditioned stimulus—response reaction has been established—if that is not reinforced with the unconditioned stimulus from time to time—the response will weaken and, ultimately, disappear. Thirdly, it has also been found that new unconditioned stimuli can be conditioned to a conditioned stimulus. "That is, if B is conditioned to A, then C can be conditioned to B" (Anderson, op cit). The most important contribution of conditioning has been to give us basic scientific data on which to begin to build a theory of learning. Watson's and Hull's theories have been directly derived from conditioned-response or classical conditioning is the occurence of two stimuli events in close time proximity.

The principles of conditioning were initially established by laboratory studies. A clear presentation of these principles, along with application to school learning, is given by Staats (1968).[18] Staats pointed out two kinds of classical conditioning : 'first order' conditioning and 'higher order' conditioning. In first order conditioning, a neutral stimulus is presented almost simultaneously with the unconditioned stimulus. Pavlov used metronome to produce a tick tock sound as the neutral stimulus and food as unconditioned one. The food in the mouth leads to natural salivation in the dog and, in the process, mere sight of the food leads to the unconditioned response of salivation, a reflex in a hungry animal. After both have been presented together repeatedly the tick-tock sound of the metronome could produce salivation in the animal and the food having withdrawn gradually, only the sound of the metronome alone could elicit the response of salivation. The metronome sound is now 'conditioned stimulus', and salivation is the 'conditioned response'.

In higher order conditioning, the next step, the sound of the metronome, which produces the salivation response, now serves the same function as did the previous unconditioned stimulus—food. When a new neutral stimulus, a red circle, is presented immediately before the metronome sound, the sight of the red circle alone, after repeated pairings with the metronome, eventually elicits the response of salivation.

18. Staats, A. W. Language—Learning and Cognition. N.Y. Holt, Rinehart and Winston, 1968.

These principles of classical conditioning may be stated more formally. That means, wherever a stimulus that elicits a conditioned response occurs in close time proximity with a new neutral stimulus (which is not conditioned) there is a resulting tendency for the new stimulus to elicit the response (due to association). Further, when the new stimulus—now the conditioned stimulus—elicits the conditioned response, it may be manipulated with another neutral stimulus with the result that the response is brought under the control of the second previously neutral stimulus.

(b) Operant Conditioning

In operant or instrumental conditioning, on the other hand, the response must be made before a positive reinforcer, such as a reward, is given or before a negative reinforcer, such as an aversive stimulus. is removed. Thus is operant conditioning, when a response is followed by a reward, there is a tendency for the response to be repeated. Conditioning in which the animal performs a particular task, makes a particular movement or emits a particular response and is rewarded for doing so—the emphasis being on the animal manipulating its environment as opposed to its relatively passive role in classical conditioning. The term was introduced by B. F. Skinner (Skinnerian Psychology). Operant conditioning experiments involve long series of trials, with cumulative records of the rate and number of responses being plotted on graphs.

In instrumental conditioning procedures the conditioned response is instrumental in doing something for the organism. The response is typically instrumental in procuring or perpetuating the reward of some kind or in avoiding or diminishing punishment. The nature of instrumental conditioning is basically dependent on operant behaviour of the learner which is again a different respondent behaviour. Skinner proposed that two classes of responses should be distinguished, a class of elicited response (respondent) and a class of emitted (operant) responses. Responses which are elicited by known stimuli—such as meat powder in the mouth of the dog producing reflexive saliva secretion—are classified as 'respondents'. The second class of responses which need not be correlated with any known stimuli are 'emitted' responses and are designated 'operants'. They are situational and not elicited by recognized stimuli. Related to two types of responses, there appears two types of conditioning. The conditioning of respondent behaviour is assigned to Type S, because reinforcement is correlated with 'stimuli'. In classical conditioning on the other hand eliciting respondent behaviour the conditioned stimulus (sound of the metronome) is presented together with the unconditioned stimulus (meat powder) and thus elicits the response (salivation).

The conditioning of operant behaviour is assigned to Type R, the letter R designates correlation with reinforcement. It is the 'response' which is correlated with reinforcement. In operant conditioning experiment, the animal has to press a lever which releases the door to reach to the food. For a hungry organism this response may be strengthened by following it with food. It is not the 'sight' of the lever which is important, it is the pressing of the lever, which is to be noted. The conditioned response, i.e. pressing the lever, is a response which causes the reinforcer to appear—the reinforcing stimuli only helps emitting the response. In operant or instrumental conditioning, reinforcement cannot follow unless the conditioned response appears; reinforcement is 'contingent' upon the response, (Hilgard and Bower, 1977, op cit). In instrumental conditioning, the response is one which must become associated with conditioned stimuli through 'learning'. Therefore, it is a learning principle and is applicable to human learning behaviour. According to Hilgard (1977) most human behaviour is operant in nature. "The behavior of eating a meal, driving a car, writing a letter, shows but little of respondent character".

In this connection, it may be noted that higher order conditioning (Staats, 1968, op cit) is also possible in operant conditioning experiments, with both positive and negative reinforcers. The conditioned reinforcer in the positive conditioning which increases the probability of repetition of response is known as secondary reinforcer. Such a secondary reinforcer, once its reinforcement property is established, may generalize to reinforce responses other than the one with which it was initially associated.

The main generalizations about operant conditioning may be summarized. When a positive reinforcer closely follows a certain response, the probability that the response will occur again is increased. Same thing happens with negative reinforcers, and, when the reinforcer is removed, the response that led to removal will also tend to increase. Higher-order conditioning occurs in instrumental conditioning in the way that when a neutral stimulus is paired with a positive reinforcing stimulus, the neutral stimulus, after repeated pairing, itself acquires reinforcing power. Secondary reinforcers are usually social and is used in human learning mostly.

The proponents of operant conditioning do not accept the idea that learning occurs merely through associating two events in close time contiguity. They, in addition, insist on a reinforcer to strengthen the response.

Forgetting and Conditioning

Psychologists who explain learning in terms of conditioning usually do not use the word "forgetting". They refer to the weakening of responses as "extinction", based on the assumption that responses are strengthened through reinforcement and may be weakened through nonreinforcement. Reinforcement strengthens a response but effective reinforcement is dependent on a variable ratio schedule. We shall discuss this in details in Skinner's theory.

Some Aspects of Conditioning

From the study of conditioning several phenomena have been isolated that are of great significance for the understanding of conditioning and learning.

1. 'Stimulus Generalization'

Stimulus generalization is vital to the understanding of much human learning and performance. The general procedure for demonstrating stimulus generalization is relatively simple. An individual is conditioned to respond to a particular conditioned stimulus. After the response to a particular stimulus becomes established, the stimulus generalization involves the individual presentation of stimuli that vary in the degree of their similarity to the original conditioned stimulus. Stimulus generalization is said to have occured to the extent that these stimuli elicit the previous response. The strength of the response to stimuli of varying degrees of similarity or closeness to the original conditioned stimulus is used as a measure of the gradient of stimulus generalization. Research findings have indicated that the degree of closeness and similarity between the original conditioned stimulus and the test stimuli is positively correlated with the response strength. The greater the similarity, the greater the response strength and the greater the discrepancy between two stimuli, the less the strength of responding causing less learning. It is an important factor in human learning because generalization may extend to objects, persons, stimuli or situations having something in common with the situation to which the individual had been originally conditioned. This means that we are probably being conditioned in some way in everything of life's situations and in this way we develop our attitudes, prejudices, biases as well as perceptual and conceptual meanings of life and living. Stimulus generalization differs from individual to individual and individual difference in stimulus generalization is significant.

2. 'Reinforcement'

From the discussion on instrumental conditioning we know what reinforcement means. The consequences of the conditioned response are said to reinforce the response. So these consequences are called reinforcers, and the obtaining of these consequences is called reinforcement. In Pavlov's experiment of classical conditioning with dog , the meat powder in the dog's tongue was the reinforcement for the salivary response as well as the unconditioned stimulus for it. In negative instrumental conditioning the reduction in pain is the reinforcer and in positive conditioning any reward or satisfying situation is a reinforcer. The use of positive reward in education and training of children has long been recognized as an effective procedure. By reinforcing the desire or by correct responses, parents and teachers guide and direct the social and academic behaviour of the children under their management.

The effects of reward and punishment on behaviour are commonly recognized. Thorndike formalized these observations in his "law of effect", which stated in essence that those responses that were accompanied or followed by satisfaction to the organism tend to be repeated and those that resulted in discomfort or dissatisfaction for the organism tend not to be repeated. Thus, a great number of things in the life situation have been found to be either positively or negatively reinforcing. It is the essential condition of learning and conditioning. When the principal controlled variable in the learning situation is reinforcement, the reinforcement—at least indirectly—is presumed to have something to do with the learning that is basic to the consistent performance. The schedule of reinforcement will be discussed in details in Skinner's theory in the subsequent chapters.

3. 'Delay in reinforcement'

In the deliberate use of reinforcements, they should occur as closely following the responses that they are to perpetuate as is possible. The most effective use of reinforcements is when they follow closely the desired responses. The delay of reinforcement probably acts to decrease its effectiveness in human as well as in lower animals.

4. 'Secondary Reinforcement'

The stimuli used to establish higher order conditions are said to acquire reinforcing value. They are called 'secondary reinforcement' because they have never been directly associated with the originally effective stimulus but become effective in eliciting and maintaining a conditioned response. The concept of secondary reinforcement is an important one because it can be used in accounting for learning in which there is no apparent primary reinforcement.

5. 'Extinction'

If a conditioned stimulus is repeatedly presented after a response has been established to it, and the conditioned stimulus is never again reinforced by being paired with the unconditioned stimulus, the conditioned response gradually disappears. The progressive decrement in responding resulting from non-reinforcement is called 'extinction'. The massing of non-reinforced trials has been found, in general, to be the most effective way of extinguishing conditioned responses. When training is carried on a regular reinforcement schedule, extinction is rather rapid and, when it has been on variable schedule, it is much more resistant to extinction procedure.

6. 'Spontaneous Recovery'

An apparently extinguished response may reoccur after some time has elapsed since the last extinction trial. Spontaneous recovery is the characteristic of learned behaviour after a series of extinction trials followed by rest or distraction. One interpretation of the phenomenon of spontaneous recovery has to do with the concept of 'inhibition' (Hull, 1943)[19]. Response inhibition is assumed to build up as a

19. Hull, C. L. Principles of Behavior, Appleton-Century-Crofts. N.Y. 1943.

function of unreinforced conditioned responses and to dissipate with rest. Thus, if the conditioned stimulus—and any stimulus to which generalization may have occured—is not encountered for some time, the inhibition diminishes and the response may again occur on the presentation of the appropriate conditioned stimulus. The precise nature of spontaneous recovery is likely to depend upon the strength of conditioned response, the number of extinction trials, the spacing of extinction trials and the number of times extinction and reconditioning have already occured.

7. 'Discrimination'

When a particular stimulus situation is to be selected to respond to, it is essential to learn to discriminate among many stimuli. The process of discrimination can be viewed as the process of breaking down or controlling generalization. Discriminaition involves responses to one stimulus being reinforced and responses to others are not reinforced and thus extinguished. When the response is eventually made to one stimulus and not to others, the organism making response has learned to discriminate. The intelligent behaviour of a student in academic or a social situation requires his ability to make rather subtle discrimination.

Principles of Learning Theories : Complex Learning

In addition to conditioning and trial and error, complex learning involves forms like imitation, cognitive and conceptual learning, problem solving, social learning, creative learning, and cumulative learning within the parameter of "obsevational" and "meaningful learning". Each of these forms (principles) contributed to the formulation of theories of learning employed by different psychologists in conducting experiments in their own manner.

I. OBSERVATIONAL LEARNING

'Imitation'

Imitation has much in common with the process of identification. Imitation refers to the copying of specific ways of acting or patterns of behaviour while identification refers to be like another person and even merge with the model's personality : Imitation of another's behaviour may be a partial means of identification. Identification is significant educationally when the person imitated acts as a model. It is more important as a source of motivation than it is a form of learning (Kagan,

1958; Payne and Mussen, 1956)[20]. The models children observe and imitate are classified as 'real life', 'symbolic', and 'representational'. At home, real life models for younger children are parents and relatives. Teachers and other persons in the community are the real life models for many school children. Models presented through oral or written instructions and pictures or through a combination of verbal and pictorial devices are 'symbolic'. Models presented by audiovisual means, particularly television, are 'representational'.

In the schools and in many homes much attention is given to 'exemplary models'. Such models demonstrate prosocial behaviours, those that are considered desirable by the adults responsible for the education of the children. The socializing aspects of education is probably more critical than is generally assumed. Much socialized behaviour and antisocial, undersirable behaviours are acquired through imitating models. Sometimes imitation of television models may cause disaster to children and family. A child may imitate in order to obtain things or for just fun of it, or for chivalrous activity demonstrated by television models. Imitation is more a form of learning than is identification.

The fact that people and some lower animals do imitate is beyond doubt—sometimes the process is conscious and sometimes unconscious. But there seems to be no convincing evidence of instinctive imitation in man. Imitation is an observational learning. An observer attends to and imitates a model. He produces behaviours overtly or covertly for the first time matching the behaviours of the model. For that the behaviour imitated must be within the capacity of the imitator. People learn to imitate by simple or instrumental conditioning and by trial and error as a means of satisfying their needs. Imitation is also a product of learning and is a means of facilitating further learning.

Some factors affecting imitation

Some factors are associated with imitation. One of these is the consequences of the response to the model and to the observer. Another is characteristic of the observer. Consequences of the responses may be examined in terms of rewards and punishments. Imitation is facilitated when the model, in

20. Kagan, J. The Concept of Identification, Psychol. Review, 65, 296-305, 1958; Payne, D.E., and Mussen, P.H. Child Relations and Father Identification. Journal of Abnormal and Social Psychology, 52, pp. 358-362, 1956.

the presence of the observer, is rewarded for certain behaviour. Imitation is hindered when the model is punished or disregarded.

Characteristics of the observer are also related to imitative behaviour. The more imitative are those persons who lack self esteem and competence because they have experienced too few rewards of their own. They are dependent on the model more for matching behaviour than those who believe themselves to be similar to the models in some attributes and are self-confident. Being emotionally aroused probably increases the likelihood of imitation. Such arousal can come through the stresses of external situations or for some other extraordinary circumstances like use of drugs etc. But it should be noted that imitation is one of the means of learning and not an end in itself; it is not simply a tendency to copy blindly the action of others. Imitation is a more effective means of attaining prestige, social acceptance and security, developing conforming behaviour as well as achieving motor and social skills. Imitation makes such behaviours easily and more effectively possible than by blind trial and error process.

Now the question is : how does imitation operate ? Some imitation is the result of simple conditioning. Such imitation, like most causes of simple conditioning, is inclined to be mechanical, stereotyped and often irrational. It develops on the basis of simple contiguity of stimuli. Much of the imitation of lower animals is probably learned by such simple conditioning. For the very young children also, simple conditioning is at the root of imitative behaviour. Mother's fear of insects develop fear in her children through simple conditioning. Some of the imitative responses proved to be useful, but many are not. Many of them are acquired without the learners being aware of the fact.

On the other hand, imitation can be acquired on the basis of trial and error, and instrumental conditioning. Such learning is based largely upon the reinforcement of activities that are like the activities of others who are present or the actions seen and heard (observational learning). These observed activities are copied and perpetuated because they were rewarded or were pain-avoiding in their consequence. This has already been mentioned in the earlier section. Imitation is a kind of social learning, it will be discussed as a part of social learning theory in details in the theory section.

II. COGNITIVE LEARNING

Cognition is "Knowing". Cognitive processes include perceiving, remembering, recognizing, judging and reasoning. These categories involve the entire group of processes whereby information about the world is acquired, remembered, recognized or transformed so that it may be applied in situations other than the ones in which the original learning occurred (Bruner et al. 1956)[21]. Cognitive processes can function at all levels of awareness. It is a conscious experience, and always involves some degree of awareness. As a result of learning, a person may abstract a principle based on his awareness, forming a percept and behave in terms of that principle, without being able to formulate it verbally. High levels of awareness and the verbal formulation of perceptual and conceptual principles facilitate their development and transfer to other situations. The cognitive processes include perceiving, learning, retention, recalling, recognizing, conceptualizing, judging and reasoning, acquisition of percepts and concepts and their use in problem-solving and creative processes. Percepts and concepts are the products of learning. They represent the retained and organized effects of past experience. Sometimes they are derived from formal education, but they are also distillations from the totality of one's experiences. According to James (1892)[22] experiences at first may seem to be consisting of a "buzzing, blooming confusion". But he assures that perception, retention and recall are organizing and transforming processes.

Cognition always represents some degree of generalization and abstraction (learning) forming concepts and percepts. Conception and perception, as product of learning, involve responding to objects, people and situations in terms of their similarities rather than their differences. As compared with concepts, percepts are more specific, more stimulus-bound and closely tied to immediate sensory experience.

Perceptions and cognitions also have behavioural implications. Cognitive processes are the intellectual or knowledge components of experiences and are, therefore, capable of learning. They accompany an affective consequence, either pleasant or unpleasant and contain some explicit or implicit predictive implications that evoke certain behavioural gestures.

21. Bruner, J.S. Structures in Learning. N.E.A. Journal, 52, 26-27, 1963.
22. James, William, 'Psychology'. Henrv Holt and Company, N.Y. 1892.

That equates the cognitive process with the develop-ment of attitude.

We have already mentioned that the cognitive processes are organizing processes. While organizing, the cognitive processes use learning in the way of establishing an order in them. A person's cognitions are indicative of how he has learned to break his experiential world into parts and then tie up these parts together to form the whole process corres-ponding to the culturally transmitted patterns. It is assumed that these patterns are internalized by the person when acquired as part of one's socialization. These patterns are nothing but organized experiences, (product of learning) in the form of concept and percept which are conscious and self-organizing. Some of this organization is reflected in our language patterns. Therefore, Bruner and others (1956)[23] stated that "perception and cognition always go beyond the information given in the immediate situation. Perception represents sumtototal of the relevant retained and organized effects of the past experience". These effects manifest themselves in terms of associative meanings, conceptual and perceptual categories.

It has already been stated that cognitions are products of learning as well as means of further learning. It differs from acquisition of skills and motor responses only in degree. However, there are differences between rote learning and meaningful learning, between the acquisition of specific motor responses and the development of perceptual patterns, between the learning of isolated facts and the patterning of concepts into a hierarchy of conceptual systems.

Conditioning, trial and error, imitation and insight are all involved in cognitive learning, of which insight can be equated with cognitive learning, because insights by definition,, are cognitive processes. Insightful learning is cognitive learning. So is reasoning, as contrasted with blind, rote or mechanical learning. Cognitive learning extracts, stores, retrieves and makes use of information provided by each experience in problem-solving and in rational control of behaviour. Formal education attempts to make learning more cognitive and less mechanical and blind.

---

23. Bruner, J.S., Goodnow, J.J., and Austin, G.A., "A Study of Thinking". John Wiley and Sons, N.Y. 1956.

'Problem-Solving (Reasoning)'

Learning involving reasoning—popularly known as problem-solving—which makes use of concepts in ideational problem-solving process. Practically all forms of learning can be conceived of as problem-solving process. They may be motor, ideational or both. The development of insights is the key issue here. It involves the discovery and understanding of the principles necessary for problem-solving. Cognitive learning is concerned with both ideational and creative problem-solving. Cognitive learning in problem-solving needs analysis of problem and influence of "mental sets". The "mental set", as used in cognitive learning to solve problems, refers to a preparatory adjustment or "response readiness" which predisposes the individual to respond in a given way cognitively.

In the creative process, the problem considers perceptual and conceptual systems and mental sets as crucial. The starting point for most learning and problem-solving is some source of motivation. The motivation for creative problem-solving seems to be dominantly intrinsic and autonomous. Reinforcement is involved in developing and sustaining creative activity. Although creative problem-solving and thinking is said to be divergent rather than convergent in nature, both elements are present in ideational and creative problem-solving. "Psychological freedom" is conducive to creativity. These are all discussed in details in the chapter on creative ability.

"Insight"

Achieving a sudden, apparently instantaneous solution to a problem, characterized by perceiving relationships between different parts of the problem which had not been perceived before, is termed as "insightful learning" by the Gestalt psychologists. Insight is a common subjective experience among humans as well as in animals. The principle of insight in learning will be discussed more in the theory section run on.

CHAPTER VI

Theories of Learning

We have already emphasized the fact that history of psychology and the history of learning have advanced almost parallely. Human interest in psychology has a long history. At least since the time of ancient Greeks in the West and ancient 'rishis' (seers and philosophers) in the East, philosophers in their own characteristic ways have been speculating about topics that are now considered part of psychology. It was not until 19th century, however, that attempts have been made to study these topics experimentally. The first psychological laboratory was founded by Withhelm Wundt in Germany in 1879 and various evidences of research in mental processes followed establishing modern psychology on a definite institutional footing, on the basis of scientific enquiries.

The psychologists, unlike the early philosophers, rested their inquiry about how do we think, feel, learn and know and make decisions and act on them, but not on inferential basis but actually testing them in laboratory conditions. The kind of psychology developed in Germany, became to a great extent the standard for the rest of Europe and America where experimental psychology flourished gradually in accelerated speed. The later psychologists in America became more interested in objective behaviour as well as conscious experiences. They were interested in what people 'did' as well as what they thought or felt. J. B. Watson was the pioneer in this field of psychology who also presented his view on learning in behaviouristic way.

Watson's Behaviourism in Learning Theory

Early in the twentieth century objective behaviourism became the main feature in American psychology and came more and more in conflict with the German tradition. Pressure increased to break the traditional mould and to develop a psychology that was directly oriented towards objective behaviour and practical usefulness.

John Broadus Watson (1878–1958)

It was through his vigorous attacks on traditional psychology and his attempt to build a radically different system that a new stance in psychology appeared in the American psychological proceedings. Watson's opposition to admitting anything subjective into psychology led him to reject much more than the study of consciousness. His psychology came to be known as "Behaviourism" with a categorical objective stance.

The reason for the name 'behaviourism' was clear enough. Watson was interested only on Behaviour, not in the conscious experiences. Human behaviour was to be studied as objectively as behaviour of machines. Consciousness was not objective, therefore, not scientifically valid and could not be meaningfully studied was the thrust of Watson. He meant nothing more abstruse than the movement of muscles. What is speech (he said) ? —Movement of the muscles of the throat. What is thought ? —Sub-vocal speech, talking silently to oneself. What are feeling and emotion ? —Movement of the muscle of the gut. Thus, Watson disposed of mentalism in favour of a purely objective science of behaviour.

Another of his targets was the analysis of motivation in terms of instincts. He opposed the instincts which were considered innate and, therefore, imbibes the character of mentalistic nature. He asserted that our behaviour is, on the contrary, a matter of 'conditioned reflexes', that is the responses learned by what is now called 'classical conditioning'. He said that we do not show aggression or sociability because we are born with an instinct to do so, but because we have 'learned' to do so through conditioning. He believed all we inherit is our bodies and a few reflexes, differences in ability or personality is differences in learned behaviour. Thus, Watson was in several respects a strong exponent of 'environment' as against heredity in the familiar nature-nurture controversy. What we are depends entirely (except for anatomical differences) on what we have "learned". And since what can be learned can be unlearned,— this contention meant that the human nature, either in general or in a particular person, was greatly subject to change— "There is no limit to what a person, properly conditioned, might become".

Watson's Interpretation of Learning

He regarded all learning as classical conditioning. We are born with certain stimulus-response connections called 'reflexes'. These reflexes, according to Watson, are the entire behavioural repertoire that we inherit. However, we can build a multiplicity of new stimulus-response connections by the process of conditioning, first described by Pavlov—"that if a new stimulus occurs along with the stimulus for the reflex response, after such pairing the new stimulus alone will produce response". This conditioning process, according to Watson, is how we learn to respond to new situations (by chaining of responses). Such conditioning, however, is only part of the learning process. We must not only learn to respond to new situations, we must also learn new responses. Thus new and complex behaviour is acquired through "serial combination of simple reflexes"—a complex sequence of stimulus-response connections. There arises the questions, like : How does complex learning, then, take place through serial conditioning ? Or how does a particular sequence of stimulus-response connections will be formed ? Watson had two answers for these questions. One answer was to say that the stimulus-response connections that make up the skilled act are conditioned reflexes. Each response produces sensations that become conditioned stimuli for the next response and thus the whole sequence of conditioned stimuli-response connections is formed. This formulation gave Watson the satisfaction of having reduced complex habits to their simple building blocks-conditioned reflexes. However, he did not try to explain it further and left the work for the physiologists to explain that. It was, in fact, more apparent than real.

Watson's another explanation of this form of learning is in terms of 'frequency' and 'recency'. The principle of frequency states that the more frequently we made a given response to a given stimulus, the more likely we are to make that response to that stimulus again. Similarly, the principle of recency states that the more recently we have made a given response to a given stimulus, the more likely we are to make it again. In order to explain the occurrence of a particular stimulus in a complex sequence, Watson says that, during learning, many different responses occur to the stimulus, but that many of the learned responses drop out. The responses that change the situation gain in frequency and recency and the particular stimulus-response unit in the sequence is then complete. All of these statements about the learning of new responses are left rather underdeveloped in Watson's treatment.

Even the theory of learning of emotional responses forwarded by Watson is not tenable, though he made a little concession to heredity in this case. He recognizes three innate patterns of emotional reaction—fear, rage and love (primary emotions) which are not feeling according to Watson but are same as reflexes—patterns of movement of internal organs. But, in reality, emotions are more complicated than what is usually meant by reflexes. Emotional learning, he emphasized, also involves conditioning of these three patterns of emotional response to new stimuli.

Long-lasting influence of Watson

"Watson's great contribution to the development of psychology was his rejection of the distinction of body and mind and his emphasis on objective behaviour. This battle was so effectively won that most of the later learning theories are in the broader sense of the word behaviourist framework". (Hill, 1977, ibid). But Watson was much as thorough than he might have been in dealing with the detailed problems of learning. They are mostly incomplete and inconsistent in his treatment of complex learning. But he opened the door for later psychologists to enter the realm of behaviourism in order to explain impact of learning. Therefore, it has remained for others to try to build, within the behaviouristic framework, a more complete theory of learning.

Pavlov's Classical Conditioning

Watson's reliance on classical conditioning had been a direct effect of the experimental conclusions reached by Pavlov in his physiological laboratory in Russia. "One cannot mention conditioned reflexes without thinking of the distinguished Russian physiologist, Ivan Petrovich Pavlov (1849-1936), who gave them their name." (Hilgard, 1975, p. 62). His investigation on conditioned reflex has influenced Watson and later learning psychologists like Guthrie, Skinner and Hull. The classical experiment was carried on with meat powder in the experimental dog's mouth producing salivation which is considered as 'unconditioned reflex'—a physiological phenomenon. The meat powder or food is the 'unconditioned stimulus'. Then another stimulus—the sound of metronome (or any other arbitrary stimulus)—is combined with the presentation of the food. After repetition, eventually, if time relationship is correct, the sound of the metronome will evoke salivation independently of the food. The sound then becomes 'conditioned stimulus' and the response to it becomes the 'conditioned reflex'.

The mechanism by which animals learn, i.e. receive information, store and relate subsequent behaviour to this information is one of the basic areas of experimental psychology. Although the precise mechanism of learning is still not understood, a major advance in theory came as the result of the experiments conducted by Pavlov. In a conditioning experiment an animal is placed in a rather passive situation, with a simplified environment and a limited number of things for it to do. In his classic experiment Pavlov used 'hungry' dogs which will naturally salivate at the sight of the food. The automatic reaction—'food/salivation', he called 'reflex' and assumed it to be instinctive. In the next stage of experiment he rang a bell at the moment that the food was presented to the dog and after a number of presentations—'bell/food/ salivation', he found that he could omit the food and get bell/ salivation. This new link he called 'conditioned reflex', and proposed that it must be the fundamental unit of learning.

In a brilliant series of studies he was able to show the enormously predictable nature of conditioning experiments and plot, in graphical form, the effect of different variables on the conditioning. For example, the bell and the food had to be presented reasonably close together for the conditioned reflex to be set up and probability of it being set up was a function of how closely the two stimuli were paired—if the bell preceded the food by too great a margin, conditioning will be slow or would not take place at all. He was also able to plot the parameters of 'reconditioning'. He showed the process of 'extinction' by means of not presenting food after the bell in repeated trials until the animal ceased to salivate to the conditioned stimulus-bell. These experiments and results may seem simple and obvious to us today, but their real and historical significance was the fact that Pavlov had shown that a process such as learning—which has previously tended to be looked upon in a rather mystical way—could not only be studied in the laboratory, but could also be shown to follow relatively simple and describable laws.

The theory and concept underlying the process of conditioning were the laws of association "when the laws were stated in quantitative form, there came a strong tendency to emphasize continuity of elements as having priority over the principles of similarity and contrast. Physiological explanations tended to rest primarily on contiguity". (Hilgard, P. 63 ibid). The law is : "When two elementary brain processes have been active together, or in immediate succession, one of them, on reoccurring tends to propagate its excitement into the other". (James, 1890, p. 566)[1] . The same principle had been working in Pavlov's conditioned reflex mechanism.

The notable accompanying events discovered by Pavlov were : 'Reinforcement', 'Extinction', 'Spontaneous Recovery', 'Generalization of Excitation' and 'Inhibition' and 'Differentiation', in developing his theory. Some of these we have discussed in the section—principles of learning theory in the earlier chapter. The rest will be discussed in the light of conditioned reactions.

'Reinforcement'—The simple conditioned reflex begins with its acquisition through repeated 'reinforcement' (presentation of food and satisfaction of the animal) i.e. the repeated following of the conditioned stimulus by the unconditioned stimulus and response at appropriate time intervals.

'Extinction'—When reinforcement is discontinued and the conditioned stimulus (CS) is presented alone, unaccompanied by unconditioned stimulus (US), the conditioned response (CR) gradually diminishes and ultimately disappears. This process is called by Pavlov as 'experimental extinction'.

'Spontaneous recovery'—An amazing event that takes place, is however, after some time has elapsed following extinction without further repetition of any kind, the conditioned salivation returns and the event is called 'spontaneous recovery' of the extinguished reflex. This has immense importance in the theory of learning and forgetting.

The phenomena of spontaneous recovery and forgetting are interrelated. Pavlov was the first physiologist to report about spontaneous recovery while experimenting with conditioning of reflexes (salivation in dogs in particular). Following experimental extinction of a conditioned response (CR), the

1. James, William. The Principles of Psychology, N.Y. Holt, Rinehart and Winston—63, 1890.

CR showed some recovery if the dog was removed from the apparatus and allowed to rest in his home cage for a while before being returned to the experimental situation and tested. The CR has "spontaneously recovered" without any special reconditioning by the experimenter. Later works showed that the amount of recovery increased was the increment with the length of the rest interval between sessions. This proved the existence of psychological factors (security, nervousness etc.) involved in physiological reaction of the instinctive reaction. Pavlov and others had also performed experiments in which the CR had been repeatedly extinguished over consecutive daily sessions. They reported that the amount of recovery of the CR became progressively less as the extinction session proceeded and, finally, CR ceased totally (a learned reaction). This event seems to be similar to 'spontaneous regression' pointed out by Ebbinghaus (1885) in his learning and memory experiments, mentioned earlier. "The amount forgotten increases with the time that has elapsed since the end of practice, and the amount of session-to-session forgetting becomes progressively less as daily practice on a task continues". (Hilgard, p. 392).

'Generalization of excitation and inhibition'—In the process of conditioning, the response can be evoked by a broad bank of stimuli of more or less similar nature, that is those which are conditioned stimulus-specific. The CR will occur on a test to a neighbouring stimulus to an extent dependent upon the similarity of the test stimulus to the training stimulus. This is called 'stimulus generalization'. (This has been discussed in details in the previous chapter on the principles of the theory of learning). Stimulus generalization occurs due to training and not only the stimulus generalization but generalization of inhibitions follow training in extinction.

The inhibitory phenomenon within conditioning, first described in connection with extinction, became of great interest to Pavlov. A classification of various types of empirical manifestations of inhibition have been summarized by Hilgard and Marquis (1940) as follows :

A. External Inhibition

Temporary decrement of a conditioned response due to an extraneous stimulus, such as a sudden accompanied loud sound reduces conditioned salivation to a light (conditioned stimulus).

B. Internal inhibition

Internal inhibition develops slowly and progressively when a conditioned stimulus is repeatedly presented under one of the following conditions :

1. *Experimental extinction*—The weakening of response to a conditioned stimulus which is repeated a number of times without reinforcement.
2. *Differential inhibition*—A conditioned response given originally to either of two stimuli is restricted to one of them through the reinforcement of one and the non-reinforcement of the other. The non-reinforced negative stimulus becomes inhibitory.
3. *Conditioned inhibition*—A combination of stimuli is rendered ineffective through non-reinforcement, although the combination includes a stimulus which alone continues to evoke the conditioned response. The other simile in the combination are conditioned inhibitors.
4. *Inhibition of delay*—If a regular interval of sufficient duration elapses between the commencement of a conditioned stimulus and its reinforcement, during the early portion of its isolated action the conditioned stimulus becomes not only ineffective, but actively inhibitory of other inter-current activities.

C. Disinhibition

Temporary reappearance of an inhibited conditioned response due to an extraneous stimulus. This may be considered as an external inhibition of an internal inhibition.

Pavlov's contribution to learning theory involves the following learning problems :

1. **Capacity** : The capacity to form conditioned reflex is the action of the nervous system : hence there are some congenital differences in learning ability.
2. **Practice** : In general, the conditioned reflexes respond and strengthens due to repeated reinforcement, but, while providing learning, care should be taken to avoid accumulation of inhibition even in repeated reinforcement.

3. **Motivation** : Motivation is the most important factor in inducing conditioned reflexes, for example, in the case of the experiment with dog, the first condition is that the animal must be 'hungry', as 'drive' is important condition in instrumental conditioning.

4. **Understanding** : Though a physiologist, Pavlov uses subjective terms like understanding or insight and says, "when a connection or an association, is formed, this undoubtedly represents the knowledge of the matter". He did not ignore the mentalistic concepts in learning. He affirms a relationship existing in the external world.

5. **Transfer** : Transfer is the result of generalization in learning whereby one stimulus serves to evoke the conditioned reflex learned to another.

6. **Forgetting** : Forgetting is a consistent phenomenon in learning and is emphasized by Pavlov not in terms of retention of forgetting but in physiological term like extinction. He did not deal with forgetting as such in the laboratory Repeated conditioned reflex experiments on the same dog were greatly overlearned. Hence forgetting was not considered as a laboratory problem, but extinction was. Therefore, decline of CR through experimental extinction was dealt with and Pavlov concluded that conditioned reflexes (CR) are temporary which are evidences of forgetting. But then he recognized the distinction between forgetting and extinction (which is a weakened CR). Extinction is frequently followed by spontaneous recovery as a reflex and therefore, forgetting is not total.

The important contribution made by Pavlov is to make his study purely objective and leading psychology to behaviourist tradition, though he himself remained strictly within physiology. But from within his own campus he exerted great influence on contemporary psychology, and learning theory, in particular, enormously, and opened new vistas for learning psychologists.

Guthrie's Contiguous Conditioning Theory

Guthrie is one of those learning psychologists who interpreted his theory of learning in the same behaviouristic fashion and maintained the tradition. Edwin, R. Guthrie (1886–1959) remained closest to Watson's original position of Behaviourism and therefore, his interpretation of learning sounds much like Watson's idea of behaviourism. Yet in some respects his system seem to follow Thorndike and Pavlov in the sense that on the one hand his learning theory rests on the objective stimulus-response association psychology and on the other uses the conditioned response terms coming from Pavlov. It was somewhat later that the conditioned reflex of Pavlov might serve as a useful paradigm for learning and he wrote a number of books emphasizing the standpoint of behaviourism in learning and psychology. This exposures influenced some follower psychologists among whom Guthrie was an important one – the result of his work and faith in behaviourism was published in the book "General Psychology in Terms of Behaviour (1921)", jointly written by him and Smith, S[2] .

Among the theories of learning, Guthrie's is one of the easiest to read in his own words, but nonetheless difficult for someone else to discuss. It is easy to read because he wrote in an informal style, making his points with homely anecdotes rather than with technical terms and mathematical equations. But his casual presentation was apparent, its deep meaning contains the germ of a highly deductive theory of learning.

Guthrie's basic principle of learning is similar to that of conditioning principles that was basic for Watson, but stated in a general form. Guthrie describes his theory and its basic principles in his book "Psychology of Learning" in 1952. In describing the contiguity of cue and response he formulates one law of learning, from which all else about learning will be

2. Smith, S. and Guthrie, E.R. General Psychology in Terms of Behaviour, N.Y. Appleton—Century—Crofts, 1921.

comprehensible. The law is stated by him in the following language : "A combination of stimuli which was accompanied by a movement will on its recurrence tend to be followed by that movement". (p. 23) Winfred, F. Hill, in his book "Learning" (op cit) paraphrased it as follows : "If you do something in a given situation, the next time you are in that situation you will tend to do the same thing again". This principle is more general than classical conditioning in that it says nothing about the unconditioned stimulus—it says that the response accompanying a stimulus is likely to follow the stimulus again. In classical conditioning the response occurs with the (conditioned) stimulus during training because the unconditioned stimulus elicits it. This sequence, of course, fulfils Guthrie's conditions of learning. As long as the conditioned stimulus and the response occur together, learning will occur.

Guthrie's statement is apparently very simple, which avoids mention of drives, of successive repetitions of reward and punishments and only mentions about the combination of stimuli and movements. But this one principle serves the basis of a very intriguing theory of learning—when interpreted loosely, is the source of all interpretations of learning and its management, interpreted rigorously, it becomes the chief postulate of a deductive theory. Its proper interpretation, in fact, needs a second statement to complete the basic postulates about learning and he writes : "A stimulus pattern gains its full associative strength on the occasion of its first pairing with a response" (Rev. ed. 1941)[3] (p. 30).

The statement is rather paradoxical and the first difficulty with this principle is that one often does many different things in the same situation and improves upon with practice. Which one will occur next time remains indefinite. This challenge is no problem for Guthrie and he simply replies, "the last one" (learning the recent one). Here the emphasis is upon some kind of "recency principle" of Watson. Because, if learning occurs completely in one trial, that which was last done in the presence of a stimulus combination will be that which will be done when the stimulus combination next occurs, for it refers to the last response of a succession rather than to recency in

3. Guthrie, E.E. The Psychology of Learning (Rev. Ed.) Harper and Row, N.Y., 1952 and 1941.

time. He accepted the recency principle ignoring the principle of frequency of Watson in order to forward a simple theory of contiguity. Like other sophisticated theorists, he did not proceed by denying familiar forms of learning. He wanted to show that complex learning can be derived from these basic postulates—that each form of learning (insightful or purposive or problem-solving) requires no new principle to explain it but can be explained basically by primary law of association of contiguity.

Guthrie's belief in contiguity is irrespective of the time interval between the conditioned stimulus and unconditioned response—the time interval which is considered as most important in conditioning experiments. The cue, in the conditioning process, is more important than the original stimulus, according to Guthrie. He defended strongly the strict simultaneity of cue and response in the process of conditioning to occur. Guthrie brought in the movement factor to fill in the time gap between the presentation of stimulus and response to it made by the animal. He argues that an external stimulus will give rise to movements of the organism—these movements, in turn produce Kinesthetic stimuli and a bond or association is made between the stimuli and response separated by time interval and the gap in between has been filled up by movement. Therefore, the association is formed between the simultaneous events, the time interval remains insignificant in the process of conditioning to Guthrie.

He cites example of "delayed response" made by the animal in support of his contention—that the animal learns deliberately delay its response to a signal in order to get reward. The signal cues off a chain of adjunctive behaviour or movements (as he terms them) that usher the animal directly into the point of reinforcement. There is a strong preference for movement-produced stimuli as the true conditioners in Guthrie's system. Guthrie makes no use of the concept of reinforcement. The aspect of Guthrie's theory that has been most attacked in his lack of concern with success and failure, with learning to do the "right" thing. He does not say that we learn to make those responses that work, or that obtain reward. He says that something we do in a situation becomes learned as a response to that situation and acts as a cue to a different situation, so that it becomes the last thing done in the old situation and the cue becomes a stimulus for the response to be made in another simultaneous event. The two events are associated with movements produced. The movement-produced stimuli which act as conditioners permit the integration of habits within a wide range of environmental change in stimulation, because these stimuli are carried around by the organism (Hilgard, 1977, p. 92, op. cit).

As regards practice, in learning, Guthrie thinks; that practice brings improvements through repetition of movements (kinesthetic) and not as a goal achievement. To other learning theorists, according to Guthrie, success, improvements and achievements, all refer to acts or outcomes to learnings and not to movements as he suggested. The prediction of movements in practice in acquiring a skill is important to him because acquisition of a skill does not depend on a single movement but a number of movements made under a number of different circumstances—a complicated skill calls for practice in all the different situations. Guthrie's theory emphasizes the importance of movements in practice because, he maintains, that practice produces its consequences, not according to a law of frequency, as suggested by Watson but according to the simple principle of attachment of cues to the movement. Therefore, a skilled task needs practice because it is composed of a large number of habits involving different kinds of movements.

Guthrie's interpretation of forgetting is similar. Habits do not weaken with disuse. They are replaced by other habits. But forgetting—like acquisition—is gradual because of the many specific stimulus-response connections that make up a complex habit. Hence it is possible to make one definite prediction from Guthrie's interpretation of forgetting. We can predict that a habit will be better retained if it has been practiced in different situations (that is, in the presence of a number of different stimulus combination). Forgetting in the theory of Learning is the counterpart of retention and, therefore, original learning and interfering learning follow the same rule. Conditioning experiments explain forgetting as a fact of extinction. Guthrie did not consider extinction as a decay in habits strength due to mere non-reinforcement but due to associative inhibition, i.e. through learning of a interfering factor producing incompatible response. As stated above, he explained forgetting in the same way, i.e. if there is no interference with old learning, there would be no forgetting.

Guthrie also suggested methods of breaking habits by accelerating its replacement. He suggested counter-movements to occur in the presence of the cues to the habit. Guthrie's breaking of habits have been adopted by the psychotherapists in the form of behaviour modification techniques. The modern behaviour therapists have picked up and applied the techniques in helping their patients overcome certain debilitating behaviour problems. One such method is called "systematic desensitization" (Wolpe, 1958)[4] .

The impression one gets from most of Guthrie's writing is that human behaviour is a mechanistic matter. Behaviour is rigidly controlled by stimuli and changes in the stimulus response connections follow simple mechanical laws. However, Guthrie has been more receptive than Watson to such concepts as desire and purpose. He recognizes that much behaviour has a goal directed character, but he interpreted it in rigorously physical terms. Guthrie reminds us to look at the particular response that is being made and particular stimuli that are eliciting learning and not rely too much on rewards and punishments. Because both Watson and Guthrie totally avoided the concept of reinforcement (which is the key point in learning process of modern learning psychologists) and insisted only on the mechanistic way of interpreting human behaviour and learning, they are, therefore, called "contiguity theorists" (Winfred, 1977, ibid.)

Thorndike's Connectionism

Edward L. Thorndike's (1874-1949) contribution to learning psychology is of major importance because his theory is the starting point of explaining the process of child learning which he thought is similar to animal learning. He, therefore, deduced his theory of connectionism from the observation of animal behaviour in the laboratory. He observed that human infants are as impulsive and dependent on the pleasure and pain as consequences of their actions as the animals. He also discovered that animals learn in the same mechanistic way as the infants do. This theory was first announced by Thorndike in his book "Animal Intelligence" in 1898. His theory is usually studied in two parts. The earliest writings on learning of Thorndike was mere associationism—learning at that period

4. Wolpe, J. Psychotherapy by Reciprocal Inhibition, Stanford Stanford Univ. Press, 1958.

was considered to be based on association between sense impressions and impulses to action (responses). Such an association has been termed by Thorndike as a "bond" or a "connection", which are responsible for making or breaking of habit (a learned response to a specific stimulus). Hence Thorndike's theory comes to be called as "Connectionism", and is recognized as the original S-R (bond between stimulus and response) psychology of learning.

The elementary form of learning of both lower animals and human being was considered by Thorndike as 'trial-and-error' learning (selecting and connecting response to the stimulus). The principle of trial and error has already been described in the last chapter. This concept has been introduced by Thorndike to explain the strategy apparently underlying animal behaviour in learning. In his experiments of trial-and-error, typically when confined to a "puzzle box" (problem situation) the animal makes a series of movements, more or less random, but one or more of which will ultimately help to escape. Thorndike argued that all learning proceeded on this basis—the successful responses being rewarded and thus learned or established, the unsuccessful ones being unrewarded and failing to be learned. The trial-and-error learning is supposed to be more or less automatic with the animal being unconscious of what he is doing or how it is actually effecting the escape or achieving its goal. A true mechanist of his day, Thorndike sought to provide a 'mechanistic' account of animal learning—a simple behaviour. (For further details of experiment see Hilgard, 1975).

Thorndike was a pioneer in experimental animal psychology who first introduced the idea that pleasure and pain consequences of our acts are important determiners of behaviour. In order to establish his contentions, he took animals into the laboratory, presented them with standardized problems and made careful observations of how they solved those problems. His most widely quoted study was with cats in the puzzle box. After the experiments were carried on in the laboratory, he concluded that the cat's learning to pull the string involved not an "intelligent" understanding of a relation between string pulling and door opening but a gradual "stamping in" of the stimulus-response connection between seeing the string and pulling it. Similarly rejection process operates simultaneously and the unnecessary and unrelated behaviours are "stamped out" by the animal. This gradual learning was typically graphed as a "learning curve" with the time clapsed before successful responses plotted on the vertical axis and successive practice trials on the horizonal axis. A learning curve can be drawn from the repetition of a performance by a well motivated subject which shows progressive improvement. If a measure of success on each trial is plotted, the success measure being the ordinate and the amount of practice upto including the given trial being the abscissa, we have a learning curve. The learning curve rises or falls according to the measure adopted. The learning curve rises if the measure is amount accomplished per trial or per unit of time; and falls if the measure is errors per trial. Thorndike (1913)[5] gives a large collection of such curves and discusses many questions of proper measurement. To obtain a complete learning curve we should start with no previous training and continue,, till the subject reaches the limit of his ability, most actual curves are cut short at both ends since we neither start from absolute zero of practice nor do we carry the subject to his absolute limit.

The slope of the learning curve indicates the rate of improvement. If this rate were constant through the learning, the curve would be a straight line. Almost any learning curve shows on the contrary a negative acceleration; it flattens out as practice advances—the rate of improvement decreases, interesting is the general shape of the curve which exhibits the course of improvement throughout the learning process. Horizontal parts of the curve, showing no improvement led to assume three levels in the course—the initial level, the intermediate level and the final level. It is possible that the 'plateau' occurs at the final level. A plateau in the learning curve may occur due to both physiological or emotional factors of the subject with the time elapsed before successful response plotted on the vertical axis and successive practice trials on the horizontal axis. Such curves typically show high values initially, declining to low, relatively stable values near the end of 10 to 20 practice trials. The characteristic curve reveals when performance in a learning task is plotted against time, till complete mastery (as below figure 6.1). The most common form is S-shaped (ogive), denoting a slow improvement in

5. Thorndike, E. L. Educational Psychology : The Psychology of Learning Vol. 2, New York, Teacher's College—29, 31-37, 60 Lemcke and Bnechner, 1913.

early trials, followed by a notable acceleration, which is, in turn, replaced by a flattening of the curve or 'plateau'.

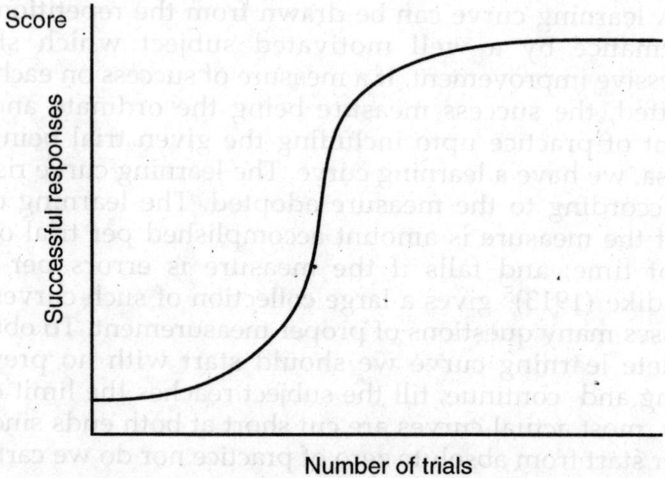

Fig. 6.1

At the time Thorndike published these studies, they are radical in two respects : their careful observation of animal behaviour under controlled conditions and their concern with the gradual strengthening of stimulus response bonds. They were Thorndike's answer to the argument about whether animals solve problems by reasoning or by instinct. By neither, said Thorndike, but rather by gradual learning of the correct response through the process of 'stamping in' and through the process of 'stamping out' of unsuccessful ones. Whole process is automatic and mechanistic which helped Thorndike to formulate his first law of learning—"the law of effect". Thorndike says nothing about the animal's feeling, but only about what animal does. Thus, he adheres to the concern of behaviourism with what individuals do. His language may sound subjective, but his meaning is as objective as Watson's. He was a pioneer of objective psychology, but he incorporated within his objective psychology of learning the "law of effect", and thus became, in fact, the first reinforcement theorist—allowing the role of motivation in learning for the future learning theorists to apply.

"Thorndike formulated his mechanistic law of effect in the following terms : responses to a situation which are followed by a rewarding state of affairs will be strengthened or stamped in as habitual responses to that situation : responses which are unsuccessful will be weakened or stamped out as responses to that situation. Rewards, or success or failures, were thus introduced as providing a mechanism for selection of the more adaptive response." (Hilgard, 1975, p. 31).

Thorndike's law of effect had cast profound influence upon his thinking about human learning which contains, in addition to "effect, readiness and exercise". He says, "Both theory and practice need emphatic and frequent reminders that man's learning is fundamentally the action of the law of readiness, exercise and effect" (1913). The law of exercise is also known as the law of use and disuse in terms of strengthening of connection of stimulus and response. Strengthening increases the probability that the same response will be made when the situation occurs and depends upon the regular exercise (practice). The law of disuse gradually introduce forgetting due to decrease in strength or lack of connection between stimulus and response.

The law of readiness, in brief, is an accessory principle going along with law of effect, which characterizes the circumstances under which a learner tends to be satisfied or annoyed. These conditions were explained by Thorndike in terms of neuronal units "conducting impulses (conduction units) rather than in terms of mental phenomenon". He thinks that it is a bodily impulse or the attractive stimulus which causes readiness in the responses of the action sequence making the chain of performances. This law refers to fatigue of situation effects; e.g. if a person is already stuffed with food, being forced to take another bit is positively aversive. "Thorndike's readiness is a law of preparatory adjustment, not a law about growth" (Hilgard, 1977, p. 33).

In addition to the above three major laws of learning. Thorndike forwarded five subsidiary laws of learning :

(1) Multiple response,

(2) Set or attitude,

(3) Pre-potency of elements,

(4) Response by analogy,

(5) Associative shifting.

These subordinate laws, in fact, involves principles adopted in learning. "The multiple response principles means that in order to produce the desired response, a number of varied responses must occur (varied reaction)."

"The second principle is that learning is guided by a total attitude or "set" of the organism."

"The third principle states that the learner is able to react selectively to prepotent or salient elements in the problem." (ibid)

"The fourth principle states that the response to a new situation occurs with reference to a previously learned or known situation and familiarity plays an important role to master a new piece of learning."

"The fifth principle is the direct application of Pavlovian conditioned response theory." The law states that shifting of stimuli can take place by substituting a conditioned stimulus for an unconditioned one. Thorndike believes that "we may get any response of which a learner is capable associated with any situation to which he is sensitive" (1913, p. 15). The principle of associative shifting of stimuli can produce amazing experience of learning—same response to a completely new stimulus, provided the organism is presented with stimulating situations throughout the shifting process. The technology of teaching-machine programs have utilized successfully the above principle of associative shifting in teaching-learning situations.

Skinner's Operant Conditioning Theory

As against classical conditioning of Pavlov which emphasizes physiological reflexes and the role of mechanical conditioning in learning, Skinner's operant conditioning emphasizes the role of satisfaction in the light of Thorndike's law of effect.

Skinner was a staunch behaviourist and tried to avoid such mentalistic concepts as 'satisfaction' and replaced the term as *reinforcement*—an objective phenomenon. Skinner's theory of learning therefore, is also known as the theory of 'instrumental conditioning'—reinforcement being the instrument. His analysis of learning, behaviour is a "functional analysis", which operates in identifying and isolating environmental variables and learning is a product of such functions.

Skinner's theory consists of a collection of concepts and principles and research strategies to explain and analyse a complex behaviour. He believed that any complex behaviour, like thinking or problem-solving, when properly analysed will be interpretable in terms of complex interplay of the elementary concepts and principles involved in them. But this analysis Skinner conducted by following absolutely behaviouristic methodology, completely ignoring the mentalistic and cognitive explanation of behaviour or any behaviour to be caused by inner psychic forces. But only significant departure from traditional stimulus-response psychology of his predecessors (Watson, Pavlov and Thorndike) he advanced a division between respondent and operant behaviour in terms of responses—stimuli being less important.

Skinner proposes that two types of responses can be distinguished—a class of elicited responses and a class of emitted responses. Responses elicited by natural stimuli are called "respondents" and emitted responses are designated "operants". Hilgard, (4th ed. p. 209) writes : "The operant-respondent distinction drawn above was to dominate learning theory for some 30 years. It was called "two-factor" and it laid claim to a number of correspondences. Responses of glands and internal organs (respondents) were distinguished (by hypothesis) by being (a) elicited by innate, unconditioned stimuli, (b) controlled by the autonomic nervous system, (c) involuntary, (d) characterized by minimal response produced feedback, and most importantly, (e) able to be classically conditioned (Type S) but not operantly conditioned (Type R). In stark contrast, responses of striated, peripheral muscles (operants) were distinguished by being (a) sometimes emitted, without identifiable stimuli, (b) controlled by the central nervous system, (c) under voluntary control, (d) characterized by distinctive proprioceptive feedback, and (e) able to be operantly conditioned but not classically conditioned".

The components of the responses elicited by the reinforcer, becomes conditioned and occur in anticipation of it. Therefore, in instrumental conditioning, the placing of reinforcer is very important i.e. how the reinforcements are scheduled. In order to emphasize the role of reinforcement Skinner introduced a process in experiment known as conditioning of "superstitions"[6], —a phenomenon described in terms of

6. Skinner, B. F. Superstition in the pigeons. J. Exp. Psychol. 38, 167-172-209-10, 1948.

operant reinforcement. Skinner noticed in the behaviour of the pigeons that when the reinforcement is first delivered, the pigeon's pecking follows the sterotyped ways for some time, so that this "operant" becomes strengthened. Skinner noticed a number of learning the superstition sequences by human adults are exposed to random, noncontingent reinforcement. The significance of superstition in learning is that whenever a reinforcement is delivered to an organism, it strengthens whatever operant behaviour is in progress at that time.

Reinforcement can be described as a stimulant, as when a person or an animal is rewarded, that is, reinforced, for what it does—the same behaviour will tend to be repeated with increasing frequency. Skinner showed the effect of reinforcement through a specially prepared box (Skinner Box) and conducted experiments with the pigeons following the principles of the law of effect of Thorndike. When a pigeon is placed in the Skinner Box for the first time, it behaves erratically and exhibits "emotional behaviours". After a period of practice, the bird is allowed to get "adapted" and undergoes "magazine training" to behave as the experiment demands. At this point, if food is made contingent upon pecking the "Key", the bird will show a number of irrelevant behaviours for a considerable period at first and when, ultimately, abruptly, it will peck the Key a single time allowing the tray consisting of food to reach the pigeon. Once the pigeon takes food from the tray brought by it by pressing the key and getting the reward all by his own effort, the process becomes remarkably orderly and predic-table. It is almost certain that the bird on restricted diet will soon peck the key again and again and that, in a relatively short period of time, the pecks on the key will occur at a moderate and stable rate allowing a graph to be plotted. By introducing the term "reinforcement" Skinner had restated the Law of effect to include the word "reward" or Thorndike's own phrase, "satisfying state of affairs", which meant to include all of the things which can be classified as rewards. "Skinner's definition of 'reinforcement' is as follows, "a reinforcer is anything or any event that increases the likelihood of responses that immediately retain it" (Anderson and Faust, 1975)[7].

---

7. Richard, C. Anderson and Faust, Gerald, W. Educational Psychology, Dodd, Mead and Co. N.Y. 1975.

The process of operant conditioning is integrally related with the reinforcement because it is through reinforcement that operant conditioning is being strengthened. The conditioned reinforcers are also called "secondary reinforcers". It is through the conditioned reinforcers that the organism learns the behaviour which operates in his environment. A reinforcer can also be artificially applied but it produces a 'natural' or physical consequence of behaviour in the form of response. When a reinforcer is no longer reinforced in repeated performances continuously, the process of 'extinction' appears. All the accessory processes due to reinforcement or non-reinforcement or delayed reinforcement have been discussed in the previous section.

A reinforcer which serves an obvious biological function is called a 'primary reinforcer'. A stimulus which accompanies or slightly precedes such a primary reinforcer may, therefore, take on the power to reinforce. Such stimuli are called 'conditioned reinforcers'. These are the secondary reinforcers which are the effect of learning and are acquired.

Schedules of Reinforcement

A caution is needed in the application of reinforcement to produce desired response. The reinforcement of operant behaviour in ordinary life is not regular and uniform. Therefore, in order to acquire desired responses, "intermittent reinforcement" is necessary not only in the laboratory conditions but also in real—life situations. The intermittent reinforcement used in laboratory by Skinner in a controlled condition, led to the discovery of two main classes of intermittent reinforcement viz. 'interval schedules' and 'ratio schedules'. A third type of reinforcement has also been used by him strictly according to the time interval and known as "fixed interval schedule" where the food for the pigeon will be available only after a fixed number of responses after lapse of a designated or fixed interval of time, measured from the preceding reinforcement or from the onset of a "trial stimulus". This arrangement controls the number of reinforcements delivered per hour to the animal. Fixed Interval (FI) schedules produce lawful and orderly results. Sometimes the FI schedules are varied by 'variable intervals' (VI) schedules, in which a range of intervals from very short to very long are used in a random, variable order. The VI schedules show that average performance is remarkably stable and uniform and are found to be unusually resistant to extinction.

Anderson and Faust (1975, ibid) summarized the use of intermittent schedules and states: "If an intermittent schedule of reinforcement is gradually introduced, a pigeon can be made to peck a key at a higher rate than it will maintain under continuous reinforcement. Perhaps more important because of its practical implications, intermittent schedules sustain performance indefinitely with little reinforcement. If a schedule has predictable features, then performance will be periodic, its exact features determined by the particular contingencies of reinforcement that are in effect. If, on the other hand, the pigeon is reinforced on a variable and, therefore, unpredictable schedule, remarkably stable rates of performance can be sustained. The general conclusion to be drawn from the research on schedules of reinforcement is that the rate and consistency of an organism's performance are precisely controlled by the frequency and contingencies of reinforcement".

The reinforcements used in the laboratory led Skinner to deduce the operant strength in the animal learning process. Various schedules helped the operation of instrumental conditioning and thus contributing to the methods of primary learning. The success in the laboratory learning process guided Skinner to deal with a procedure which he called functional analysis, which we have discussed before. Nevertheless, a functional analysis is concerned with the lawfulness of the relationships and the manner in which these relationships fluctuate under specified conditions—the reinforcement and the various schedules are thus very important class of events in the functional analysis of behaviour. They express how do the reinforcement and their scheduling affect operant strength. Two other such classes of events are 'drives' and 'emotions'.

Drive, basically, is something which pushes an animal or a human into action. Drive, therefore, is functional and operational. Skinner used the term drive to mean a set of operations (such as withholding of food for certain number of hours, or reducing the organism's weight, which have effect upon rate of responding to a stimulus. A drive, according to Skinner, is not a stimulus, or a physiological state or a mental state, but refers to certain classes of operation and may be called as a behavioural state which is affected by reinforcement. Drive, according to Skinner, is dependent on deprivation; for example, hours of food deprivation are important in determining the rate of responding in a Skinner box and thus is related to reinforcement (in terms of the length of time interval) eliciting operant conditioning. Experimental studies made by Skinner with the 'Skinner box' illustrates the kinds of relationships between 'drive' and 'operant conditioning'. Deprivation of food is the medium through which these relationships are established. Deprivation involves withholding something for a period of time. It is the condition in which a reinforcer is denied or unavailable, so that activity or behaviour is restricted for the time being. Consequently, deprivation increases the efficacy of appropriate reinforcer inducing drive and thereby producing an increase in alertness and restlessness. The effects of deprivation are found when the reinforcer has been withheld, releasing more activities. Drive then becomes an operant reinforcer for further activities. Deprivation is opposed to satisfaction, which, on the other hand, leads to cessation of activities. Therefore, drive itself is not a stimulus but acts as an operant behaviour of a reinforcer.

In the same manner, as above, Skinner advances his opinion to establish the state of emotion, not as a class of responses but a set of operations. Emotion functions as causing changes in response. He emphasized that emotional responses can be conditioned (like Watson) and called them 'conditioned emotional responses' (CER), a phenomenon which he demonstrated with electric shock suppressing appetitive behaviour. The same phenomenon (CER) had also been demonstrated by Pavlov in advancing his theory of classical conditioning.

Most of the later psychologists, however, thought that CER is due to motivational competition between conditioned anxiety and appetitive motives.

Hull's Deductive Theory

Hull's theory of learning is the most ambitious of the connectionist theories we have discussed so far. Clark, L. Hull. (1884-1952), a professor of Yale University, was the most influential learning theorists of his time. Originally an engineer, later becoming psychologist, he made effective use of his engineering training and engineering outlook in formulation of psychological theories later on. His engineering mental make-up was evident in his desire to construct an 'elaborate, formal, precise structure of psychological theory'. In him we see the full flowering of the connectionist reinforcement tradition in developing his hypothetic-deductive system. The system he followed was strict behaviourism and, therefore, falls into the family of Guthrie and Skinner—three of them combined to apply force and power to Watsonian behaviourism. Hull's theory is fundamentally mechanistic, totally devoid of consciousness, but with some exceptions. Hull's central concept of learning theory is 'habit'. He derived most of the information about habit from his experiments with conditioned responses. His theory of learning has two highly significant characteristics—'elegancy' and 'drive-reduction'—each consisting of distinctive features. Hull's theory conforms to the requirements of science and logic which was the demand of his time and so gathered fame as 'elegant'.

Secondly, Hull's theory of learning is a drive-reduction theory based on the assumption that life process is tension-producing and the organism's endless effort to reduce this tension is learning to make compromise with the processes of living. In the process, "the organism finds itself in disequilibrium with its environment, that is, it finds itself deprived of something it needs". (Skinner, p. 404 ibid). As illustration, we can cite the physiological need for food (hunger is the drive, here). Drive then becomes the "tension state" associated with the need. In order to fulfil the need the drive instigates the organism to become active and the drive is 'energized'. The movement and the energized activity produces its own stimuli and its own responding (instrumental conditioning) satisfying the need and thereby reducing the drive. The responses here, becomes reinforced and the reinforcement of a response causes it to be learned, since it is tension reducing.

Basic elements in Hull's theory

A. Hull's theory is essentially a stimulus-response theory. But since the stimulus-response bond occurs in an observable situation, causing a change in the organism, Hull postulates, firstly, certain *intervening variables* and called them *symbolic constructs*. Actually, the observable intervening variables are not new constructs but may be considered as elaboration of Woodworth's S-O-R concept and its different interpretations. The S-O-R signifies that the stimulus (S) affects the organism (O), and what happens as a consequence is the response (R), depends upon O as well as S. The stimulus-response theory in the experimental conditions considers only input (the environmental influences on the organism)-output relationship, (output being the organism's response). But in between, there remains all sorts of contingencies of reinforcement, such as deprivation schedules, prior practice and others. These variables are capable of producing different responses. An understanding of the effect of these variables would help us to deduce new phenomena.

B. "Reinforcement, the primary condition for habit formation". Hull emphasized the role of reinforcement as the primary condition of habit formation. Hull used the contribution of reinforcement in terms of law of effect of Thorndike rather than of Pavlovian way. This means that he considered reinforcement to be used as instrumental conditioning. Reinforcement that Hull considered was primary reinforcing state of affair leading to drive reduction. Gradually Hull shifted his original position from primary reinforcement to secondary reinforcement as the latter in instrumental conditioning came into greater and greater prominence in reinforcement theories. In considering Hull's theory of reinforcement it should be noted that Hull had identified "drive" and "drive-stimulus" to convey the same idea and "drive-stimulus reduction" as similar to "need-reduction".

C. Anticipatory goal responses : Most of the primary behavioural laws in Hull's system were derived from either classical or instrumental conditioning (Learning under the control of reinforcement) and are not confined to simple conditioning, rather deals more with discriminatory learning, maze-learning, all forms of verbal and rote memorization, tool using and so on. Hull proposed a number of intermediate mechanisms, derivable from the basic laws of his system. One of such intermediary variables is the notion of anticipatory goal responses.

He assumed that the stimuli at the goal stage was present at the initial stage too. These stimuli include the internal drive, environmental stimuli present both earlier as well as during reinforcement, persisting up to the goal state and also the stimuli aroused by the organism's own movements. Hull assumed that all of these stimuli become conditioned to the goal response. This anticipatory goal responses are already achieved prior to reaching the goal and are considered as fractional goal responses. These fractional antedating goal responses (designated by Hull as *ra's*) are very important integrators, in Hull's system. Guthrie used the same concepts in formulating his theory but not as explicitly as done by Hull. (Hilgard, p. 155, op. cit).

The fractional anticipatory responses give rise to stimuli (*sg*) which can be conditioned (because they are response producing *ra*) to differential responses and so aid in eliciting them. These *rg-sg* stimuli are used by Hull in describing the further mechanisms of 'secondary reinforcement', 'the gradient of reinforcement' and the 'habit–family hierarchy'; *sg*, according to Hull, can be a mechanism of wider generality in addition to *rg* and is capable of getting connected to earlier stimuli in an instrumental sequence.

Hull established his theory of deductive reasoning – a formal system on the basis of adequately defined terms and certain basic postulates.

The basic postulates of Hullian Theory

The postulates

The original postulate of Hullian theory is known as Mathematico-deductive theory of rote learning. Hull, however, organized and classified the arrangements in 1943 in a more systematic way, which he states as follows :

A. The external cues which guide behaviour, and their neural representation

Postulate 1. Afferent neural impulses and the preservative stimulus trace.

"Stimuli impinging upon a response give rise to afferent neural impulses which rise quickly to a maximum intensity and then diminish gradually. After the termination of the stimulus, the activity of the afferent nervous impulse continues, in the central nervous system for some time. (Hull, 1943)."

Postulate 2. Afferent neural interaction.

Afferent neural impulses interact with other concurrent afferent neural impulses in a manner to change into something partially different. The manner of change varies with every impulse or combination of impulses. (ibid).

B. Responses to need; reinforcement and habit strength

Postulate 3. Innate responses to need.

Organisms at birth possess a hierarchy of need—terminating responses which are aroused under conditions of stimulation and drive. The responses activated by a given need are not a random selection of the organisms responses but are those more likely to terminate the need (ibid).

Postulate 4. Reinforcement and habit-strength.

Habit-strength increases when receptor and effector activities occur in close temporal contiguity provided their approximately contiguous occurance is associated with primary or secondary reinforcement (ibid).

C. Stimulus equivalence

Postulate 5. Generalization.

The effective habit-strength aroused by a stimulus other than the one originally entering into conditioning depends upon the remoteness of the second stimulus from the first on a continuum in units of discrimination thresholds. (Just noticeable difference) (ibid).

D. Drives as activation of responses

Postulate 6. Drive Stimulus

Associated with every drive is a characteristic drive stimulus whose intensity increases with strength of drive. (ibid)

Postulate 7. Reaction potential aroused by drive.

Habit-strength is sensitized into reaction potential by the primary drives active at a given time.

E. Factors opposing responses

Postulate 8. Reactive inhibition.

The evocation of any reaction generates reactive inhibition, a disinclination to repeat the response. Reactive inhibition is spontaneously dissipated in time.

Postulate 9. Conditioned inhibition.

Stimuli associated with the cessation of a response become conditioned inhibitors.

Postulate 10. Oscillation of inhibition.

The inhibitory potential associated with every reaction potential oscillates, in amount from instant to instant.

F. Response evocation

Postulate 11. Reaction threshold

The momentary effective reaction potential must exceed the reaction threshold before a stimulus will evoke a reaction.

Postulate 12. Probability of reaction above the threshold.

The probability of the response is a normal function of the extent to which the effective reaction potential exceeds the reaction threshold.

Postulate 13. Latency.

The more the effective reaction potential exceeds the reaction threshold, the shorter the latency of response.

Postulate 14. Resistance of extinction.

The greater the effective reaction potential, the more unreinforced responses of striate muscle occur before extinction.

Postulate 15. Amplitude of response.

The amplitude of responses mediated by the autonomic nervous system increases directly with the strength of the effective reaction potential.

Postulate 16. Incompatible responses.

When reaction potentials to two or more incompatible responses occur in an organism at the same time, only the reaction whose effective potential is greatest will be evoked. (ibid).

These 16 postulates form the basis of Hull's theory of learning. His systematic behaviour theory involves the system as a chain of symbolic constructs. Six major symbolic constructs may be identified as follows : (which are inferred as intervening variables).

1. **Reinforcement.** Habit Strength ($_SH_R$) is the result of a reinforcement of stimulus response connections in accordance with their proximity to need reduction (Postulate 3 and 4).

2. **Generalization.** Generalized habit strength ($_SH_R$) depends both upon direct reinforcement of an S–R connection and upon generalization from other similar S′–R′ habits. (Postulate 5)

3. **Motivation.** Reaction potential ($_SE_R$) depends upon the interaction of habit strength and drive (Postulate 6 and 7).

4. **Inhibition.** Effective reaction potential ($_SE_R$) is reaction potential as reduced by reactive inhibition and conditioned inhibition (Postulate 8 and 9).

5. **Oscillation.** Momentary effective reaction potential ($_SE_R$) is effective reaction potential as modified from instant to instant by the oscillating inhibitory factor associated with it (Postulate 10).

6. **Response evocation.** Responses are evoked if the momentary effective reaction potential is above the threshold of reaction. Such responses may be measured according to the probability of reaction, latency of reaction, resistance to extinction, or amplitude (Postulate 11 to 16)[8] .

From the above statements, it can be surmized that "Learning, according to Hull, depends upon contiguity of stimulus and response closely associated with reinforcement defined as need reduction (or in secondary reinforcement associated with a stimulus that itself has been associated with need reduction). That the growth of learning is based upon the increment of habit strength with each reinforcement and it is a constant fraction of the amount remaining to be learned. This can be referred to the fractional anticipatory responses giving rise to Stimuli (SG)r when the goal is partially reached releasing a number of environmental stimuli persisting from both earlier and during reinforcement. Further, the upper limit M of the association between S and R depends on the amount of reward (need–reduction) and the delay of reward. It concerns temporal relationship between CS onset and the UR in classical conditioning. Hence, basically, Hull's theory is an associationistic theory—association by contiguity, which is similar to Guthrie's.

8. From Hilgard, p. 161, op cit.

DRIVE

The next important role in Hull's theory is the role of Drive, because :

(1) Primary reinforcement is not possible without some drive—internal or external and consequently it cannot evoke secondary reinforcement. Primary reinforcement requires a strong D to enable the subject to learn, or else secondary reinforcement will not occur because the secondary reinforcement can only be evoked when association between the stimulus and primary reinforcement has been established.

(2) Without drive there could be no response, for drive (D) activates habit-strength into reaction potential. Hull assumed that drive (D) multiplied habit-strength, so that a "zero-drive" state implied that no SER could exceed the reaction threshold. (Hilgard, p.164)[9] .

(3) Again, without the distinctiveness of drive stimulus (SD), there could be no regulation of habits by the need state of the organism. The organism will not learn to select the proper line to respond to the different directions for the requisite need state.

Hull provides an equation that will express the relationship among reaction potential, habit strength, and drive, based on the assumption that drive interacts with habit strength in some multiplicative fashion to produce reaction potential.

$$sE_R = sH_{ER} \times D$$

Inhibition

Hull's inhibitory postulates were not very original but are deduced by him from the physiology of fatigue and Pavlov's ideas about "internal" or conditioned inhibition generated by conditions of non-reinforcement, specifically during the extinction trials. For Hull, as for Pavlov, SIR was a 'learned response', responded to active inhibition—a deliberate learned opposition to a particular response. Hull, of course attempted a drive-reduction interpretation of SIR (inhibition postulate). He thought that when fatigued IR, gets in, in spite of the R, or

9. Hilgard, p. 163.

reaction being very effortful, it would generate much aversive drive leading to fatigue (IR). Then stopping or quitting the response would be reinforced by the immediate reduction of fatigue. The process suggests that SIR is really based on "an associative habit for the stopping of R" (reaction). Hull very hastily has drawn such a conclusion which he could not prove equation-wise—what he had successfully done in the case of habit and habit-strength. Moreover, subsequent conceptual and empirical studies by later psychologists attacked Hull's notion of inhibition in a strong way. Hull, however, ignored such criticisms and maintained his contention till the end, when in 1952 he forwarded his theory and interpretation of final behaviour system.

Derived Intermediate Mechanisms

Hull assumed that behaviour system is non-physiological, complex due to environmental influences and are analyzable into simpler mechanisms. Hence Hull's system has been classified as a `reductive' system, in that more complex phenomena are deduced on the basis of simpler and more basic phenomena and relationship, and thus they are also "reduced". By being reduced they become so different and simple that sometimes these cannot be perceived to be coming from the postulates. In order to bridge the gap, Hull assumed in the postulates and corollaries the presence of some derived intermediate mechanisms which would also explain the connection between "laboratory experiments and the more familiar behaviour of the organisms adapting to a complex environment". These mechanisms, he assumed, would facilitate the emergence of many more varieties of behaviour. Two such intermediate mechanisms referred by Hull to explain complex learning behaviour were 'the gradients of reinforcement' (the goal gradient) and the 'habit–family hierarchy'.

The goal gradient is the term used by Hull to describe the observation that an animal speeds up its activity as it nears a goal. It also refers to the observation that when an animal is learning a goal-directed sequence, those aspects closer to the goal are first learned. A goal response can easily be achieved by combining recognition of a "short primary gradient" and "secondary reinforcing stimuli" scattered along the route towards goal. From the observation that "a long chain of behaviours will be reinforced and strengthened to a lesser degree than will behaviour components closer to the goal, Hull and Spense derived the goal-gradient". (Hilgard, p. 172). The principle behind it was that responses nearer to the goal would be more strongly conditioned than those further removed. The `goal-gradient' of Hull is opposed to the time gradients involved in classical conditioning experiments.

Habit-Family Hierarchy

Another mechanism—the habit-family hierarchy—is an important means of learning deduced by Hull, not originating in the postulate but as an intermediate mechanism. It is derived from a more basic principle of learning and carries great weight in the deduction of further behaviour phenomena. It is a phrase coined by Hull to refer to the mechanism by which the organism in a complete environment selects one response in preference to another. Hull found that the natural environment of learning is often not very simple and consists of a number of alternative means and the correct path has to be chosen for the organism to reach the goal. How to encounter these complex problems is often left to the organism to find out. A given complex environment for learning may provide multiple routes between a starting point and a goal. The organism learns alternative ways of moving from a common starting point to a common goal position where it finds need–satisfaction. These alternatives constitute a family of equivalent responses—called a habit-family—because of an inferred integrating mechanism. The most suitable response in this situation has to be selected from this family hierarchy. The likely response will be the one that heads the 'habit-family hierarchy'. If this is blocked, number two in the hierarchy is elicited. The most suitable response incurs the habit strength and is integrated in the habit-family.

Hull describes the process as inferred integrating mechanism. This takes place as an integration into a family hierarchy by way of the fractional antedating goal reaction, present in each alternative response being performed. The fractional antedating goal reactions become conditioned stimuli (SG) to which all overt responses are conditioned, possessing a derived gradient of reinforcement. They also constitute alternative means and compose a family with hierarchical arrangement. The means now become responses and the responses which are more strongly conditioned (secondary reinforcement) to SG than others have now been comfortably chosen.

Hull, in 1937, writes that "if one number of a habit-family hierarchy is reinforced in a new situation, all other members of the family share at once in the tendency to be evoked as reactions in that situation. This makes possible the explanation of response equivalences and other appropriate reactions in novel and problematic situations, such as those found in insight and reasoning experiments". The habit-family hierarchy, thus, forms a chain of operative responses and, thus, if one is blocked the next in the hierarchic order takes its place.

Hull's comprehensive systematic deductive theory of learning opened up far-reaching vistas to explain problem learning, evoke insightful thinking and learning by reasoning to solve a complex situation. It casts immense influence in developing social learning theories and their applications in school situations.

Outlines of Social Learning Theories (non-associative)

The dictionary meaning of social learning is the process of acquiring knowledege by observation or imitation. Various patterns relevant to an individual's interaction with his group or society. (Evans 1978).

Socialization means the process by which an individual learns the rules of the society. More specifically, it refers to the learning of patterns of behavior expected of one by society as a whole and by the segment of the society—sex, race, religion, culture, social backgrounds etc.—of which one is a part. The deliberate efforts and processes which help such learning constitutes the contents of social learning theories.

Social learning theory is a form of cognitive learning different from Skinnerian and other behavioristic contentions and are, therefore, not dependent on the principle of conditioning only. Social learning theory was advanced systematically by Bandura (1969, 1971)[10] and Mischel (1968)[11] and N. E. Miller and Dollard (1941)[12], Rotter (1954)[13]. They advanced their theoretical positions through a balanced

10. Bandura, A. Principles of Behavior Modification, Holt, Rinchart and Winston. N.Y. 1969
    " Social Learning Theory. General Learning Press, N.Y. 1971.
    " Psychological Modelling. Conflicting Theories. Aldine Atherton, N.Y. 1971.
11. Mischel, W. Personality and Assessment. Wiley, N.Y. 1968.
12. Miller, N. E. and Dollard J. Social Learning and Imitation. New Haven Yale University Press, 1941.
13. Rotter, J. B. Social Learning and Clinical Psychology. Englewood Cliffs, N. J. Prentice Hall, 1954.

synthesis of cognitive psychology with the principles of behaviour modification. They emphasized the development of personality, social and personal competences which evolve out of the social conditions within which learning occurs. The main issue of this theory, as has already been pointed out, is that only associationism in human learning is not tenable and that classical and operant conditioning are not sufficient for explaining initial learning of all behaviour.

They emphasized that a learner is an observer and he imitates a model who manifests the behaviour that is new to the learner. Their primary contribution thus is the explanation of the learning of new behaviours or responses through observation, and imitation which they refer to as vicarious learning.

Ausubel (1963)[14], on the other hand, refused to accept that human learning can be explained by the principle of condi-tioning. He believed that humans assimilate, relate, organize and store information for further use. His theory is known as Subsumption theory emphasizing the function of central nervous system in learning.

Bandura's observational learning theory indicates that learning would necessarily show the following effects to the observer :

(a) A modeling effect.

(b) A disinhibitory effect.

(c) An eliciting effect.

Cumulative learning

Gagne (1970)[15] developed a model of "cumulative learning" describing eight types ranging from the learning of simplest associations between two things or events through learning to solve problems. Gagne agrees to accept associative learning for elementary learning effort but he thinks that complex concept learning or learning the principles or rules and problem-solving cannot be explained only through any of the conditioning principles. We shall discuss it in the later section of this chapter.

---

14. Ausubel, D. P. : The Psychoiogy of Meaningful Verbal Learning. Grunne and Stratton. N.Y. 1963.
15. Gagne', R. M. : The Conditions of Learning. Holt, Rinchart Winston, N.Y. 1970.

A model of Cumulative Learning

Gagne' has synthesized knowledge concerning various types of learning and has formulated a model of cumulative learning. According to Gagne, the effects of learning are cumulative. The higher level skills that man possesses are gradually developed. That individuals first learn the capabilities that build successively on one another and gradually develop and help the individual acquire knowledge. Gagne, while working with cumulative learning, recognized that, to foster the capabilities, identification of eight types of related learning is necessary.

The following eight types of learning consist of starting from simplest, signal learning to most complicated problem-solving. Gangne in his book (1970, ibid) has shown the hierarchy of difficulty level as :

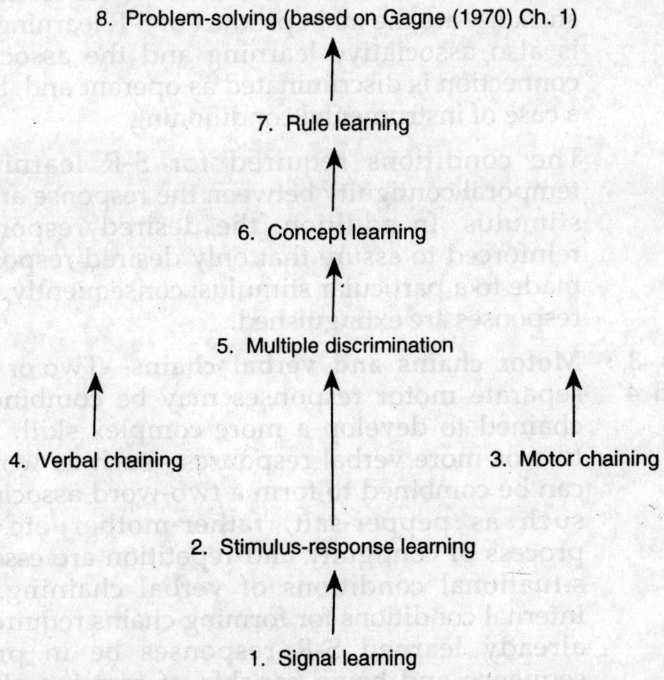

Gagne not only classified different types of learning but also considers the conditions—internal and external—of the learner and learning situations.

Brief description of each type of learning and the related conditions are presented below :

Type 1 : **Signal learning**—Signal learning corresponds directly to classical conditioning. Learning to respond to signals is common form of reflective behaviour—both in animals and human infants. Signal learning uses the same mechanism of classical conditioning, two stimuli occurring simultaneously.

The primary condition involved in signal learning is the time proximity of the conditioned and unconditioned stimuli. Gagne explains signal learning in terms of contiguity and repetition.

Type 2 **Stimulus-Response (S-R) Learning**—precise movements of the muscles in response to specific stimuli that have become discriminated from other stimuli—are the main product of S-R learning. This is also associative learning and the associative connection is discriminated as operant and, hence, a case of instrumental conditioning.

The conditions required for S-R learning is temporal contiguity between the response and the stimulus. In addition, the desired response is reinforced to assure that only desired response is made to a particular stimulus; consequently, other responses are extinguished.

Types 3 : and 4 **Motor chains and verbal chains**—Two or more separate motor responses may be combined or chained to develop a more complex skill. Here, two or more verbal responses—such as words—can be combined to form a two-word association, such as pepper-salt, father-mother etc. The process of contiguity and repetition are essential situational conditions of verbal chaining. The internal conditions for forming chains require that already learned S-R responses be in proper sequence and being capable of forming chains. Verbal chaining will also occur due to reinforcement which must immediately follow the chained response.

Type 5 : Discrimination learning—The complex discrimination learning also follows the same principle like S-R learning and proper acquisition of S-R chain responses will lead to mastery of complex discrimination learning. The essential situational conditions are the same as S-R learning i.e. contiguity and repetition.

Type 6 : Concept Learning—Similarly, concept learning has been explained by Gagne following the same S-R principle. But the important feature of concept learning is that, having attained a concept, one is able to identify other examples of the concept without further learning. This is typical of concept learning only. All other types that we have seen do not possess such characteristic. In the earlier types, each new association, chain or discrimination must be learned as and when it is encountered. To attain a concept the individual must have some prerequisites, such as capability of discrimination and capability of making common response. For example, to learn the concept "dog" the child must discriminate between a dog and other objects and must perceive the commonality of two dogs.

The learned discrimination between dogs and other organisms and things must be available to the learner in close temporal contiguity. So that they can be reinstated to form a concept of "dog". Some repetition of the learning sequence as well as confirmation of the correct responses are also essential for learning concepts. Concept learning is very important for gaining organized knowledge.

Type 7 : Rule learning—Gagne defines rule in S-R terminology as a chain of two or more concepts. Rule learning must corroborate with a statement made. It is differentiated from rote learning in making correct responses or, rather, exactly same responses as is given in the statement presented for learning. It is presumed that rule learning helps problem-solving in future. Essential to rule learning are having the concepts embodied in the rule and the capability for making the responses specified by the rule. This means that rule learning provides capability for forming verbal chains. It is a simple associative process.

Type 8 : **Problem-solving**—This is the culmination of all the forms of learning, in the sense that when an individual learns to solve a problem his learning reaches the highest stage of gathering knowledge. It enables an individual to acquire new ideas independently and is itself an achievement on the part of the learner. But learning to solve problems is a gradual process involving defining a problem, suggesting a hypotheses and establishing a related one and varifying the final hypothesis and achieving a solution.

Klausmeir et al (1975, op. cit) describes problem-solving learning type (starting with needed rules) needs the ability of the individual to recall and apply them to the problem. These two are the essential prerequisites of problem-solving. They are the internal conditions. The external conditions include making the component principles available to the learner in close temporal contiguity aiding the learner to recall the principles and providing cues to guide thinking. They then become almost verbal instruction to the learner.

Much has been already stated about concept learning in the development chapter of this book. The reader can refer the related materials about concept learning from the chapter, if necessary. The interested reader may also refer Gagne's experiments with several curriculum projects applicable to school learning involving all the eight types of learning mentioned above.

The basic learning theories have been discussed briefly as we consider learning from behavioural point of view. In recent times, there seems to be a shift of emphasis from merely formulation of laws to the techniques involved in school learning. The school learning is not only a learning process, it is a teaching-learning process. Therefore, more emphasis is laid on meaningful learning than on mere theorizing. Textbooks, reference works, use of computer and other mechanical devices, sound, films and other instruction materials are used extensively in schools to present information to the students.

As a result, new theories have been presented by the modern educational psychologists, namely, "The Information-Processing Theories" of behaviour. They deal with meaningful learning in the classroom situations and are interested in working with mechanical devices.

The modern trend in the teaching-learning situation is the extensive and intensive use of new techniques in psychological theorizing. Consequently, in formulating theories, they started using a format of 'program' and arrange the learning materials and methods in the form of program-learning, that run in high-speed computers. The emphasis of this theorizing has been shifted from describing the nature of behaviour to the nature of processes or "actions". The aim of this enterprise is to get such a programmed computer to go through a series of actions which, in some essential ways, resemble or simulate the cognitive and behavioural actions of a real subject performing the task. The students study the materials and try to relate the new information to what they already know.

Two dimensions of learning processes are fundamental in this theory (cognitive and meaningful learning theory). These two ways are 'reception learning' and 'discovery learning', on the one hand, and meaningful and rote learning on the other — both ways furnishing a cognitive structure with organized sets of facts, concepts and generalization. In rote learning the students only get reception and no discovery, while in discovery learning all that is to be learned are presented in the final form and the learner gets some information independently. This information is then integrated into the existing cognitive structure and reorganised and transformed to produce a new or modified cognitive structure.

The information-processing theory uses reception and discovery process through programmed model. The first stage is characterized by reception and discovery learning, in which information to be learned becomes available to the learner. In the second stage, the learner acts on the information in an attempt to remember it so that it will be available thereafter. If the learner attempts to retain the new information by relating it to what is already known, meaningful learning occurs.

The same approach has been adopted in programming of the computer so that it goes through the same steps (after the model) that one would if he is to make a verbal deduction from the theory. The computer does the job mechanically in short time and with no errors. The computer programms are generally problem-solving and help simulate learning. They demonstrate how past learning can be utilized in solving new problems, as described in earlier paragraphs. The information processing theory categorically has a cognitive bias.

The historical antecedents of this theory show that both the technique and the mode of thinking have been imported into psychology from engineering, introducing a new line of research and work—a practical one—known as educational technology. Educational technology uses a number of charts, models, visual aids and computers to aid information processing.

As the working of information processing is computer-dependent, learning also uses the same descriptive languages as computer, the computer-simulation approach. The stimuli, data, instructions are all called "information" and are input or read in the computer; the computer reads out or exposes outputs either in printing or in any other mode the machine permits. This is the information processing mechanism. For the operation of this mechanism, it is essential, first of all, to prepare the learning programmes. Verbal learning and concept learning, meaningful learning are thus programmed in such a way that the theorists, while deciding these working processes, remain cautious and concerned more with describing and modelling experimental results than with actually producing an intelligent machine.

Simulation of how an actual subject might learn and improve his performance is not the goal, how effective learning can take place through the information processing is the ultimate goal—the former is only the first step to the final goal.

CHAPTER VII

Personality

The history of personality study rolls down from being entirely philosophical to being absolutely humanistic. To ask what is personality is asking for a complete picture of a human being, who even himself does not know what he is and what he would be finally. To answer what is personality, therefore, remains an utter confusion. Some would say that it is an ineffable mystery—a shaft of creation, an incarnation. Since no man can transcend his own humanity, he cannot hold the full design of personality under a lens. The radical secret will ever elude us. Some say that personality is a product of nature. It is a nervous-mental organization which changes and grows while at the same time remaining relatively steadfast and consistent. The task of science is to explain both stability and the change. Both views individually or together are correct but paradoxical.

Another line of thinking rests in viewing personality as a self-enclosed totality, a solitary system, separated not only in space from other living systems, but also marked by internal urges, hopes, fears and beliefs. He is unique, has his own pattern, his own unique conflict runs his own course of life and then dies alone.

But others think that personality is social in nature, wide open to surrounding world. It owes to the perception and relationship with each other and is maintained through nurture freely given by others. They view personality as "affiliative, symbiotic and sociable. Culture cooperates with family in moulding its course; and that no man is an island." (Allport 1981)[1].

Allport's own approach is naturalistic but open-ended. His search for personality is psychological and the method

1. Allport, G. W. Personality and Social Encounter, Selected Essays. University of Chicago Press, Chicago, 1981.

applied is developmental as he believes that man has immense capacity for growth and development.

The common approach to the study of human personality comes from literature and psychology, which, when reconciled, provides scientific humanistic frame for that study. In the early twentieth century three great revolutions have occurred in Western psychology on man's thinking about his own mind. These are, first, Freudian psycho-analysis, with its discovery of the depth (emotion and motivation) and primordial impulses of mental life. Second, Watsonian and Skinnerian behaviourism with its discovery of the accessibility of mind to objective study. Third, Gestalt psychology with its discovery of the essential orderliness and self-regulatory activities of the mind. Consequently, the same period has witnessed the discovery—on the basis of series of research studies—that human personality is an accessible subject for scientific probing. Freudian, Behaviouristic and Gestalt psychologists have all contributed to such probing and experimentations.

The mid-part of the twentieth century noticed that the study of personality has been influenced by four basic provinces of research—the natural sciences, the biological sciences, the social sciences and humanistic discourses. From the biological sciences came the colossal impact of scientific methodology and also from the biological sciences came 'high standards and exacting methods' of research, as well as evolutionary, genetic and organistic point of view without which the study of personality would have been theoretical and sterile. It would otherwise have been more scholastic, epistemological and metaphysical than subject for experimentation and testing.

The social sciences provided the study of man and his mental processes within his own province through observable behaviour. The anthropologists, social anthropologists and sociologists insist that mind takes its form almost wholly in response to cultural demand and a person fashions his personality make-up accordingly. They, therefore, emphasized personality study to be culture-bound. The study of personality is, lastly, gently influenced by the humanistic approach. This is the underlying current of treating man as a person who is a product of philosophy and literature. Personality is the substantial concrete unit of mental life that exists in forms that are definitely single and individual. (Allport, 1961)[2]

Then arrived the psychologists with their interest in exploring and defining personality, known as personologists. They depicted personality from adopting a Holistic approach. In order to consider this approach we start with the premise forwarded by Spinoza (in Allport, 1961) : "I have made a ceaseless effort not to ridicule, not to beweil, nor to scorn human actions but to understand them." According to Allport, the scientific study of personality centers round one subject, 'the person', where person is understood to refer as much to an 'activity' as to a 'thing'—an ever progressive motion engaged in giving itself a new form assuming a dialectical at the same time a dichotomous relation between entities and processes (thing and activity Kagan, 1916)[3] Personality, in Eastern culture, is more a realization of inner potential or self that unfolds gradually with conscious effort (activity) than an entity (a being). The process can be further illustrated—for example, the day and night are seen by Westerners as static poles or distinct realms, but the Easterners see it as sub-processes that tend toward each other. They have less difficulty in seeing that objects are also events, that the world is made up of processes as much as entities. Their thinking is more dialectical than dichotomous.

Nevertheless, person is also 'human being' whose personality has to be taken into account while dealing with personality in general. A human being—a person—is not only a being who 'does' something to evolve, but also suggests something which he 'is'. Two important ideas are involved in it—'constructivism' (that persons or systems constitute which is a construct reality) and 'developmentalism' (that organic systems evolve through eras according to regular principles of stability and change). Both these ideas insist on a recognition that behind the form (or thing) there exists a process which creates it or which leads to its coming into being (Kegan, 1982)[4].

---

2. Allport, G. W., Pattern and Growth of Personality, Holt, Rinehart and Winston, N.Y. 1961.
3. Kagan, J. A. Conception of Early Adolescence. In Twelve to Sixteen : early adolescence ed. J. Kagan and R. Coles. N.Y. 1972.
4. Kegan, Robert : Ego Psychology-Clinical. Evolving of Self : the problem and process in human development. Harvard University Press. Cambridge. Mass. 1982.

The scientific study of a person has a long history. The study started with the psychology of the normal and integrated person. The schools of thought varied with the psychologists who either favoured stimulus-response, or psychoanalysis or differential psychology, typology or factor-analysis. In the interval much welcome progress have occurred. Many recent writers belonging to several new movements have had a beneficial impact. Among them, existentialism, phenomenology, client-centered therapy, ego psychology movements emphasizing the influence of culture on personality, social anthropology as well as the ongoing process of social formation of personality and self-actualization are major contributors to this dynamic subject.

The great personologist Gordon. W. Allport (1961) depicts his view about personality and writes : "..... The basic problem remains unchanged. This problem, as I see it, is to discover the proper balance between uniform factors and individual morphogenic factors in personality. Let me explain what I mean by referring to the science of biology. Molecular biology shows increasingly that life substances are identical across species. The building blocks of life, vegetable and animal—turn to be strikingly uniform in terms of nucleic acids, proteins, molecules and enzymatic reactions. Yet a sparrow differs from a pine tree, a man from a sparrow, and one man is very unlike another. The challenge of morphogenesis (accounting for pattern) waxes more and more acute as we discover commonalities in life ..... The more we search out and discover what is uniform in human nature, the more urgent it becomes to account for uniqueness in the form and pattern of the whole .... Our emphasis, therefore, is upon the inner organization of motives, traits and personal style ....." (Allport, ibid)

But the growing and bulging literature of personality study and a bulk of new researches world over have opened up new dimensions, like,

(1) Personality a matter of roles;

(2) Inter-personal relations;

(3) Incidents within socio-cultural systems etc.

They are to be considered in the scientific pursuit of personality. But personality as the internal coherent system of a person is the very essence of it and cannot be neglected. Allport emphatically proclaimed that individuality is the self-contained system of the individual, though it expresses itself in the social milieu, but its uniqueness is an amazing phenomenon. Therefore, Allport conceived personality as a 'patterned and growing system'.

The view of human beings as self-contained unitary individuals who carry the uniqueness deep inside themselves, like pearls hidden in their shells, is the very basis of personality. (Burkitt, 1991)[5].

The critics defying the contention call this idea of a 'person' as a 'monad'—that is a solitary individual divided from other human beings by deep walls and barriers. The psychologists defending the role of society in making up individual's personality faces the problem that this understanding of people as monads—a self-sufficient, self-contained being poses a central problem because his social bonds are not primary, but only of secondary importance. The very idea divides the society and the individual and thereby presenting another dichotomy. Now, the question is, how, then, these two identities can be related.

Alongside this dichotomy and also related with it, there exists another problem in understanding the social nature of individuality. A self-contained person feels separated from the others with whom they live and who make up their society. Not only the interrelationship is in distress, they also feel divided within themselves, riven between the selves, they encounter others as if with an armour that protects and separates him and push him deep down inside. People often believe that they present a 'face' to others and hide their true feeling inside. The connection between our actions and thoughts, on the one hand, and our emotions on the other, are severed and appear to dissipate. There is a feeling as though not only are we divorced from others, but from our selves as well. In such a situation we feel a pull inside us between our rational consciousness and our inner emotional stress leading to conflict.

Therefore, the exponents of the theory of "social selves", like, Ian Burkitt (op cit), a British psychologist, views society and individuals as not two separate entities, for humans are always in social relations from the moment they are born and

5. Burkitt, Ian. Social Selves. Theories of Social Formation of Personality. Sage Publications. New Delhi, 1991.

they remain part of a network of other people throughout their lives. The fact that we feel isolated from others, and also from ourselves, reveals something about the type of social relations in which we live in the world. It does not express anything about our essential nature as human individuals. In his theory he develops a coherent understanding of humans as social selves, notwithstanding the development of individual self or personality. He moves beyond what he calls dichotomous or dualistic vision of society and individuals and advances to see humans in terms of their essential social relations with others. According to him, it does not lessen the notion that humans are individuals, but grapples with the possibility of understanding individuality as socially based. By proposing such a theory, he thinks that the individual—a 'social self'—will not face the dichotomy or dualism or conflict between conscious rationality and emotion, between needs and unconscious strivings. The emergence of social self would help the individual to share with other people—lessening his conflict. The many facets each one of us have in our personality leading to individual difference, are differentiated and divided in the way we relate with other people : they are not pregiven aspects of the self with which we are born.

Burkitt (1991, op cit) first followed George Herbert Mead (1863-1931), an American philosopher and social psychologist, in developing his theory of "social selves" (an ethogenic theory). Mead, he concludes, refuses to see any aspect of self as asocial, yet at the same time he does not reduce the individual to the level of a cultural cipher. Mead demonstrates how individuals develop their subjectivity in the network of social interaction and meanings and that this subjective attitude has both a moral and cultural aspect as well as a personal and innovative sense and application through the 'I' that develops in the social self. This 'I' can only arise in and from social communication, where we first get an objective sense of our own self. That objective idea of self is what is known as 'me'—self as an object.

At the later stage, Burkitt was greatly influenced by Marxism and followed Marxian principles of division of labour in forming personality in social relation and interdependence. Burkitt thought that a more rounded theory of social selves could be developed from theories influenced by Marxism. In Marxist theory the essential social relations and activities in which humans are engaged are those that transforms the actual or real world we live in. For Marx, this is the reason why men are to be seen as social beings. It would be impossible for people to meet their needs and survive in the world were it not for the power of transformation generated by social activity and, more specifically, by social labours. The level of productive power required to change the natural world could never be generated individually. For Marx, it is only in the capitalist society where individuals are separated from the means of production. When these become owned as private property, people feel themselves to be isolated "individuals" alienated from the society and the essential social relations the members form together. Yet capitalism does witness a society of most advanced social relations and socially developed productive forces : it is the type of relations that exist in capitalistic society that makes individuals feel isolated and powerless. But even isolated individuals of capitalistic pattern of society are still social beings, their personalities develop within the social relations embedded in capitalistic structure.

Lucien Se've (1978)[6] chose to take as the starting point for his psychology of personality this notion of humans as necessarily connected and socially so related that transforms the real. For Se've the development of the personal capacities of each social individual takes place within productive activity organized by the division of labour. Each person can only develop to the level of productive forces created in the society, for these constitute the social heritage which individuals appropriate in their personal development. It is not through gene that people inherit the talents necessary to the continued existence of humanity, instead they are handed down and transformed from generation to generation through social relations. It is not the individual, but social relations which are the basis for the real life processes in which the personalities develop. This view has its roots firmly planted in the theories of Marx.

Burkitt concludes that the image of humans as monads, as isolated and self-contained individuals is totally inappropriate for the study of personality and replaces the monad concept with his theory of social selves. The basic insight of his theory is that everything which is unique and personal about

6. Se've, Lucien, Man in Marxist Theory and the Psychology of Personality. Brighton, Harvester Press, 1978.

our identity does not radiate from within the self as something pregiven or innate. Rather, the basis of human difference and individual identity is to be found within the society in the social relations that exist between individuals. Human individuals can only make themselves into a subject to the extent to which they have become an object. That is to say, to the extent they have realized their own world around them, or by making them into a distinct entity in the eyes of others. There is no basic division between the society and individual. Individual is essentially a social being. Individual is a social being, a society affecting the individual and the individual affects the society. This interrelationship is a dialectical one that affects the object—the individual person. In this respect the self is the new dimension which is created in the active relationship between humans in their natural environment. Originally in these relations there is no self; just the bodies of human animals who seek to satisfy their needs and protect themselves socially. As the group becomes more organized in methods of production and communications, basic instinctive reactions and needs are brought more into scope of social organization and conscious reflection. The state of self-conscious 'individuality' is not innate or prior to society, but only comes into existence through social relations.

Nature of Personality

With these two concepts of personality let us now reflect into the basic nature of personality from both points of view.

From the nature of personality, point of view personality is the term commonly used in everyday life to designate a person. Personality refers to the *distinctive* characteristics of the person —characteristics that essentially manifest themselves in different life situations. In order to describe the nature of personality we shall consider first some definitions (traditional as well as modern). Jim McMartin (1995)[7] defines personality starting with a common usage :

(1) "Personality refers to all those psychological characteristics of the individual—emotional, mental, spiritual —in which she or he consistently differs from other people".

This is the common sense definition at personality without probing into the inherent technical implica-

7. McMartin, Jim. Personality Psychology. Sage Publication. New Delhi. 1995.

tions. But this definition fails to consider how do an individual's emotional, mental and spiritual characteristic are organized or interrelated. The individual behaves as a whole, entire person and not as fragmented characteristics. Thus, personality refers to some sort of unifying tendency or force integrating all our distinctive abilities, interests, skills, feelings etc. This consideration leads to the second definition.

(2) "Personality is the dynamic organization within the individual of those psychophysical systems that determine his or her characteristic behaviour and thought." This is Jim McMartin's definition which has been derived from G. W. Allport's definition (Allport, 1961 p. 28 op cit) with the author's own analysis:

(i) Dynamic Organization signifying integration and organizational processes as essential components of the normal personality.

(ii) Psychophysical signifies personality as both mental and physical.

(iii) System means the complex interrelations of our emotional, cognitive and spiritual characteristics. Allport says : "each individual carries with him his past relations with the world, his emotional dispositions and his own expectancies for the future." (p. 264 op cit).

(iv) Determine signifies all the emotional, physical, cognitive and spiritual systems exerting a directive influence on all the manifestations of personality. As Allport succinctly puts it,. *"Personality is something that does something."* (p. 29. op cit).

(v) Characteristics are our distinctive actions, thoughts and feelings.

(vi) Behaviour and thought are the blanket terms to cover anything a person does. This includes our feelings, hopes, aspirations, wants and personal meanings of life.

Allport holds that personality is what a person "really is" (p. 35). To Allport, then, personality refers to an individual's internal psychological structure as distinct from how she or he may appear to other people at any given point in time.

From the above analysis, McMartin (1995, op cit) summarises and forwards his own definition as follows, which highlights the significance of personality development and growth over the life span :

"Personality is the developing *system* of those distinctive emotional, cognitive and spiritual *attributes* that manifest themselves in the individual's characteristic behaviour at any point in the life course."

The terms in this definition are :

(1) **Developing** : the most significant term of this concept of personality. Personality is living process, not a static thing—to make explicit the idea that a person's future self may be organized in ways quite different from her or his past self.

(2) **System** : Same meaning as Allport's.

(3) **Emotional** : a person's feelings—conscious or unconscious.

(4) **Cognitive** : a person's thoughts ideas and beliefs—whether they are consciously realized or not.

(5) **Spiritual** : the meaning a person gives to her or his life and the world she or he lives, whether it is recognized or not.

(6) **Characteristic behaviour** : A science of personality requires observations from which theoretical influences are drawn.

(7) **At any point in the life course** : any stage of life—developmental changes underlying emotional, cognitive and spiritual attributes—from childhood through adolescence to adulthood.

Theoretical approaches to Personality

The term personality, according to Allport, refers both to the mind-in-particular and mind-in-general. The purpose of the personologists is to discover general principles of development, organization and expression of personality. The outstanding characteristic, Allport views, is his *individuality*. He is the unique creation of forces of nature. There was never a person just like him, and there will never be again. Individuality is the supreme mark of human nature. An individual, throughout his lifespan, manifests his own special pattern of physical and mental traits.

There are three basis of defining personality as inherent in him—(a) external effect, (b) internal structure and (c) positivist direction. The external effect depends on other's opinion about the person—his social effectiveness. Thus, the popular conception of personality refers to a certain cluster of traits that is socially pleasing and effective.

Origins of the term Personality

The term *personality,* in English closely resembles the "personalitas" of medieval Latin. In classical Latin *"persona"* alone was used, which originally meant "mask" (signifying the modern definition of personality as external appearance that a person puts up and not the inner organization). But "persona" even in ancient times, came to mean among other things, the player behind the mask and an assemblage of inner and personal qualities. Personality not only embraces all biological dispositions. impulses, tendencies, appetites and instincts of the individual—both innate and acquired by experience, but also includes the entire mental organization of a human being at any stage of his development—every phase of human character, intellect, temperament, skill, morality and every attitude that has been built up in course of one's life. Personality is the organized aggregate of all psychological processes pertaining to the individual.

The positivists like McClelland view personality as the most adequate conceptualization of a person's behaviour in all its detail that the scientist can give at a moment of time (McClelland, 1951)[8] . The positivist argue that we cannot know the "multiform dynamic unity" of a person. What we know of a personality is merely his "operations".

By revising his earlier definition G. W. Allport in 1961 edition of his book gives his own definition as :

"Personality is the dynamic organization within the individual of those psychophysical systems that determine his characteristic behaviour and thought."

The key concepts in this definition as analysed by Allport himself are :

Dynamic Organization : The central problem of psychology is mental organization (the forming of patterns of hierarchies of ideas and habits that dynamically direct

8. McClelland, D. Personality, Sloane. N.Y. 1951.

activity). Integration and other organizational processes are necessary to account for the structure and development of personality. The term also implies the reciprocal processes of *disorganization.*

Psychophysical : This term explains that personality is neither exclusively mental, nor exclusively neural or physical. Its organization entails the functioning of both mind and body in some inextricable unity.

Systems : A system is a complex of elements in mutual interaction, e.g. a habit, a sentiment, a trait, a concept which are all a style of behaving. These systems are latent in the organism even when not active. Systems are our "potentials for activity", says R. R. Sears (1951)[9].

Determine : Personality is something and does something. The latent psychophysical systems, when called into action, either motivate or direct specific activity and thought. All the systems that comprise personality are to be regarded as *determining tendencies.* They exert a directive influence upon all the adjustive and expressive acts by which the personality comes to be known.

Characteristics : All behaviour and thought are characteristic of a person and are unique to him.

Behaviour and thought : These two terms are a blanket to designate anything whatsoever an individual may do. Chiefly what he does is to adjust to his environment. They are modes of adjustment to grow and to survive.

The environment of an individual involves two types—one, his physical environment surrounding him, and two, the behavioural environment in which he interacts. The interaction in a social environment helps the individual to develop his social behaviour and facilitates socialization which ultimately leads to the all–round development of personality.

Allport differentiates between character and temperament which are commonly used as synonymous with personality.

Character : Personality and character are two fascinating terms, often used interchangeably, although the first is of Latin origin, the second of Greek, meaning engraving. Character is the

---

9. Sears, R. R. A Theoreitical Framework for Personality and Social Behaviour. American Psychologist. 6. 476-483./95/

mark of man—his patternization of traits or his life-style. As the significance of the term character gradually evolved the two terms—character and personality—came to be interpreted almost in the same way, almost synonymously. Character, in fact, has acquired a special connotation implying an ethical standard and makes a judgement of value. Character expresses the idea as to how far a personality is socially effective or ineffective. Therefore, Allport humourously defined "character as personality evaluated and personality as character devaluated".

Temperament

A person's temperament is determined largely by the "body humours" (glandular secretion). Therefore, temperament means "a constitution of habit of mind especially dependent upon or connected with physical constitution." Temperament, today, often goes under the name of "constitutional psychology".

Temperament—like intelligence and physique—might be used to designate a class of "raw-material" from which personality is fashioned. Just because temperament heavily leans upon gene-determination, therefore, it is that aspect of personality structure which depends mainly on heredity. As Allport describes it : "Temperament refers to the chemical climate or internal weather in which personality evolves........." Temperament refers to the characteristic phenomena of an individual's emotional nature, including his susceptibility to emotional stimulation, his customary strength and speed of response, the quality of his prevailing mood and all peculiarities of fluctuation and intensity in mood—these phenomena being regarded as dependent upon constitutional make-up and, therefore, largely hereditary in origin."

But temperament is not something unamnable to changes. They are dynamic in nature and, like physique and intelligence, temperament can also be altered (within limits) by medical, surgical or nutritional influences in the course of learning the life's experiences throughout the living process. Alteration is possible but not unlimited—restricted within the constitutional make-up.

Theories of Personality and Personality Development

Personality is a process of development which takes place throughout the individual's lifespan, making him a complete man. He is a product of both heredity and environment—influenced by the processes of nature and nurture. The relative importance of these two factors have led different psychologists to adopt different theoretical bias in order to explain the nature and development of personality. In this context four main approaches of personality have been discussed briefly in this book. The four approaches are summarized as :

1. Personologistic/Holistic theory—represented by G. W. Allport
2. Psychodynamic theory—represented by Sigmund Freud, Erik Erikson (neo-Freudian)
3. Cognitive/Learning theory—represented by B. F. Skinner
4. Humanistic/Existential theory—represented by Abraham Maslow.

Holistic theory—G. W. Allport

We have already dealt with the nature and definition of personality described by Allport in the earlier sections. Allport's theory, also known as trait theory, takes an integrative approach towards personality and its development. According to him, personality is a broad and comprehensive concept covering the organization of an individual's predispositions to behaviour and his unique adjustment to his environment. Traits are the constructs or personal characteristics, emotions, motivations, values, goals and ways of perceiving. They constitute all aspects of personality structure and they become personality characteristics or traits. The traits are used explicitely and implicitely to refer to a wide range of properties of a person. The traits, therefore, are designated as surface traits or depth traits. Nevertheless, these diverse uses have one feature in common; underlying all is some kind of *dispositional construct* in Carnap's (1936)[10] sense of the term.

To put the matter more precisely, a trait ordinarily implies a tendency towards behaviour associated with a particular person under a given set of conditions. Most commonly, this behavioural tendency refers to a disposition to act on the part of a person. Accordingly, personality has been explained by Allport as : personality "is" what a person "does". Therefore,

10. Carnap, R. Testability and Meaning. Phil. Sc. 3. 419-471. 1936.

traits can be response tendencies, or motives or stimulus characteristics. The first two refer to dispositions towards action on the part of the person himself, the last to tendencies to evoke response in others.

In a response tendency the specific behaviour elicited is relatively invariant. Every time the response tendency is activated, the person tends to do exactly the same thing. There is no modification of response in order to achieve a particular goal or end-state. Hence, it becomes a trait and a trait seldom has any deviation. The crucial criterion for a response tendency, then, is not whether the behaviour is adaptive or non-adaptive (it may be either), but whether the particular behaviour evoked tends to be the same under similar stimulus conditions.

Motives often underly a trait of a person. Motives reveal the goal or end-state of a behaviour which remains invariant and not the mode of response; the person may resort to a variety of actions to achieve the goal and stick to the variation until the goal is achieved. The persistent effort he puts is due to the response tendency underlying the trait he has.

In case of motives, then, the specific behaviour manifested constitutes an instrumental act that may vary markedly from one situation to the next. The motives and response tendencies are the essential characteristics of a trait. The other characteristic of a trait is its stimulus property. The difference between the former two and the stimulus property of a trait is treated by Allport as "biophysical" and "biosocial" characteristics.

All the genotypical and phenotypical traits or personality characteristics combine to form a personality. The genotypical traits are the traits inherited by the person and phenotypical ones are acquired by him through life-experiences and with interaction with others. The relationship between the traits are sometimes intrapersonal and sometimes interpersonal. The unique combination of traits makes every individual a unique person, not quite like any one else. Personality is the concept or construct that describes the uniqueness and totality of an individual as a social being. This means that personality is the unique organization of traits in the individual as reflected in how he reacts to himself and others and in how others react to him and also how he meets frustrations and conflicts—that is how he adjusts to environment.

Living involves a continuous series of adjustments between satisfaction of individual needs and demands of the environment including demands of other people in group and society. To adjust means to change in some way appropriate to certain requirements.

Personality structure is primarily represented by Allport in terms of trait. He also asserts that behaviour is motivated or driven by traits. Thus, structure and dynamics or development of personality are for the most part one and the same. (Hall and Lindzey, 1978)[11]. Allport made a number of conceptual and terminological changes in his theory. He considered the small segmented concepts like specific reflexes as important as the concept of cardinal traits of some importance for understanding behaviour. He thought that these processes referred to by these concepts operate within the organism in a hierarchical fashion so that the more general takes precedence over the more specific. He especially emphasized the importance and utility of the following concepts in the development of personality—conditioned reflexes, habits, traits, self and personality—in hierarchic order.

Of all the above concepts the major emphasis is on the theory of traits along with attitudes and intentions in the formation of personality. "Indeed, Allport's theory is often referred to as a trait psychology". (Hall and Lindzey, ibid) The traits, in his theory occupy the position of the major motivational construct. "What the need is to Murray, the instinct to Freud, the sentiment of McDougall, the trait is to Allport." (ibid)

In Allport's 1937 publication of the book, 'Personality : A Psychological Interpretation' (1937) he has distinguished between individual and common traits. In 1961 a trait has been defined by him as a :

"Neuropsychic structure having the capacity to render many stimuli functionally equivalent, and to initiate and guide equivalent (meaningfully consistent) forms of adaptive and expressive behavior."

The term trait was used to designate common traits and a new term *personal disposition* was introduced to designate the individual traits.

11. Hall, Calvin Springer and Lindzey. Gardner. Theories of Personality. John Wiley and Sons., Inc. Canada. 1978.

A personal disposition or morphogenic trait is defined as a "Generalized neuropsychic structure peculiar to the individual with the capacity to render many stimuli functionally equivalent, and to initiate and guide consistent (equivalent) forms of adaptive and stylistic behaviour" (1961, p. 373). A trait may be shared by a number of individuals and not unique—not peculiar to the individual but as much within the individual as the disposition is. The same trait (common trait) can be expressed in different individuals or groups of individuals, whereas the individual trait or personal dispositions are each person's "unique patterned individuality."

The traits or dispositions cannot be observed directly but can be inferred from behaviour. "These tendencies are not all time active, but are persistent even when latent, and have relatively low thresholds of arousal." (1961, p. 374).

The traits and dispositions are differentiated from *habits*, which are also determining tendencies but are less general than traits. The trait, to a considerable extent, represents the outcome of combining or integrating two or more habits. Same with *attitudes*. An attitude is also a predisposition, unique in kind, may initiate or direct behaviour and is the product of genetic factors and learning. Nevertheless, the distinction between the concepts are, first, the attitude is linked to a specific object or class of objects while the trait or disposition is not. The difference is of generality. A trait is much more general than the attitude; the latter may vary in generality from highly specific to relatively general—not as generalized as a trait is. Second, the attitude implies evaluation (acceptance or rejection) of the object or idea towards which it is directed, whereas a trait in its expression is never evaluative—it remains a general trend behind the expression.

Allport's idea of generality of traits faces the questions. Whether all dispositions possess roughly the same degree of generality, and, how to distinguish between the varying degrees? In answer, he suggests a three-tongued classification of traits into *'cardinal. central and secondary dispositions'*. The most general of the three are the cardinal dispositions and are revealed by the individual in almost all performances and behaviours and are not commonly shared by many. More typical are the central dispositions, which represent tendencies highly characteristic of the individual. The central dispositions within an individual are not many in number and they are often called into play, and are very easy to infer. The secondary dispositions are more limited in occurrence, less crucial to a description of personality.

Some traits are clearly impelling, have a crucial motivational role than others. The traits do vary in exerting influence upon directing the individual into action or instigate behaviour. Another essential nature of the traits is that they do not exist within the individual independent of each other. A trait is identifiable not by its rigid independence but rather by its focal qualities. They remain so interwoven that they cast simultaneous influence in guiding a behaviour. There is no sharp boundary that delimits one trait from another.

Allport further points out that his theory of traits does not necessitate a complete consistency. He suggests that there are multiple, overlapping traits simultaneously active which may lead to inconsistency of individual's behaviour. The integration comes because of the subtle congruent nature of the traits which unite to give various behavioural manifestations of the individual and leads to personality integration. But it is not implied that any or every personality is perfectly integrated. Dissociation and disorganization exist in every life. But there is ordinarily more consistency than disorientation in a normal personality.

The Proprium

Allport was early recognized as an "ego" or even "self" psychologist. In 1943 (The Ego in the contemporary psychology) and again in 1955 (Becoming : basic considerations for a psychology of personality) he revived the many meanings of ego and self. The concept raised so much controversy that Allport later on revised his opinion and introduced a new term 'proprium' to replace self or ego. He proposes that all of the self or ego functions be called propriate functions of the personality. These (including bodily sense, self-identity, self-esteem, self-extension, sense of self-hood, rational thinking, self-image, propriate striving, cognitive style and the function of knowing) are all true and vital portions of personality (Hall and Lindzey, 1978). Together they may be said to comprise "the proprium". It is in this region of personality that attitudes, intentions or motivations remain consistent. The proprium is not innate, but develops in time.

Allport identifies seven aspects in the development of proprium (1961, Ch. 6). During the first three years, three of these aspects make their appearance : a sense of bodily self, a sense of continuing self-identity and self-esteem or pride. Between the ages of four and six, two other aspects appear, the extension of self and a self-image. Sometimes between six and twelve the child develops self-awareness that it can cope with its problem by means of reason and thought. During adolescence intentions, long-range purposes, and distant goals emerge. These are called *propriate strivings*. These seven aspects of selfhood constitute proprium.

Psychoanalytic Theory

Another theory of personality emerged not from psychology, but from psychopathology, introduced by Sigmund Freud, which eventually was developed by him as a complete system of normal psychology. His theory was a product of his clinical experiences with neurotic persons—spread over a period of forty years. Freud presented his ideas on the organization, dynamics and development of normal personality. Freud himself regarded psychoanalysis primarily as a system of psychology and not merely a branch of abnormal psychology or psychiatry.

By training Sigmund Freud was a physician concerned with trying to understand the genesis of the symptoms of his suffering patients. This attempt led him to search for missing links and transformations that had occurred earlier in the development of an individual's personality.

Freud's long life, from 1856 to 1939, spans one of the most creative periods in the history of science. Freud as a biological scientist was greatly and immensely influenced by Charles Darwin's *Origin of Species*. This book revolutionized man's traditional conception of human being as totally different from animals. The evolutionary doctrine made man a part of nature, sharing animality with other animals. The year following the publication of Origin of Species, when Freud was four years old, Gustav Fechner founded the science of psychology and demonstrated that mental processes could be studied scientifically and that they could be measured quantitatively. These two scientists (Darwin and Fechner) had a tremendous impact upon the intellectual development of Freud.

Other noteworthy influences on Freud came from the then physicist—Hermann von Helmholtz, who formulated the principle of the conservation of energy. This principle, in effect, stated that energy is a quantity and can be transformed but cannot be destroyed. When energy disappears from one part of a system it tends to appear elsewhere in the system. This was a momentous discovery in the field of dynamics. The ongoing researches on energy and dynamics not only led to the new discoveries in the field of physics and physical appliances, but also furnished new conception of man and his psychic energy.

Darwin conceived man's animal heritage, Fechner proved that mind of the man is measurable—the new physics, however, made possible an even more radical view of man—that man is an energy system and that he obeys the same physical law's as a part and parcel of nature. This new physics profoundly influenced Freud's creative and scientific bend of mind. As a medical student he was interested in human physiology and could discover that the living organism is a dynamic system to which laws of physics and chemistry apply. Freud was greatly indoctrinated by the new dynamic physiology.

Twenty years later Freud's singular genius discovered that laws of dynamics could be applied to man's personality as well as to his body. (Hall, 1956)[12]. When he made this discovery, Freud proceeded to create a dynamic psychology that studies the transformation and exchanges of energy within the personality.

Although Freud was trained in medicine and received his medical degree from the University of Vienna in 1881, he never intended to practice medicine. He wanted to be a scientist, but, as destiny would lead him, he was forced to take up the practice of medicine. But, in spite of the compelling duties to be performed as a doctor, he found time for neurological research. But in a way it was fortunate that Freud was forced to practice medicine, because his constant and pressing contact with patients stimulated him to think in psychological terms and create dynamic psychology. He specialized in the treatment of nervous disorders under the watchful guidance of

12. Hall, Calvin, S. A Primer of Freudian Psychology. George Allen and Unwin Ltd., London, 1956.

Jean Charcot in France who was having some success with hypnosis, particularly in the treatment of hysteria. Freud learnt Charcot's method but was not quite satisfied with the process. He was rather attracted to another Viennese physician's method of cathartic treatment—Joseph Bruer's cathartic method or "talking-out-your-problems" form of therapy. Eventually both these doctors became good friends practising in consultation with each other.

But Freud, later, deviated from the cathartic method that was in practice and developed a new and improved therapeutic technique, the "talking-out" or "free association method". By using this method he could probe deep into the patient's mind and deal with the knowledge about the underlying causes of abnormal behaviour. More and more probing into the depth of the mind of the patient revealed the dynamic forces at work which were responsible for creating abnormal symptoms. Freud became convinced that most of these forces are unconscious, and that most part of human mind occupies the unconscious region. This was the turning point in Freud's scientific life.

Putting physiology and neurology aside, he became a psychological investigator. "The room in which he treated his patients became his laboratory, and the couch his only piece of equipment, and the rambling of his patients his scientific data" (Hall, 1956, p. 7).

Structure of Personality

The psychdynamic approach to personality arises from the clinical practice of Freud and later adopters (Neo-Freudians) of this orientation. It is chiefly but not exclusively concerned with *emotional responses* and *emotional conflicts* aroused by changing events of everyday life. Even Carl Jung and Alfred Adler—two staunch disciples of Freud—later on diviated from Freud's concepts of psychoanalysis, the former emphasizing the lack of meaning in adult life as a contributing cause of emotional difficulties and the latter (Adler) emphasizing "identity crisis" of the person.

But, nevertheless. Freud's ideas of the sources of conflict could never be overlooked. Firstly, because our whole life is an anxiety state with some interludes. Freud's views help us to understand thoughts and behaviour under conditions of anxiety. Secondly, Freud's view of the flow of psychic energy help us to understand why and how individuals in a collective setting simultaneously experience and react to powerful irrational forces.

It is noteworthy to mention here that Freud was also a social critic. He believed that society which has been fashioned by man, reflects to a great extent man's irrationality. As a consequence, each new generation is corrupted by being born into an irrational society. The influence of man on society and of society on man is a vicious circle from which only a few hardy souls can free themselves (Freud's opinion). He thought that only by re-educating psychologically the parents and teachers the effective agents of reason and truth can be assured. Freud's social criticism is presented in his book *Civilization and its Discontent*. Thirdly, his view helps dealing with conflict—both external and internal. One root cause of conflict is the human tendency to distort experiences (intrapsychic). The Freudian explanation of 'transference' and other defense mechanisms help us to understand and deal with this phenomenon at the individual, group and institutional levels.

Freud opened up an entire new realm of human functioning —our unconscious mind. He discovered unconscious conflict between instinct and civilization as it is incorporated in the other parts of our personality. The conflict between the primitive drives and today's complex world is embodied in Freud's map of our personality.

The instincts are the biological ones which man shares with animals as hereditarily transmitted by evolution. Freud accepts this notion of Darwin and thinks that "the primary drives of human beings are also the residues of evolution—mental remnants of the early era : such as 'stress reaction', that ready the body to fight or flee. Freud noted that these and other mental remnants of this early era or prehistoric past, continue to send out the same messages that were sent eons ago." (Segal, 1997).[13]

These are the basic components of mind which constitute the basic structure of personality. The rational influence in personality pattern and consequent human behaviour have been the basic model of most of the personality theorists, but Freud's basic model of personality remains important by

13. Segal, Morley. Points of Influence. Jossey–Bass Publishers. San Fransisco. 1997.

identifying the conflict between three universal forces : instinct, morality and reason. The three psychic subsystems are named by Freud—id, ego and superego. 'Id' represents the raw instincts—primordial, primitive, irrational, inborn impulse—libidinal in character. The 'ego' represents reason and, therefore, essentially rational and realistic in character. The 'superego' represents morality, and, therefore, ethical in character and amenable to social sanctions. These subsystems do not exist as particular organs but as patterns of interaction within the brain and between the brain and the rest of the body. They, therefore, manifest themselves as bodily cravings. Freud thinks that the formation of personality takes place at the point where these subsystems interact. (Segal, 1997 op cit)

Organization of Personality

It has already been mentioned that the total personality as conceived by Freud consists of three major systems—id, ego and superego. These three systems (the tripartite systems of mind), in a normal mentally healthy person, remain unified and form harmonious organization. They work uniformly and cooperate with each other to cradle the person's functioning in a satisfying and efficient manner and successfully adjusting with the environment. The individual constantly interacts with the environment in order to satisfy his needs and desires. The environment either satisfies his desires or frustrates him as occasion arises. When the three systems of personality are at odds with one another the person is said to be maladjusted. He is dissatisfied with himself, and with the world—thus his efficiency is reduced.

1. The ID

The id, characterized as a reservoir of primitive instincts and drives—is present at birth. It is the force that presses for immediate gratification of bodily needs and wants. As for example, an infant when he is hungry (basic need) cries and becomes quiet and stable as he gets the supply of milk to appease his hunger. The sole function of the id is to provide for the immediate discharge of quantities of excitation (energy or tension) that are released in the organism by internal or external stimulation. This function of the id fulfils the primordial or initial principle of life which Freud calls *pleasure principle.* The aim of the principle is to rid the person of tension or to reduce the amount of tension to a low level in order to keep it as constant as possible. Tension is experienced as pain or discomfort, while relief from tension is experienced as pleasure or satisfaction. The aim of the pleasure principle may be said, then, to consist of avoiding pain and finding pleasure. This is regarded as Freud's Hedonistic philosophy.

How does an id develop? Id is the resident of the unconscious level of mind. In its earliest form the id is a reflex apparatus that discharges immediately by motor pathways any sensory excitation reaching it. Thus, when a very bright light falls upon the retina of the eye, the eyelid closes and light is prevented from reaching the retina. The organism is equipped with many such reflexes through which tension is reduced. But all tensions are not always discharged by such reflex actions, or else there would be no need for any psychological development beyond that of the primitive reflex apparatus. Many tensions occur for which there is no appropriate reflex discharge, instead appears other physical responses of psychological nature (e.g. crying) manifesting frustration and discomfort. These experiences stimulate the development of id. The new development that takes place in the id as a result of frustration is called *primary process*—the first step of the development of id. The primary process is described by Freud as the process which produces a memory image (e.g. feeding bottle while hungry in case of a baby) of an object that is needed to reduce a tension. The primary process attempts to discharge tension by establishing what Freud called "an identity of perception". Freud meant that, in this case, the id considers the memory image to be identical with perception itself. Freud calls id as the true psychic reality, the inner world, and the primary subjective reality of a person which exists before he experiences the objects of the external world because id remains deep into the unconscious.

Freud believed that id is also a product of evolution—a biological instinct. He believed that experiences that are repeated with great frequency and intensity in many individuals of successive generations become permanent deposits in the id. New deposits are made in the id during the life of a person as a result of the *mechanism of repression*. Id is in this sense archaic, not only from the point of view of racial history, but also archaic in the life of the individual. It is the foundation upon which the personality is built.

The essential and characteristic nature of id has been summarized by Hall (1956, op cit) as, "The id retains its infantile character throughout life. It cannot tolerate tension. It wants immediate gratification. It is demanding, impulsive, irrational, asocial, selfish, and pleasure-loving. It is the spoiled child of the personality. It is omnipotent because it has the magical power of fulfilling its wishes by imagination, fantasy, hallucinations and dreams. It is said to be oceanic because, like the sea, it contains everything. It recognizes nothing external to itself. The id is the world of subjective reality in which pursuit of pleasure and avoidance of pain are the only functions that count." It is the obscure and inaccessible part of personality (equated with unconscious) and what little is known about it has been learned from the study of dreams and neurotic symptoms. "Id is impulsive—it does not think, it only wishes and acts" (Hall, 1956, p. 21). The id is equivalent to the English usage "it"—which has no sense of proportion and direction.

The Ego

The second psychological system—*the ego*—develops when the id comes in contact with external reality or environment. The id has to depend on external reality for the satisfaction of other demands and needs that are gradually increasingly growing within his mind. In order to accomplish the missions of satisfying different kinds of new needs arising from within it is necessary for him to take into account the environment—either by accommodating himself to it or by asserting mastery over it—to obtain from the world that which he needs. The person conducts these transactions between id and the world by forming a new psychological system, *the ego*. Because ego develops as a result of interaction between the person and external reality, therefore, the ego is naturally guided by *reality principle* and restrains the so long dominant pleasure principle of id. Ego restrains id because it resides in-between unconscious and conscious levels of mind. Ego acts as a watch-guard in the door way of the preconscious level.

The now powerful reality principle comes in constant conflict with the naked pleasure-seeking desire of the id. Reality means that which exists. The aim of the reality principle (as Freud observes) is to postpone the discharge of energy until the actual object that will satisfy the need has been discovered or produced. This helps him to recognize reality and also to tolerate painful experiences coming from frustration. The postponement of action means that the ego has to be able to tolerate tension until the tension can be discharged by an appropriate form of behaviour. The reality principle does not drive out the pleasure principle altogether but the pleasure principle has been temporarily suspended in the interest of reality. Eventually reality principle leads to pleasure and the id incorporates the sense of reality.

In the well-adjusted person the ego is the executive of the personality, controlling and governing the id and the super ego as well, and maintaining commerce with the external world in the interest of the total personality and its far-flung needs.

The reality principle is served by a process which Freud called *secondary process* because it is developed after and overlays the primary process of the id. The secondary process consists of discovering or producing reality by means of a plan of action that has been developed through thought and reason (cognition). The secondary process is equal to a thinking or problem-solving process. Ego helps *reality testing* through the secondary process. This process helps the ego and the person to be able to separate the subjective and objective worlds. The most significant contribution of the ego development in the person is the development of cognitive abilities in the personality. The secondary process helps the individual to distinguish between fantasy and reality.

Although the ego is largely a product of an interaction with the environment, its limits of development is determined by heredity and follows general rules of development. This means that every individual has inborn potential of thinking and reasoning. The realization of these potentialities are brought about by experience, training and formal education.

The Superego

The third major institution of personality—*the superego*—is the moral or judicial branch of personality. It develops out of ego by internalizing the parental standard of ethics and moral judgment, and, therefore, remains at the conscious level. The superego thus formed becomes the moral code of the individual. It represents the ideal rather than real and it strives for perfection. The child, during his process of development, assimilates the parent's standards regarding what is good and virtuous and what is bad and sinful. The sanctions provided by the parental authority are internalized by the children which helps forming their own intenal authority by means of a process called "identification"—a psychic mechanism stated by Freud. This process falls in the domain of personality dynamics, which enables the child to form its own superego. The child learns that he not only has to obey the reality principle in order to obtain pleasure and avoid pain, but that he also has to try to behave according to the moral dictates of his parents. The child remains dependent for relatively longer period of his growth and development, and the long time favours the formation of superego.

The superego has two aspects or subsystems, the *ego-ideal* and the *conscience*. The ego-ideal corresponds to the child's conceptions of what his parents set as good standard—morally good. The parents often set such standards of virtue to the child by rewarding him for the behaviours they prescribe in correspondence with the social sanctions. That becomes an ideal for the child's ego which receives a boost as he is rewarded either verbally or by getting material gifts. Then his superego gets strengthened as ego-ideal. Conscience, on the other hand, corresponds to the child's conceptions of what his parents feel is morally bad. These are established in the child through punitive experiences they receive from the parents. "Ego-ideal and conscience are the opposite sides of the same moral coin." (Hall, 1958). The rewards or the punishments are the measures by which the parents control the formation of superego in children. They may be physical or psychological in form.

The superego represents traditional values and ideals of society as they are handed down by the parents to the children either in physical or psychological terms. The superego of the child is, in fact, the superego of the parents who had incorporated the social values in the form of their superego. In addition to the parents, other agents of society—teachers, senior citizens, civic laws, social sanctions—any one who in the position of authority over the child contribute to the formation of superego of the child. Superego in the personality may be said to be the product of socialization and the representative of cultural tradition.

There is no sharp boundaries between the three systems and are not separate entities, but only signify the mental processes, functions, wishes and mechanisms and dynamisms within the total personality. The ego is formed out of the id (when id comes in contact with reality) and superego is formed out of ego (when the parental and social authority and sanctions are internalized). They continue to interact and blend with each other throughout life.

Development of Personality—psychoanalytic view

Freud believed that human development proceeds as a series of universal stages that all individuals pass through from infancy to childhood. He believes that the foundation of personality is laid within the five years of an individual's life and that the personality develops with growing chronological age which pass on through various stages.

These stages are largely determined by an innate tendency to reduce tension and achieve a pleasurable experience. This innate tendency arises out of the operative process of the three systems of personality—id, ego and superego and their interaction with one another as well as with the environment. These three systems are again produced by the *psychic energy* the individual prossesses. The human organism is a complicated energy system, deriving its energy from food it eats and expending it for such purposes as circulation, digestion, nervous conduction, muscular activity, perceiving, remembering and thinking. It is essentially same as physical energy working in the physical world. The form of energy which operates the three systems of personality is called psychic energy and works like any other form of energy and helps psychological process to behave. The bodily energy is transformed into psychic energy, and vice versa. According to Freud, all of the energy used for performing the work of personality is obtained from the *instincts*. Instinct, as defined by Freud, is an inborn condition which imparts direction to psychological process and it has a source, an aim and an impetus. The principal sources of instinctual energy are bodily needs or impulses. There may be as many instincts as there are bodily needs of which Freud especially mentioned to great groups of instinct which direct development of personality and on-going process of life of the individual. They are *life instincts* or Eros that are in the service of life and death instincts, Thanatos those are in the service of death. Life instincts are the mental representatives of the bodily needs whose satisfaction is necessary for survival and propagation. The life is continued through sex instincts and so they are at the core of life instinct. Sex instincts play important part in the psychoanalytic theory of personality. The principal derivative of the sex instincts is *love* which orrginates in life instinct and often neutralizes *late* which is a derivative of death instinct.

The form of energy which is used by the life instincts is called *libido* by Freud. In his earlier writings, Freud used the term libido to denote sexual energy, but when he revised his theory of motivation, libido was defined as the energy of all the life instincts. It is the libido which develops throughout the stages of childhood leaving parts of it fixated to the respective stages forming building blocks for the foundation of personality.

Each stage of personality development consists of its unique characteristics supplied by the libidinal energy. The libido finds its sources of satisfaction in various bodily zones which are called *erogenous zones*. The mouth, the anus, the genital organs are the chief erogenous zones producing bodily needs demanding satisfaction. The sex instinct is at play at the time of achieving gratification which it achieves through secretion of sex hormones from sex glands. The sex instincts arise independently of one another in the life of the individual at each stage but at puberty they normally become synthesized in the service of reproduction. The oral region, the anal region and the genital regions give psychological satisfaction and pleasure when is stimulated in certain ways. Each erogenous zone is particularly sensitive to erotic stimulation at various times in the developmental sequence. Freud described these stages as "psychosexual" to indicate that development is the outcome of the successive focusing on and reduction of tension in various erogenous zones which predominate at different times in life. Each stage is associated with a particular conflict due to libido-fixation, which must be resolved before the child moves psychologically to the next stage.

There are two reasons why difficulty may be experienced in leaving one stage and going on to the next. Firstly, the child may not be able to satisfy the demands others make at a particular stage; in this case the child's own needs will also not be satisfied and the resulting conflict, according to Freud, can leave a permanent residue of frustration in the individual's psychological make-up. Alternatively, the needs may be so well satisfied that the child is not willing to leave the stage and as a result the characteristic behaviour of that stage may continue, manifesting the behaviour which is not age-like. Thus, either frustration, or over-indulgence or a combination of the both is presumed to result in some *fixation* at a particular stage of development, although, chronologically, the individual has already passed through it.

Presumably, all individuals have some psychological investment of energy which remains at each stage through which they pass, when the amount is relatively small (i.e. libido-fixation is less strong), the individual is expected to behave occasionally in the same way as the individual matures. On the other hand, when the substantial investment of energy has been made at an earlier stage, the individual's personality may become dominated by those techniques of obtaining satisfaction or reducing tension that were used at the earlier period (strong libido-fixation). This instigated Freud to surmise that early childhood experiences of a person play very important rọle in determining the nature of his later personality development.

Psychosexual Development

The psychosexual development, according to Freud, consists of five stages—the oral stage, the anal stage, the phallic stage, latency and genital stage.

Oral Stage (from birth through approximately the first year of life) :

Throughout this period the infant's mouth or the oral region is the prevailing source of pleasurable sensation—the sensation associated with sucking. At the same time, the infant is physically and psychologically immature and remains to be cared constantly by others. Therefore, this stage of the infant's life is characterized by *dependence* and its function is *incorporation* i.e. taking things in. But, psychoanalytically, these acts represent durable or potentially durable style of interacting with the world. Thus, Strupp (1967)[14] points out "that the focal point of the child's personality organization at this period is not necessarily the mouth per se but the total constellation of immaturity, dependency, the wish to be

---

14. Strupp, H. H. An Introduction to Freud and Modern Psychoanalysis. Woodburry. N.Y. Barron's Educational Series. 1967.

mothered, the pleasure of being held, the enjoyment of human closeness and warmth" (p. 23).

Freud believed that the individuals who become fixated at the oral stage are likely to develop an optimistic view of the world, to have relationship in adulthood that are primarily dependent in character, specially friendly and generous, but to expect in turn the world to "mother them". The oral stage ends when the child is weaned, and with weaning comes the conflict. The more difficult it is for the child to wean and more intense is the accompanying pleasures, the greater will be the proportion of libido left at this stage. The oral stage derives pleasure from two processes—oral sucking and oral biting producing loving and aggressive tendencies.

Anal Stage (from about one to three years of age) :

At this stage, the focus shifts from oral to anal zone, with its function of elimination and retention along with accompanying pleasure. The infant, at this stage, experiences direct attempts by parents to interfere with the pleasure obtained from excretory functions. The resultant conflict of this stage is between the demands from society and the sensation of pleasure associated with the anus.

Various aspects of the anal period may be related to later behaviour. If children view their feces (Waste product) as possession (because it is basically food which gave the infant pleasure originally), toilet-training experiences may be the foundation for a host of attitudes about possessions or valuables. (Baldwin, 1967)[15]. Excessive cleanliness or being pedantic also are viewed as stemming from toilet training. The other psychological features that may arise at this stage involve the development of shame, shyness or impulsiveness etc. On the other hand, if parents' demand for toilet training are met by the child with relative ease, the basis for self-control is established. The difficulty with toilet training at earlier stage—which the child refuses to accept and if it is repeatedly disapproved by the parents whenever the occasion arises, the child shows hostility and aggression of some form. Later on, at the adult stage, such an individual may express stubborn and hostile attitude and related behaviour in his social interaction.

15. Baldwin, A. L. Theories of Child Development, Wiley, N.Y. 1967.

The anal stage, like the oral phase has two stages—anal expulsiveness and anal retentiveness. The severe cases of anal retentive child often manifests stingy and stubborn behaviour in adult life.

Phallic Stage—four years of age

The phallic stage is also known as pregenital stage, indicating that at about four years of age the child's pleasure seeking libidinal desire centers round the genital region, as reflected in the child's curiosity about his own sex organ and that of others, inspection of the same organ, sometimes touching the place and sometimes resulting in masturbation. Psychologically, this is the period when Oedipal desires arise and the period is characterized by oedipus complex, specially in the male child. Freud postulated the electra complex in female child but the theory was not comprehensively established. The oedipal phase is physically and psychologically important because, it is in phallic stage the sex–role identification takes place. The child thus becomes conscious of his/her own sex role which continues up to adulthood and then throughout life. The sex role identification is necessary for moral and social development in future.

Latency and Genital Stage

The final two stages postulated by Freud—latency and genital stage—are of less importance to understanding the early foundation of social and emotional behaviour. These two stages appear at the end of childhood. Freud himself considered these two stages of less importance and rather insignificant to the development of the basic structure of personality (Baldwin 1967, op cit). At the end of five to six years of age the physical and psychological developments contributing to the foundation of formation of personality is almost complete and all the developments take their natural course at and from this period of childhood. Freud says that this is a time when libido lies dormant up to the end of early childhood and becomes active again at the preadolescent stage and is propelled during early and late adolesence.

The latency years are described as a relatively stable and serene period because most of the phallic conflicts get resolved for the time being, but which may reappear at puberty. During the latency period the child acquires varieties of social and cultural skills. But at the onset of genital stage the libido is seen as being reactivated and the child's liking for same-sexed friend is directed toward hetero-sexual objects. The strong fixations of early psycho-sexual stages are gradually successfully repressed to lead the individual well on the way to establishing fruitful relationships with other members of the society including adult ones. The happy child faces the real world effectively and that leads him toward the normal development of personality.

The basic assumptions of psychodynamic theory as presented by David Laster (1995)[16] are :

1. The first basic assumption that Freud made was that all behaviour is determined, that is, they are all motivated behaviours. This is known as the *principle of psychic determinism.* All behaviours include observable and also internal desires.
2. The second assumption is that some of the desires motivating human behaviour are unconscious. This instigated Freud to advance his theory of unconscious and the levels of consciousness—the structure and dynamics of personality. Unconscious is the repertory of our psychic energy and instincts with their driving force.
3. The thrid assumption is that there are two components of Freud's feature of personality development—
   (a) We form derivative desires; for example, from mother's breast milk to all other liquids we take later in life, such as, drinks, Coca-Cola, tea, coffee, alchohol etc.
   (b) Formation of derivative desires gives control and enables us to deal with the loss at early years. Forming of derivative desires also involves cathexis. Cathexis is the process of learning about an object or a desire—learning to like and appreciate it.

A note on libidinal development related to personality development

Freud's conception of libido, which is the cathected energy of the sexual instinct getting attached to an object, has a

16. Laster, David. Theories of Personality. Taylor and Francis. U.S.A. 1995.

physical as well as a psychological aspect of pleasure seeking. At the initial stage of personality development the pleasurable activities center round the stimulation and manipulation of bodily zones of the infant and is of narcissistic (self as object) in character. The expenditure of psychic energy involves mainly there erogenous zones—viz. oral, anal and genital region. As the infant's personality develops the accompanying psychological pleasure gets cathected and fixated upon other objects in the environment.

At the oral stage two chief sources of pleasure derived from the mouth are those of tactual stimulation obtained by putting things in the mouth, and biting (stimulation of the lips and oral cavity by contact with objects like mother's breast or nipple of the bottle or pacifier). Oral aggressive pleasure comes later in developmental stage with the eruption of teeth. The baby holds these pleasure-giving objects till his pleasure is gratified and leaves when it disagrees. The mouth, therefore, has at least five main modes of functioning : (1) taking in, (2) holding on, (3) biting, (4) spitting out, and (5) closing. Each of these modes of functioning is a *prototype* which are transferred to produce later personality traits. By a prototype is meant an original mode of adjusting to a painful or disturbing state. It serves as a model for later adaptations—the child, once learned, would make similar adaptation when, similar occasion arises later in life. For example, the mode of 'taking in' through mouth leads to acquiring knowledge, or love or power, through other sense organs in future life and incorporating them as personality traits. Freud, furthermore thinks that the mouth is a prototype for acquisitiveness, holding in for tenacity and determination, 'biting' for destructiveness, 'spitting out' for rejection and contemptuousness and 'closing' for refusal and negativism, whether these traits will develop and become part of trait or not depends upon the amount of frustration or anxiety experienced by the individual child in connection with his own prototypic experience.

Similarly, at the anal stage the toilet traing (cleaning after defecation) is a pleasure-producing and also a frustrating prototype for the child. The methods employed by the mother or nurse in training the child and her attitude at that time about defecation cleanliness, control and responsibility may determine the nature of the influence that toilet training will have upon personality and its development. A person naturally resists having a pleasurable activity interfered with and regulated. If the interference is too strict and punitive, the child may retaliate by intentionally soiling himself. As he grows older such a child will get hostile even with frustrating authority figures by being messy, irresponsible, disorderly, wasteful and extravagent. Strict toilet-training procedures may also bring about opposite kind of reaction formation, like meticulous neatness, fastidiousness, tediousness, compulsive orderliness, disgust, fear of dirt (in extreme case), strict budgeting of time and money and other over-controlled behaviours. Constipation, psychologically, is a common defense against elimination. On the other hand, mother's soft and pleasing training during this period may result in the development of pleasing attitude in the child.

The third important pleasure zone of the body consists of sex organ and its stimulation. Along with the bodily pleasure a corresponding psychological pleasure is also experienced by the baby—whether a boy or a girl. The stage characterized by such desire for pleasure is called the phallic stage, which is again specifically characterized by intensification of erotic longing in the child for parents who are the main sources of the child's satisfaction for his hunger, comfort and love. Therefore, as the child enters this stage of development a series of important changes in his/her object-cathexes are initiated.

The sex organs being different in the male and female children the events at the phallic stage show different characteristics.

Prior to the emergence of the phallic period, the boy or the male child loves his mother and identifies with his father. This love intensifies and almost converts into a sexual love-urge due to frequent hugging, kissing and caressing by the mother (which is a natural outcome of mother-instinct), when the sexual urge increases at the pre-genetic stage, the boy's love for his mother becomes more incestuous and as a result he becomes jealous of his rival—the father. This state of affairs, when the male child wants exclusive possession of mother and feels antagonistic toward the father is called Oedipus Complex (Oedipus was a Greek mythological figure who killed his father and married his mother). This is a normal phase in the process of personality development and gradually disappears as the child matures. The Oedipus complex gradually weakens and ultimately disappears in the normal course of development due mainly to a self-evoked anxiety produced by superego, which is well-formed during this period and also due to other factors like disappointment from the mother and maturation. By and by the boy renounces the mother and intensifies his identification with the father. The masculinity factor, common both in the father and the son, strengthens the bond and the son gradually takes after the father. The normal oedipal impulse helps the later attraction for the opposite sex and full-fledged adult heterosexuality at puberty. As the child's identification with the father becomes stronger and stronger, the superego of the male child gets more and more well-formed. The superego, therefore, is said to be the heir of the Oedipus complex, because it takes the place of Oedipus complex. The superego, is in fact, the internalized father-like authority figure in the child (the operative mechanism is known as Interjection).

The Electra Complex is the counter part of Oedipus complex—it is the female equivalence of the same. It is represented as daughter's love for the father which like oedipal impulse originates in the love for the mother and in due course shifed to the father as love-object. The female child's identification with the mother does not take place as early as the boy identifies with the father. Freud assumes that as the cathexis for the mother weakens in the case of a female child, the girl begins to prefer the father and compensates her urge for intense love. And by operating the mechanism of introjection the girl also identifies with the mother gradually. The whole Oedipus process is unconscious both in male and female children and a normal phase that they pass through. Both boys and girls later on face latency period, when the impulses are under the domination of reaction formation at earlier stages and gradually reach puberty, work through problems of adolescence and finally achieve some measures of stability, take their role as adult personality.

Learning theory—B. F. Skinner

Skinner is characterized as a radical behaviourist. His theory ignores internal psychic processes and focuses on the relationship of behaviour to external environment. For Skinner, behaviour is a result of its consequences. This means that the perceived consequences of behaviour determine the degree to which that behaviour is likely to reoccur. Skinner's model engenders the simple but useful image or metaphor of a machine or organism that reinforces behaviour. This image is a powerful reminder to focus upon the messages of reinforcement. Skinner's theory focusses upon the external conditions that elicit conflict. In conflict situations both parties view of the situation in win-lose terms, believing that inevitable result someone else's gain is their loss. Skinner's theory serves as a framework for identifying conditions in which all parties' interests can be supported and reinforced.

Skinner defines growth in terms of changes in behaviour and treats "inner desires" as mental functions. Skinner rather encourages personal awareness establishing procedures for individuals to monitor their own behaviour. A person who wants to get rid of his habit of smoking or extravagance or a diabetic patient's greed for sugar are all examples of specific behaviours of these individuals. In order to get rid of these behaviours or in order to bring changes in habits, Skinner insists on the individual's personal awareness procedure and asks them to monitor for a specified time. The individual would keep accurate track, without judgement, of the number of times that he smoked a cigarette, ate candy, spent money—the specific behaviour he wished to change. This encourages personal awareness, according to Skinner, which is an important aspect of psychological growth.

Skinner noticed the human tendency to repeat a behaviour the organism experiences as being *reinforced* by the environment. His unique contribution is to look at the influences and relationships between the environment, the psyche and behaviour. He starts from the premise that the organism "emits" behaviour—that a behaviour occurs. This behaviour is observable and measurable and is the starting point for a scientific study of human activity. For him, a behaviour "*operates*" on the environment eliciting another behaviour under similar situation and acts as a reinforcement. Hence the term "operant behaviour", (see Skinner's theory in the Learning Chapter), or "operant conditioning" (Skinner 1953)[17]. What this behaviour does to the environment is what makes it more or less likely that the behaviour will occur again. It acts as instrumental to successive behaviour.

Skinner, the ardent behaviourist, derived his principles from precise experimentation following objective method. He

17. Skinner, B. F. Science and Human Behavior. McMillan. N.Y. 1953.

was thoroughly convinced of the importance of objective method in laying down the principles which he established through experimental precision. He, thus, induced science to solve most complex behavioural problems and gradually acquired a steadily increasing influence on psychology and personality fields.

Skinner's influence on the field of personality was no less important than J. B. Watson's influence on establishing psychology as a science of behaviour as Skinner advocated some reforms as behaviourist. He showed more careful respect for well-controlled data and precisely highly regular relations between particular pattern of reinforcement and carefully specified response measures. In his studies of reinforcement schedules he was absolutely objective and specific in considering the resultant responses. His findings exhibited regularity and specificity—a law and order in the system.

He insisted, firstly, that behavioural law and equation must apply to each subject observed under appropriate condition. Secondly, he believed that responses and behaviours are emitted rather than elicited. His emphasis was on operants rather than respondents.

His basic assumption was that behaviour of any organism is lawful. Like Freud, Skinner emphasized on the orderliness of behaviour. By means of his writings and refined experiments Skinner has persuaded many that the principle of determinism applies to human being. He insisted that human behaviour results from identifiable variables that completely determine behaviour and, therefore, human personality is measurable. This was the first contribution of learning theory in describing personality. Skinner believed that an individual's behaviour is entirely a product of the objective world and can be understood in objective terms. The human behaviour has a cause-and-effect relationship with objective environment. This fact led later behaviouristic psychopathologists to account for an individual's neurotic behaviour and introduce an important method of treatment—behaviour modification.

The assumption that all behaviour is lawful also clearly implies the possibility of behavioural control. He thought all that is required is to manipulate those conditions that influence or result in change in behaviour. This is known as behaviour modification. In order to establish his second assumption that behaviours are controllable, Skinner was not interested to consider those behaviours which are strongly resistant to change i.e. the behaviours governed primarily by hereditary endowment. He was interested in more or less plastic type of behaviour for which change would be brought about by manipulating environmental variables (which are observable). For this purpose he proposes to adopt the method of *functional analysis*—a method where analysis of behaviour can be done in terms of casual relationship and where causes themselves are controllable. The control can be best achieved by lawfully relating independent variables or inputs into the organism, and then controlling subsequent behaviour by the manipulation of those inputs (environmental events) in such a way as to obtain a particular output (response or emitted behaviour). This is the principle which Skinner employed in explaining personality development which, according to him, consists essentially in behavioural change and learning.

Skinner shows less interest in the structure of personality because they are hereditary endowments. They are genetically determined and, therefore, rigid and fixed. Skinner considered these to occupy a distinct category because they relate groups of responses to groups of operations. They are not energy states or purposive, but according to Skinner they are considered to be causal antecedents of behaviour.

Most of Skinner's position is concerned with modification of human behaviour which he equated with personality development. He thinks personality development can be understood from the consideration of behavioural development of human organism as he grows. The human organism faces continuing interaction with environment throughout the growth period. In the process, more and more complicated interactions take place between increasingly complex environment and the human organism which induce the individual to emit more complex form of behaviour. Consistently, this interaction has been the focus of a large number of carefully managed experimental studies. The key concept within Skinner's system is the *principle of reinforcement*. Thus, his theory of operant reinforcement has evolved.

Most aspects of personality are generally demonstrated in social context. But Skinner ignored this aspect and assigns no special significance to social behaviour as distinct from other behaviours in general. Social behaviour takes place and is characterized by a dyad interaction between two persons. On the other hand, Skinner believes, principles that determine the development of behaviour in an objective environment is surrounded by animate objects. When a developing organism interacts with this environment, a part of that interaction receives its feedback which positively or negatively reinforces or punishes that behaviour and the pertinent behaviour becomes a part of the personality. Reinforcers that a person receives usually depend entirely on the person's behavioural output.

Skinner did not advance any theory of personality whatsoever or never did try to explain how the social behaviour of an individual develops. But, surprisingly, the clinical psychologists have adopted the basic attitude and approach characteristics of Skinner for the treatment of neurotic behaviour. They found that his framework can be used to understand a person's normal behaviour as well as can be applied to the study and control of pathological behaviour. According to the clinical psychologists, abnormal behaviour is assumed to be the same in its principles of development as normal behaviour. They argue that if the normal behaviour can follow the learning principles and are learned behaviours then the abnormal behaviour is also learned in the same way. In putting forward a program for the treatment of abnormal behaviour, Skinner repeatedly asserts that the goal is simply to replace abnormal behaviour with normal ones and this can be achieved by direct manipulation of behaviour. In dealing with abnormal behaviour, Skinner does not appeal to the actions of repressed wishes as done by Freud, or an identity crisis (Erikson's view), or conflict between ego and superego or other constructs. Rather, he attempts to modify the undesirable behaviour by manipulation of the environment in a manner determined by the techniques of operant and respondent conditioning.

Thus, learning theory forwards a theory of development of personality but ignores the structural aspect of personality or personality dynamics.

Neo-Freudian theory of personality—Erik Erikson

Since Freud's death, Erikson—more than any other person —has performed the function of continuing Freud's idea of personality and its development. Erikson considers himself a Freudian psychoanalyst (Hall and Lindzey, 1978, op. cit). But he is more popularly known as a neo-Freudian after Carl Jung and Alfred Adler. Erikson, in formulating his theory of personality, has followed in Adler's footsteps more than those of Sigmund Freud, though the basic assumptions of Freud's psychoanalysis remained as influential a factor in forming his theory as the ego psychology of Adler.

The most significant contributions Erikson has made in the theory of personality fall under two major headings : (1) A psychosocial theory of development from which emerges an expanded conception of the ego; and (2) the psychohistorical studies that exemplify his psychosocial theory in the lives of world famous individuals. The second area of investigation made by Erikson is beyond the scope of this book and so remains out of the present purview.

Regarding the structure and dynamics of personality, Erikson upholds Freud's view and agrees with him about the tripartite system of the mind. But, as to the personality development, he deviates from Freud's idea of psychosexual stages of libido development. He rather agrees with Alfred Adler's concept of ego development which gives a man his identity. Like Adler's, Erikson's theory applies to numerous points across the life course. Adler and Erikson agree that we all make *active contributions* to growing our personality by understanding who we are and who we want to become. It is this identity aspect of ego in the social context has been emphasized strongly by Erikson in developing his theory of psycho-social growth of personality.

Unlike Adler, Erikson holds that the effects of our early social experiences depend on 'when' they occurred. Also unlike Adler, Erikson (1963)[18] sees personality growth as following *epigenetic principles*. He accepts the bioscientist's view that development is genetically determined and it operates in stages that unfold in an invariant way and universal way. They exhibit unchanging sequence for all individuals. Epigenesis determines the "proper rate and sequence" of development (Erikson—1968)[19]. Epigenesis is an extremely

18. Erikson E. H. Childhood and Society, 2nd ed N.Y. Norton, 1963.
19. — Identity, Youth and Crisis. N.Y. Norton, 1968.

important idea. The biological theory of epigenesis is that in the course of its development the embryo is moulded and modified by environmental forces and that the mature embryo is, therefore, equipped with characteristics which were not present in the fertilized egg. At its most extreme, the theory holds that even a mother's reading habits during pregnancy will affect her child's intellectual development. (Evans, 1978)[20]. Epigenesis means that what comes later in development totally depends on all that preceded it. This interpretation has been taken by Erikson to describe epigenesis in developmental stages. According to him, our first social encounter lays the groundwork for everything that follows.

He points towards the specific maturity demands made by our cultural and social groups at each stage of life—demands that provoke us to respond adaptively or maladaptively. Each society is supposed to have its own views of the ideal characteristics of the mature individual. All of the society's socializing agents—particularly the parents—promote these valued personal characteristics. Personality development, according to Erikson, is the ongoing product of the interaction of our individual needs with social expectations.

Erikson's theory involves a total of eight stages with each stage centering on a particular crisis of development. He uses the term *crisis* to denote a developmental turning point, a decisive period during which the individual either acquires new capacities for vitality or fails to grow and thrive. A positive resolution of each crisis strengthens the growing ego; a negative resolution weakens it. Moreover, a positive resolution of a crisis at one stage increases the chances of that positive resolution of crisis at later stages.

A positive resolution, to Erikson (1968), means that a balance, a *ratio* of positive to negative experience, is favourable. But a positive resolution does not necessarily mean the crisis is settled forever. New conflict may resurrect old crises. He says : "Personality is engaged in the hazards of existence continuously, even as the body's metabolism copes with the decay" (Erikson, 1963, p. 274). There is given the description and block of Erikson's stages of personality development in the form of a chart in the next page.

---

20. Evans Cris. Psychology, A Dictionary of the Mind, Brain and Behaviour. Arrow Books Ltd. London. 1978.

Block of Erikson's Stages of Personality Development

Life Stage	Psychological Crisis	Adaptive Ego quality	Ego care pathology
1. Infancy. 0-2 yrs.	Trusts or mistrusts	Hope	Withdrawal
2. Toddler. 2-3 yrs.	Autonomy vs. shame and doubt	Will	Compulsion
3. Early school age 4-5 yrs	Initiative vs. guilt	Purpose	Inhibition
4. Middle school age 6-12 yrs	Industry vs. inferiority	Competence	Inertia
5. Adolescence	Identity vs. identity confusion	Fidelity	Repudiation
6. Young adulthood	Intimacy vs. isolation	Love	Exclusivity
7. Adulthood (middle adulthood)	Generativity vs.	Care	Rejectivity
8. Old age (later adulthood)	Integrity vs. despair	Wisdom	Disdain

The above chart has been taken from Erikson's book on Childhood and Personality, 1963.

Erikson is regarded as a "neo-Freudian" because he employs the framework of the psychoanalytic theory of Freud and follows the methods he adopted in developing psychosexual stages of personality development. But in describing the characteristics of later stages of life Erikson deviates from Freud's technique and fashions it in his own direction.

Erikson accepts the notion of Freud for the early stages of life and agrees with him that libidinal or emotional energy exists at birth and is at the core of human functioning. He also agrees with him that development passes through stages, several of which coincide with Freudian ones too. Nevertheless, he has made certain distinct deviations from Freudian stages, particularly at the maturity years. The adult years of life are obviously a continuation of much of what has gone before. But they also bring inevitable physical, social and psychological changes.

Erikson, in developing psychosocial stages, mentions three adult stages, each of which involves a psychosocial crisis.

They belong to the three last stages he referred to of a person's life. According to Erikson, the crisis that faces the young adult is to establish sharing and caring relationships with others that involve personal commitment. It is usually the time when a separate family is being established on his own and the family becoming extended, responsibility and liabilities increase. It becomes necessary for him to extend this commitment to a wider range of people to take on guiding and nurturing of the younger generation. Failure to be "generative" can result in stagnation and conflicts. If integration is not achieved, the individual suffers from despair. The old age is able to trace a decline in social interaction. The life experiences become stale leading to stagnation and life expectancies are on the way to decline leading to despair. Nevertheless, life becomes rich due to the increased wisdom through varieties of experiences, good or bad and leads to end.

Existential / Humanistic Psychology—Abraham Maslow

In the years immediately after the World War II, a popular movement known as existentialism rose to prominence in Europe and quickly spread to the rest of the world. The movement was born out of the French resistance to German occupation and its two most articulate spokesmen were Jean Paul Sartre and Albert Camus. (Hall and Lindzey, 1978, op. cit.). Sartre was a brilliant graduate of the Sorborne who was to become a distinguished philosopher, writer and political journalist. Camus, a native of Algeria, became famous as a novelist and essayist. Both were awarded the Nobel Prize in literature, though Sartre refused it !

The most ancestral figure of existentialism was the Danish philosopher, Soren Kierkgaard (1813-1855), who wrote books for existentialism. Then it was Martin Heidegger (1889-1976), the German philosopher, who had great pertinence in connecting existentialism with psychology. Heidegger was the bridge to the psychologists and psychiatrists whose views of humans is considered important. His "ontology"—philosophy of being or existence—helped him to consider that an individual is a "being in the world", and the world has its existence because there is a Being to disclose it. To him, Being and world are one.

Heidegger was a phenomenologist. The history of psychology reveals that phenomenology has played an important role in establishing itself as a science. Phenomenology is the description of the data (the "givens") of immediate experience. Phenomenology—as experienced in the works of the Gestalt psychologists—has been employed primarily for investigating the phenomena of such psychological processes as perceiving, learning, remembering, thinking, feeling etc. but has not been used in personality studies. Existential psychology, on the other hand, has used phenomenology for elucidating those phenomena that are often regarded as belonging to the sphere of personality. "Existential psychology may be defined as an empirical science of human existence that employ the method of phenomenological analysis." (Hall and Lindzey, 1978, ibid, p. 312).

The existential viewpoint explains psychological phenomena as free from the cause-effect relationship in human existence. They maintain that psychology is not like other natural sciences, the science that deals with the human being can never be bound by causality or causal relation. They reject causality, reject positivism, determinism and materialism and assert their own concepts—being-in-the-world, modes of existence, freedom, responsibility, becoming, transcendence, spatiality, temporality and many others.

Existentialism replaces the concept of causality by the term (concept) motivation. Motivation, again, always presupposes understanding (or misunderstanding) of the relation between cause and effect. The existentialists emphasize human freedom. A person is free means (as the existentialists take it) that he is dynamic—freedom is not something humans have, it is something they "are". Humans are free by nature. It is this tenet of existential psychology that makes it appealing to the humanistic movement in America and helped gaining popularity throughout the world. The psychological endeavours all over the world were naturally greatly influenced by the existential ideas which smoothly ushered in the humanistic psychology in the field. The humans became the focus of attention.

By 1950, the psychologists working in different fields of psychology started taking a review of the state, status and areas of psychological investigations. Some of them felt that psychology had become straight-jacketed by behaviourism and, thereby, lost sight of the person and human values.

Existentialism was seen by these dissidents as offering a basis for humanistically-oriented psychology.

A man-centered psychological study was already in the field—the psychiatrists, clinical psychologists and psychoanalysts were working on it and discovered valuable information about human motivation, human desires and human values. The existentialistic psychology seem to resemble psychoanalysis, though in another way. The psychoanalysts discovered the normal personality interaction behind the abnormal behaviour of the person. The new discovery was reached at by them working intensively with people in therapeutic settings and more and more favoured the development of broad concepts of humans.

Abraham Maslow was one such humanistic psychologist who thinks that if we study existentialism from the point of view of psychology, there will emerge a Third Force Psychology (Maslow 1962)[21]. To Maslow existential psychology emphasizes on two main issues :

(1) It is a radical stress on the concept of identity and the experience of identity as a sine qua non* of human nature and of any philosophy or science of human nature.

(2) It lays great stress on starting from experiential knowledge rather than from systems of concepts or abstract categories or *a prioris*.

Existentialism rests on phenomenology and therefore, uses personal subjective experiences as the foundation upon which abstract knowledge is built. He concludes by saying that existential-humanism is not a new 'ism' that could turn antipsychology or into antiscience. It would enrich psychology —it would give a push toward the establishment of another branch in the discipline psychology. His new psychology is the psychology of authentic "self" and its way of being. Maslow admits that what we call "normal" in psychology is really a psychopathology of average.

In propounding his theory of personality Maslow forwards his idea of "basic human needs" as the first basic principle.

---

21. Maslow Abraham, H. Towards a Psychology of Being. D. Van Nostrand Co. Inc. N.J. 1962.

* Meaning indispensible.

Basically, as a psychoanalyst, Maslow started from an inquiry into pathological behaviour of the neurotics. What makes people neurotic was the question for Maslow about psychopathogenesis. His own answer was that it is a deficiency disease, that it was born being deprived of certain satisfactions which he called "needs"—in the same sense as water, amino acids and calcium are needs of the body and their absence produce illness. He found (from his patients) that most neuroses involved—along with other complex determinants—ungratified wishes for safety, for belongingness and for identi-fication, as well as for close love relationships, for respect and prestige. These he considers to be the fundamental and basic needs on which the development of personality structure depends. The social gratification of these needs leads to the development of normal personality and failure to gratify the needs may lead to abnormal development of behaviours.

The second basic principle on which Maslow's theory rests is on the concept of self and motives that ultimately leads to self-actualization. The "self" or the full-fledged personality of a person is gradually developed through various stages. The development of self, according to Maslow, depends on various motives the individual is born with and their interactions. So far as motivational status is concerned, the healthy people with normally developed personality exhibit the behaviour which shows that they have sufficiently gratified their basic needs for safety, belongingness, love, respect and self-esteem, that they are motivated primarily by trends of self-actualization. Self-actualization as a motive has been defined by Maslow as "ongoing actualization of potentials, capacities and talents, as fulfilment of mission (or call it fate, destiny) as a fuller knowledge of and acceptance of the person's own intrinsic nature, as an unceasing trend toward unity, integration within the person." (Maslow, 1962)

Self-actualization as the master motive was originally master-minded by Kurt Goldstein, the pioneer of Organismic Psychology. He thought that it is the only motive that the organism possesses—self-actualization to him is the creative trend of human nature. This is the specific end toward which people strive. It is the inner determinant of behaviour of the organism. Its principles are taken from environment that is most appropriate for self-actualization. The environment intrudes upon the organism by stimulating or overstimulating it so that the organic equilibrium is disturbed and thereby upsets the organism. The organism, then, searches in the environment for what it requires to equalize the inner tension.

The person has to come to terms with the environment because it affords the means by which self-actualization can be achieved. Goldstein tells us that a normal healthy organism is one "in which the tendency towards self-actualization is acting from within, and overcomes the disturbance arising from the clash with the world, not out of anxiety but out of the joy of conquest."

Maslow as a humanistic psychologist has much in common with Goldstein. The distinctive features of his view came from the study of his patients of brain damage and mental disturbance and, later on, reflected in his description of healthy and creative persons. He feels that so far psychology has dwelled more upon human frailties than it has upon human strength. Humans deliberately make desperate attempts to avoid pain rather than taking active steps to gain pleasure and happiness. Maslow has made a number of striking assumptions regarding the nature of humans. People, according to him, has an inborn nature that is essentially good, or, at least, neutral. It is not inherently evil. The personality unfolds through maturation in benign environment and, by active effort, the person realizes his nature through interaction with it.

Maslow's another basic contention is the theory of motivation. He differentiates between basic needs and metaneeds. The basic needs are those necessary for survival e.g. hunger, affection, security, self-esteem and the like. The metaneeds are those of justice, goodness, beauty, order, unity and so forth. The basic needs are, to him, deficiency needs, whereas the metaneeds are growth needs. The basic needs are prepotent over the metaneeds in most cases and are arranged in hierarchical order. Metaneeds, on the other hand, have no hierarchy but are potent, inherent and grow in time. (Maslow, 1970)[22].

By synthesizing the basic and the metaneeds a normal person develops his personality throughout the life process. The motivations supply the nourishment for proper growth

22. Maslow, Abraham, H. Motivation and Personality. Harper and Row. 1954 and Abraham, H. Maslow. London. 1970.

and helps the person to attain his "self" and "self-actualization". A self-actualized person possesses the following characteristics, as observed by Maslow who summarized them in his book "Motivation and Personality" P. 153.

1. More efficient perception of reality and more comfortable relations with it.
2. Acceptance (Self, Others and Nature).
3. Spontaneity, simplicity, naturalness.
4. Problem-centering.
5. Quality of detachment; the need for privacy.
6. Autonomy, independence of culture and environment, will, active agents.
7. The mystic experience; the peak experience.
8. Gemeinschaftsgefiihl.

The term (no. 8), invented by Adler, is the only one available that describes well the flavour of the feelings for mankind expressed by self-actualized people. The self-actualized people, in general, have a deep feeling of identification, sympathy or affection in spite of occasional anger, impatience or disgust.

9. Interperonal relations.
10. The democratic character structure.
11. Discrimination between means and ends, between good and sevil.
12. Philosophical, unhostile sense of humour.
13. Creativeness.
14. Resistance to enculturization (i.e. transcendence of any particular culture).

The above characteristics are also the characteristics of healthy persons, according to Maslow. More or less the same characteristics have been identified by Maslow in his research work with distinguished persons. Thus, the distinguishing features of Maslow's conception of human nature coming from his studies with famous people advances a support to his theory of motivation and personality.

Maslow, in his study with renowned personalities, came across the phenomenon of "peak experience" (as he calls them), exprienced by those subjects. Maslow described peak experience as most wonderful experience of life. He discovered that the persons undergoing peak experience feel more integrated, more at one with the world. They feel more as their own boss, more spontaneous, less aware of space and time, more perceptive, and so on (Maslow, 1962).

All the above studies and his own experiences with his patients have pushed Maslow automatically to be a humanistic psychologist. His immense interest in human being helped him to uphold the human values above all. He advocates psychology to be that kind of science which is not mechanistic as represented by behaviourism, but a humanistically oriented scientific endeavour which deals with human values, humane ideas, individuality, consciousness, purposes, ethics and "higher reaches of human nature."

CHAPTER VIII

Factors Influencing Personality Development

Personality development is an enormously complicated process, influenced by a vast number of interrelated and continually interacting factors. This is evident from the major theories we have discussed before. The difference between the theories consists of the emphasis each theory lays on the relative importance of the rate and range of influence exerted either by heredity or nature and environment or nurture on the development of personality.

But many psychologists dealing with the personality development, like Kluckhohn and others (1953 p. 53)[1], who forcefully asserted that "The old problem of heredity or environment is essentially meaningless. The two sets of determinants can rarely be completely disentangled once the environment has begun to operate. All geneticists are agreed today, that traits are not inherited in any simple sense. The observed characteristics of organisms are at any given point in time, the product of a long series of complex interactions between biologically inherited potentialities and environmental forces. The outcome of each interaction is a modification of personality."

On the whole, four broad types of influence play more or less a determining role as factors which can be treated as contributing to the development of new behaviours constituting personality. The first is *biological properties*, such as genetic endowment, temperament, physical appearance and rate of maturation. The second is cultural group membership. The third—and most important factor—is the individual's personal history of experiences with others and also known as interpersonal relations. Personality is largely a product of social

1. Kluckhohn, C. Murray, H. A. and Schneider, D. M. (ed) Personality in Nature, Society and Culture. Knopf. N.Y. 1953.

learning, and a child's social interactions provide the crucial learning situations. Relationships with family and with other members of social class, ethnic and religious groups, and with teachers and peers are of outstanding significance. The fourth type of influence on overt behaviour and the personality characteristics is the *situation* that is the stimuli immediately present in the environment, and the feelings of the moment, for instance fatigue, frustration, anxiety, calm, relaxation (Mussen, 1969)[2].

All these factors are interwoven—operating, interacting, and affecting personality development concurrently. Nevertheless, we briefly discuss the biological, social and situational factors—their nature, type as reported by series of scientific researches.

Biological Factors

By and large, the influences of biological factors on personality structure are limited and indirect. The biological factors include genetic, hereditary factors, physical appearance and physique and rate of maturation. Most of these factors have been elaborately discussed in the chapter on development in this book. For personality development, the characteristics such as—aggressiveness, nervousness, timidity and sociability are strongly influenced by genetic endowment. The constitutional make-up—which is also largely determined by heredity—influences a person's personality characteristics and influences his personality development in an indirect way. The children reliably classified as active, moderately active or quiet are actually the differences attributable to hereditary endowments, although training and learning may produce noticable modifications. Here, the environment and culture provide a decisive role.

The influence cast by the physical appearance and physique have been thoroughly discussed on the section of physical development and needs no repetition. Only thing to be pointed out is that any deficiency in physical appearance or physique can be compensated by other achievements made in the individual's life.

The rate of maturing is another important factor (which has also been discussed earlier) in causing striking variations

2. Mussen, Paul, H. The Psychological Development of the Child Prentice-Hall of India Private Ltd., New Delhi, 1969.

at various ages at which the child reaches due to chronological development. The differences in behaviour is noticable in the relatively mature or immature adolescents of the same age. This difference may be due to the adolescent's exposure to different social-psychological environments. A late maturing boy looks younger than his age and is likely to be regarded and treated as immature by others, while the early maturing boy is likely to be credited with being more grown-up socially and emotionally.

But a caution has to be considered in over-emphasizing the influence of physical characters on personality development. Because, although the rate of maturing and associated factors may affect personality development, the relationship between physical make-up and psychological characteristics is not very rigid and categorical. The relationship can be influenced by a vast number of complex, interacting factors determining the individual's personality structure.

Cultural determinants of Personality

From the point of view of personality development the most significant aspect of the individual's world is his social environment. All human beings live in a society, an interacting group of people and each society has a distinctive culture, a body of stored knowledge, characteristic way of thinking, feeling attitudes, goals, ideals and value system.

Culture regulates our lives and influences the development of personality at every turn, primarily by prescribing and limiting what he will be required to acquire for the development of his personality. Such culture expects and trains its members to behave in the ways that are acceptable to the group. Each culture has its own concepts, needs and specific techniques of child rearing as well as a set of expectations regarding patterns of approved behaviour. There are cultural variations in the methods of achieving such goals as to perpetuating the group and maintaining solidarity, or for satisfying basic needs of its members. There are cultural prescriptions for different types of child-rearing according to the necessity of the various groups. Again, there are social class differences—children from different socio-economic backgrounds differ in personality structure, behaviour and attitudes. They differ with respect to achievement motivation —the basic need leading to success in life. Middle-class parents, in general, stress achievement strongly, but lower-class parents do not. Sociological analysis suggests that the lower-class child develops little capacity to "delay gratification", because, for him, the future is uncertain. Therefore, the variation in social class leads to the setting of variety of aim, modes and methods in developing social behaviour and, thereby, cause individuals to vary in the development of personality.

Family influences on Personality development

The ultimate aim of personality development is the development of social behaviour in children. Socialization is the process by which the individual infant acquires the behavioural potentialities and, eventually, those behaviour patterns that are customary and acceptable according to the standards of his family and the social group. He starts acquiring those patterns of social behaviour from the immediate environment and gradually from the wide range of extended environments.

The child's first social learning occurs at home, and his earliest experiences with his family, particularly his mother, are critical in determining his attitude toward—and his expectations of—other individuals. The mother remains most important to him because she gratifies his primary needs for food, for alleviation of his pain and source of pleasure, for warmth. The infant soon learns to search for and approach his mother whenever he is hungry, in pain and uncomfortable. If the mother is nurturant and gratifies his needs promptly and effectively, she rewards the child's "approach" responses and these are likely to be repeated. Positive approach responses then, gradually, generalize to other people as well and the child develops positive social attitude. As we have seen in Erikson's theory that the earliest interactions between mother and child lay the ground-work for child's development of trust and mistrust in the world. This leads to the trust and mistrust to be generalized to trust others when the child grows up.

Almost all the theorists of personality development maintain that early mother-child relationships influence not only a child's immediate behaviour but also his subsequent and long-term adjustment.

The child-rearing practices also are taken into account as influencing the personality development. The parental attitude (in child-rearing process) toward the child's growing independence and their reactions to exploration and the curiosity strongly influences the development of important motives, like, curiosity, and the drives for autonomy, independence, mastery, competence, and achievement, as well as intelligence. This is evident from the different cross-cultural studies of child-rearing practices and their influences on child behaviour.

Permissive and easygoing parents will allow their child to explore and investigate freely, encouraging and rewarding his curiosity and independent behaviour. As a result, their children will manipulate their environment actively, thereby developing self-confidence, spontaneity and the desire for mastery over their surroundings. Parents who severely restrict their children in exploring and manipulating their environment and inhibit the development of motivation for autonomy will ultimately lead to the child's dependent behaviour. The same result yields when the mothers become over-protective. The over-protected children tend to become submissive, compliant and, sometimes, passive.

The impact of various types of home atmosphere on the personality characteristics have been studied cross-culturally and the research results show the children from democratic homes—which are characterized by general permissiveness—frequent conversing with children, emphasis on the child's decision-making, problem-solving and helping them to rationalize behaviour—lead to strengthening their (children's) ego-strength and strong self-concept in future.

By contrast, children brought up in the authoritative (controlled, restricted) homes, homes with clear-cut rules, prohibitions and restrictions—tend to be quiet, well-behaved, shy, socially unassertive children. Those from the highly "indulgent" homes, show almost same behaviour, when they grow up, as shown by the restricted and overprotected children.

Thus, it can be surmised that the traits developed throughout the course of personality development depend, on the whole and in general, on the interaction of the biological, cultural and social factors and the congenial environment provided by the family and society.

The predictions given above (received from different research studies) are only generalizations and not absolutely conclusive. Most of the traits acquired by the child in future depend on many other factors he encounters in his own life, his own perception and reactions to them. A young child's behaviour may be swayed by the reactions his peer groups show to him. Personality change do occur frequently during childhood because, at this stage, personality characteristics are not fixed or immutable. As his world expands, the child faces and encounters many new situations and faces many a new social interactions that may produce radical alterations in personality structure and behaviour. Even simple social learning and formal training of attitudes and values in proper learning situations like school and other institutions play important role in influencing the personality change and development.